The Eagle Soars

A Story of Triumph
over Disability

as told by J. Harold Zook

Transcribed and compiled by
Marian and James Payne

VANTAGE PRESS
New York

Published by Vantage Press, Inc.
419 Park Ave. South, New York, New York 10016

Manufactured in the United States of America
ISBN: 978-0-533-14458-7

Library of Congress Catalog Card No.: 2007902383

To my family
without whose encouragement and support
this story would never have been.

—J. Harold Zook

Harold and His Family, 1978. Seated (left to right) Mary, Omar,
Fern, Harold. Standing (left to right) Mervin, Kenneth, Ruth,
Lloyd, Omar Jr., Donald

Contents

Foreword

What life means to us is determined not so much by what life brings to us as by the attitude we bring to life; not so much by what happens to us as by our reaction to what happens.

—Lewis Dunningham

We cannot control the material given to us from which to shape our lives. However, we can determine how we utilize that material to create our lives. We can accept responsibility for developing our potential to its fullest, for dreaming and seeking to realize our dreams, and for becoming all we are capable of becoming. We can give to life our best, dedicate ourselves to the work we can accomplish, and continue to become the persons we were created to be.

J. Harold Zook was born with a very rare unnamed disability that restricted his movement. As a child, he could never run and play like other children. If he fell, he could not get up without help. Throughout his life he experienced great limitations, pain, and struggle. Instead of allowing his disability to define him, Harold accepted it, rose above it, and used it to achieve a career that would be extremely outstanding for anyone.

Upon Harold's retirement, President Clinton sent him a letter congratulating him for his years in education, his contributions to excellence, his dedication, and the lives he touched.

On October 13, 2002, Harold's alma mater honored him by naming him 2002 Alumnus of the Year, awarding him the clock pictured on the following page.

Harold's final message to students and staff regarding their

Joseph L. Lapp, President of Eastern Mennonite University, presents Heritage Clock to Harold.

mascot, The Eagle, describes his spirit, attitude and his soaring above his disability. (See message on following page.)

At Harold's retirement banquet, a speaker said, "He has given three thousand percent or more to his profession. He has done this with honesty, humility, sensitivity, and a lot of other things we could come up with." Attitudes begin to develop in our youth.

At this banquet, Harold said of his parents, "My mother was an angel. She taught me everything that a young man should know about how to treat a lady and how to treat women. I've never forgotten that. I hope I've been true to her word, true to her life, and true to her inspiration to me.

"I had a great dad. He has been a great support to me all my life. He has been with me. He told me how I should be. He never allowed me to be wayward. There were times in my life when I wanted to go the wrong way. His gut told him there was something he needed to check out, and he usually did. There were very few things I got away with, and I thank him for that. He taught me a great work ethic. We learned to work; we learned to give a man an honest day's work and an honest wage. He taught me how to believe in myself. He taught me there was no obstacle in life I couldn't overcome.

"I remember some time after my brother Mervin had been teaching at Indian Valley for many years, a student asked him what was wrong with me, meaning my disability. My brother said, 'Gee, I never thought about it, that he had a disability.' That's how my dad taught us. There was no disability, there was no handicap you couldn't overcome."

Harold says, "Every man's work is a portrait of himself. The highest reward for his toil is not what he gets for it but rather what he becomes by it. My portrait is a tribute to all those who have helped me to never lose my love for life, nor my belief and willingness to face each day with anticipation, love, and happiness just for the privilege of doing so."

THE "SPIRIT OF THE EAGLE" AT INDIAN VALLEY HAS BEEN ALIVE AND WELL EVER SINCE THE SCHOOL'S BEGINNING. AS STUDENTS AND STAFF, WE COME HERE EAGER TO LEARN AND SERVE; AND THEN, ONE BY ONE, WE LEAVE THE JOY OF OUR LABOR FOR OTHERS TO CARRY ON. THEREFORE, TO EACH NEW STUDENT AND STAFF MEMBER PRIVILEGED TO BECOME A PART OF THIS GREAT SCHOOL, I CHALLENGE YOU TO PROUDLY ACCLAIM THE GREAT AMERICAN EAGLE AS **YOUR** MASCOT SYMBOLIC OF POWER, COURAGE, DIGNITY AND INDEPENDENCE.

THIS "KING OF BIRDS" — STRONG, SWIFT, MAJESTIC, MAKING HIS PLAYGROUND IN THE CLOUDS AND DEFYING THE STORM — HAS THROUGH THE CENTURIES BEEN CROWNED BY THE GLAMOUR OF LEGEND AS THE UNDISPUTED RULER OF THE SKY AND MADE THE EMBLEM OF FREEDOM, THE INCENTIVE TO VALOR AND THE PLEDGE OF VICTORY. THE GRANDEUR OF ITS FLIGHT INTO THE CLOUDS, ITS PRETERNATURAL KEENNESS OF VISION AND ITS FREEDOM-SOUNDING SCREAM NOT ONLY HAVE STIRRED THE IMAGINATION OF MEN IN EVERY AGE, BUT HELPED TO LEAD OUR OWN ASPIRATIONS TO THE CLOUDS. NO LONGER DOES ITS GRACEFUL FIGURE ADORN ONLY THE GREAT SEAL AND INSIGNIA OF A FREEDOM-LOVING COUNTRY TO SIGNIFY ITS PROWESS AND WORTHINESS, IT HAS ALSO FOUND A PROMINENT PLACE IN EACH OF OUR HEARTS SO THAT WE WHO ARE SO EARTHBOUND PHYSICALLY CAN ASPIRE TO NEW HEIGHTS SPIRITUALLY AND SEIZE UPON THIS SYMBOL TO HELP US SOAR TO EVEN GREATER HEIGHTS OF SPIRITUAL AND ACADEMIC FREEDOM.

J. HAROLD ZOOK
TEACHER AND ADMINISTRATOR, 36 YEARS

Harold's life exemplifies the spirit of Jesus and the Buddha, with a strong belief in peace and nonviolence. His faith gave him hope and strength. In his life he soared like the eagle. The hope is that this account of his achievement, in spite of his disability, will inspire all, both those with a disability and those without one, to fulfill their potential, to give of their best, and to also soar like eagles.

It takes a big leap of faith and courage to see sufferings as blessings. Through his handicaps and sufferings Harold found himself, his work, and his God. Happiness and suffering are the result of one's situation and one's consciousness of that situation.

(Note: The story is written in Harold's own words and the words of those who spoke about his life and its impact, with editing when appropriate. Comments inserted by the compilers are in italics.)

—MARIAN AND JAMES PAYNE

Acknowledgments

We acknowledge the fact that though doctors did not expect him to be able to speak following his operation two years ago, Harold was able to provide hours of taping as he recounted his life experiences. For this we are deeply grateful, since without it, there would be no story.

We appreciate the cooperation of Harold's former principal and friend, R. Brooke Moyer, who took time out of his day to drive forty-five minutes to be interviewed and taped.

Harold with James and Marian Payne

Five of Harold's brothers took time to come for taped interviews. Two of his nieces also were interviewed, and his sister provided information as well. Several of his caregivers were interviewed.

We acknowledge the many other persons, school staff, students, parents, caregivers, and others whose many written comments and interviews proved valuable.

The *Souderton Independent, Reading Eagle,* and *North Penn Reporter* newspaper accounts as well as several others mirrored public respect and appreciation for the dedication and service Harold gave to their school and community.

Harold's caregiver, Terri Buchanan, interviewed persons we could not interview, for which we are grateful. She also read the manuscript, offering clarifications where needed, which has been extremely helpful.

—Marian and James

The Eagle Soars

1
Two Rescued Lives

Sara

My most challenging achievement involved a girl named Sara. She's a beautiful girl. She had no goals, was very hard, and had an experimental drinking problem in seventh grade. Her parents tended to blame all Sara's friends for her problems yet were unable to see their own daughter was creating her own problems as well as problems for other youngsters.

I loved this girl, as difficult as she was to deal with. Her name was scribbled all over the lavatories. She was very difficult with other girls and teachers. Sara's attitude was very bad, as well as her actions and everything about her. I prayed about it. I said, you know, this girl has a beautiful smile; she has a beautiful body, a beautiful appearance that's going to be destroyed in time. So I decided to do my best. I called her in for ten straight sessions. There was no response.

I remembered Dr. Scanlon in my Lehigh University psychology course—a tremendous professor. I attended summer courses, each session being three hours in length, every day for three weeks. One day all the students came in and sat down. The rule at Lehigh was that if a professor didn't show up twenty minutes after the scheduled beginning of the class, students were free to leave. Over thirty of us students waited, thinking he wasn't coming. Then, two and a half minutes before the twenty minutes were up,

Sara on her wedding day

he walked in, and sat down at his desk without a word. He pulled out a cigarette and smoked it. He sat there just doing his own thing. These were graduate students who began getting restless. They became bolder and bolder, chiding him, saying, "First you come in late and then you sit there like an idiot." Some students became very obnoxious. My friend and I wondered what was happening. The professor seemed rather amused as he read his magazine for a full hour of the three-hour class period. Some people threatened to walk out but didn't quite have the nerve to do it since they didn't want to take a cut for the class. We were only allowed three cuts for a class.

Finally, Dr. Scanlon stood up and said, "Well, folks! This is a lesson today." This was a guidance counselor's course. He said, "Supposedly you're all in this course because you're all guidance counselors or you wish to be guidance counselors. I wanted to demonstrate to you that the way you reacted today to me is the way you will react to a student that is unresponsive to you when you deal with a child in your school." The professor made a very simple statement, or lesson, and those students felt rather strange because it demonstrated that they would be either good guidance counselors or bad ones. I remembered that lesson as I talked to Sara.

I called Sara in again, but there was no response. I called her in again, talking to her for fifteen to thirty minutes. She just stared straight ahead with no response. She wouldn't even look at me, angry because I was calling her in. Over the course of several weeks, about the tenth session after having prayed about this, I don't know why I did this, but I rolled my chair over to her chair. There were two chairs in my office—one by my desk and one by the door. She always sat on the one by the door, never on the one by my desk. I rolled my chair to her. She had her hands in her lap. Reaching over, I took her hand into my hand and said, "Sara, you're a beautiful girl. You've got more than ninety percent of the girls in this school have in attractiveness. I'm not giving up on

3

you, Sara. I'm going to call you in here every day until we can come to some kind of understanding, or you can tell me what's wrong, or you can relate to me why you're having so much difficulty." I just held her hand. She looked directly into my eyes with a glowing smile, and I lost it. I just cried and cried.

"Oh, my goodness!" she said. "What did I do? What's wrong?"

I think my crying scared her, because when I cry I can boo-hoo pretty good sometimes.

After I got my composure, she said, "Whoa! What did I do?"

"Sara," I replied, "you smiled! That's the most gorgeous smile I've ever seen in my life. You're one very beautiful girl." That was the beginning of her opening up to me about her difficulties and about why she was choosing these avenues rather than others. I felt I needed to find something to help rivet in her mind what it feels like to be good. After we had talked for quite a while and she indicated she wanted to change the direction of her life, I suggested she might want to attend the Special Olympics at a neighboring town on a Saturday to become a "hugger." She thought she could do that. I told her I knew she could do that. She would choose a child, stay with him for the day, encourage him, hug him, cheer him on to do his best. She said, "I think I can do that."

"I know you can do that," I responded. "You just get a child and that child will be yours for the day. Give lots of hugs. Encourage him to do his best."

Sara's parents took her to the Special Olympics, where she connected with one little guy for whom she was a motivator. She had the personality! She was there "gunnin' " for this guy and he won his race! She hugged him at the end of every race. He cried; she cried; there were lots of hugs! She called me at 4:00 in the afternoon saying, "Mr. Zook, that's the best day I've ever had in my life! I want to do some more of those kinds of things!"

It was a real chore to persuade teachers to put faith in Sara again. She had been so difficult, so bad. They gave me every reason in the book why they shouldn't give her a break. For every reason they gave me I countered with a reason why they should give her a break. They felt I was being too lenient with her. I began with her homeroom teacher, saying, "Sara is a new girl. She'll make mistakes, but she's trying. Just give her the benefit of the doubt."

The teacher complied and soon came back to me saying, "Wow, what a beautiful and good girl Sara is becoming." It took about a year and a half, but by the time she got through ninth grade she was a different person.

In the past, Sara had run away from home several times. That was always a very difficult thing. Her parents would call me. One rainy, cold October night, her parents called asking, "What shall we do?"

I said, "Well, you must do what your parent instincts tell you to do, but my advice is to just go about doing what you've been doing. If you're cooking, just continue on with your cooking. Don't even leave the house. Just do your thing. She'll be back."

About an hour later, she came crawling back into the house, soaking wet. I had cautioned her mother, "Just be kind to her when she returns; just love her; help her get a nice warm shower; give her a nice treat—cookies or whatever her favorite treat is, don't reprimand her. When the right time comes, sit down with her and tell her, 'Sara, I want you to know we really love you.' Then tell her how that hurt. Let her know how it makes you feel." That happened several times.

That's the kind of girl Sara was—obstinate, just trying to break you, wear you down in any way she could. Her parents didn't know what to do anymore. They were at their wits' end. They were the only parents with whom I had a three-hour conference. My principal thought I was crazy for wasting my time.

Sara's mother says, "Our famous three-hour conference . . . was the most important one in my life. I think we'd all agree it changed all of our lives. . . . We could have lost Sara and more importantly, Sara could have lost herself. . . . We wish for all troubled teens a 'Harold Zook' in their lives."

By the end of ninth grade, Sara was writing little love notes to her mother in the morning before she left for school. To this day, her parents think I'm some kind of god or something. She turned out to be a terrific girl. After she graduated from high school she became employed as an aide at a group home for mentally challenged adults. She did some real transforming work with these adults. She felt these adults were being denied opportunities human beings should have, such as the opportunity to see how it feels to put your feet in the sand at the beach, how it feels to go into the water, and how it feels to have the wind swoop through your hair. She would take these residents, one at a time, for rides in her Jeep—fast rides—and these guys would really whoop it up. When she asked to take three of them to the seashore, she was told: "Oh, you don't want to take these people out in society," which she thought was most horrible. After finally getting permission to take them to the beach, she basked in the euphoria shown by these appreciative adults.

The *Indian Creek Foundation* publication says of Sara:

> Sara is a bubbly blonde with a genuine smile and an abundance of good looks.
>
> Just out of high school, Sara had her fantasy job as a beautician. "To many of my clients their appearance seemed to be all that mattered. I wanted to do something that had meaning." Finding a job in a group home, Sara found a new person inside of herself as she worked with the residents at Kulp Road, Harleysville, and later Perkiomen Road. "Working in a group home feels like being part of a family and I guess I realized how important the work was to me when I found, like a mother I suppose, that I made sure residents were fed before I was; sometimes I even gave up my mealtime portions so they could have seconds."
>
> As she moved from a direct care to a house supervisor position, she began to realize it was important for her to find new op-

portunities for personal growth and new ways to contribute to the field of mental retardation. Sara went from this position to a full-time nursing program.

When I encouraged her to become a nurse, she demurred, saying she didn't think she could be a nurse. "Sara," I assured her, "you have all the smarts. You have a terrific bedside manner. I've been in hospitals and I know what a good nurse is and what a mediocre nurse is. You could be an excellent nurse. It would just do my heart good to see you go out and become that kind of person." She mulled it over for several years, with me continually encouraging her, until one day she said, "Mr. Zook, I'm going to give it a try." She entered training where they gave a full scholarship to the top nurse in the class. She was the top nurse every year until the last year, when she had a roommate who was nip and tuck with her, so she wanted her roommate to have the top nurse honors of the year.

That's the kind of person she is. Today she's a nurse, married to a Pennsylvania state trooper, and recently gave birth to her third child. Being an excellent nurse, she works two weekend shifts at a local hospital and gets paid for the whole week so she can be home with the children during the week while her husband is with them on weekends.

That was one of my most difficult achievements—turning this girl around. Today she's a tremendous credit to society. Her family loves her. She's a queen of the world!

During 1977, a year designated for the handicapped, I had set aside $17,000 to refurbish the chapel in the church I attend. It was the $17,000 I had offered to put in a lift for handicapped students in our school, but the school board wouldn't do it because it would be setting a precedent. I was devastated. I had gone before three school board meetings, but there were just a few people on the board at that time who didn't want to do it. I think they thought it would ruin the aesthetics of the stairwell, since it was a nice open stairway at that time. So I decided to use the money to refurbish the chapel at our church, which wasn't very appealing.

I had gotten to the place with my disability where I couldn't go up the stairs anymore to attend church services. This chapel gave me a place to worship where the service was piped down through an intercom. I felt that if I were going to use the chapel, I would refurbish it as I thought a chapel should be. My cousin's husband, Virgil Miller, was president of Souder Manufacturing Company in Ohio, which makes church furniture, so they made all the furniture for the chapel and chancel area, except the altar rail. It was an old altar rail made of beautifully grained wood. There was also an old door in the back that was about to be thrown out, but I suggested we see what was under the old finish. After the door was stripped and revarnished, it turned out to be a treasure. Everything in the chapel was done in red, white, and blue, including the draperies.

I engaged Allen Hermansader, whom I had never known before, knowing only that he was a professional church artist who did many church restorations and paintings. We became the best of friends, as I would sit for hours watching him paint cherubs and a dove of peace with an olive branch on the front wall of the chancel area.

One beautiful October day, we were outside the church talking when I said, "Al, you're a Christian. I need your help."

"What's that?" he asked.

"I need more than paintings," I explained. "I need your prayers." And I told him about this girl back at Indian Valley who wouldn't respond and that I couldn't break through to her. Tears came to my eyes and they glistened in the bright morning sun. Al was nearly finished with a beautiful portrait of Christ on which he had been working that he had brought to the chapel to show me. After listening, he took my arm, guided me back into the chapel, and while looking at the portrait of Christ commented, "Harold, tonight I will change the eyes in this portrait. I will put your eyes in this portrait of Christ because I see the spirit of Christ in you and your work."

Al had originally made the eyes brown, but he changed them to blue and finished the painting. A year or two later, Al told me he had painted one of these portraits for Sara. At Easter of that year, Al and I presented this portrait to Sara because she, in part, became the inspiration for the painting.

The artist wrote the following message on the back of the portrait that I presented to her:

Sara, I know Mr. Zook feels deeply honored to present this particular portrait of Christ entitled "Come Unto Me" to you, but may I as the artist share with you a very moving and personal experience which occurred several years ago while the portrait was still being painted.

It was a beautiful autumn morning in 1982 and Mr. Zook had been sharing with me as a trusted friend his genuine concern for you. I was deeply moved by the visual expression of his concern as well as his undaunted belief in you and immediately felt inspired to paint in the eyes of Christ that same compassion seen through the eyes of my friend, Harold. With your life and friendship, Sara, you continued to be a constant source of strength and inspiration to him. This is evidenced by the fact that you among a select few have been chosen by him to grace his personal portrait for which I have also been commissioned and feel privileged to paint.

Harold and I have become the closest of friends these many years. I personally believe his calling is a special one as he has been a blessing to so many individuals through the years.

Sara, I feel I know you personally through Harold and I pray the Lord will continue to bless you in your life's work.

Your artist friend, Allen.

My message was:

Dear Sara, What a beautiful note my artist friend has so thoughtfully written to you—a very special touch I never expected this week when he delivered this framed portrait of Christ for me to give to you today in celebration of Easter. I can assure you that a *very few* receive this kind of special recognition from a highly acclaimed artist such as Al. Writing this personal letter to you really affirms just how deeply he was moved by my personal concerns conveyed to him in confidence nearly ten years ago.

Yes, Sara, I do feel *deeply* honored to present this particular portrait to you because of its special significance for both of us. I, too, recall so well that beautiful autumn morning as we stood outside Saint Michael's Lutheran Church in Sellersville discussing my concerns for you and the difficulties you were experiencing as an eighth-grader. I loved and cared so much for you—a compassion Al obviously saw and felt. At one point that morning, my eyes began to moisten; and as they glistened in the morning sunlight, Al suddenly took me back into the chapel to show me his partially painted portrait of Christ (this very portrait) and said, "Harold, I am so deeply moved by the great compassion you show for this young lady, Sara, that I've just decided to place your eyes—their very color and expression of compassion—into this portrait." At that point the painting had brown eyes so he changed them to blue—all because of my deep feeling for you. Sara, you are and always will be very special to me. As Al said, your friendship really is a constant source of strength and inspiration to me; he knows because I've spoken so often of your attributes. Thanks for always being there (at least in thought) when I seem to need your strength and caring as well as your friendship.

An appreciative friend,
Mr. Zook

I would consider the change in Sara's life to be one of my greatest achievements. Today she is my best friend, even though she was a former student. When I was with her about six weeks ago she was still calling me Mr. Zook. I said, "Sara, it's time you stopped calling me Mr. Zook. I'm Harold now."

"Isn't that a dishonor?" she asked.

"No," I responded. "You're a friend. You're no longer a student."

Sara's parents attended my retirement dinner. When I intro-

Glory to God
A Hermansader

© Allen Foster Hermansader   "Come Unto Me"   Hermansader

duced her parents, I commented, "I don't want to be disrespectful nor do I wish to embarrass them, but these parents broke the record in the amount of hours I spent in a counseling session." Then I said, "And this is their daughter. Sara, forgive me. I don't want to embarrass you, but I want all you teachers sitting out there and all you administrators and board members to see a beautiful young lady. She was my greatest achievement." I told them a bit of how Sara was my most difficult student but my greatest joy because she became the young lady whom I dreamed she could become, adding, "She's a testimony to that as she stands here before you." She received a standing ovation.

Sara's mother says, "Harold helped me feel competent and to follow my vibes. There were times when I felt if I said the wrong thing I might lose my daughter, but he would say, 'Just follow your vibes. Your vibes have led you very well up until now. Just keep doing it.' He also gave me his phone number so we could call if we needed him. And we used it. I can remember one very cold night she was perched out in the car in our garage, I didn't know whether or not to go out and get her. When I called Harold, he said, 'Just leave her there.' When she finally came into the house on her own, Harold called her and talked with her a long time. He helped me develop the ability to listen to my kids and know from where they were coming.

"During our famous three-hour conference I learned a lot from Harold. I learned Sara was putting more pressure on herself than anyone else was. She had always been ornery, loving, wonderful, pretty, and lively. Now she wasn't that way anymore.

"We've known Harold since Sara was fourteen, when she began having problems. She would come home from school in very angry moods. At first, school personnel assured us everything was fine, but later we recognized there was a problem. It seemed she felt she was being measured by her older sister and didn't recognize her own capabilities, which may have been some of the problem. At age fourteen, she was also getting a lot of peer pressure, and being told by teachers she wasn't like her sister. They were competing in things like gymnastics.

"One day when she was being disciplined for some misdemeanor, Harold called me to have Sara picked up at school. She was very angrily tearing up notes from her purse and throwing paper all over the place. That was our first introduction to Harold."

Sara's father comments, "It was very comforting to know Harold was at the school and that he would assist the kids and us when we needed him. He was there for our two daughters and one son.

"Harold is a wonderful man, has a strong belief in God, loves children, and enjoys working with them. He's always showing that even though he is in a wheelchair, he has a wonderful heart and never allows that to be a handicap. He believes what's important is the self from within, not what a person projects. He's just a real, wonderful person.

"I think Harold contributed immeasurably to the school by being a solid rock for students to use as a sounding board which magnified itself in the community by building a wonderful generation of young adults. Seeing his former students develop into wonderful, well-rounded adults, raise their families, and celebrate with him gives him great joy. He was a tremendous example that one's character grows from within, not like a weight lifter who only builds on the outside."

Sara's mother continues, "Harold looks beyond. His character is exceptional. He is a wonderful human being, and is by no means handicapped. If anything, he might be physically challenged. He helps the students see who they are and helps the parents see who the students are. He never once thinks of anything but helping a child. He doesn't put up with any nonsense, and tells it like it is. He'll be there to help at any time, but he expects a lot from a child. He recognizes a troubled child and knows exactly how to reach that child. I don't think he ever thinks of himself, but he's always there when a child needs him.

"Harold has a tremendous love of family and God, and he loves to help children. Those three things are what have driven him. He never stops and he's never shocked. He's heard every word children can possibly utter. He never hesitates and is very strong-minded. He told me if he needs to go into a student's locker he does that, and he told me I had the right to do the same thing. Many people think they shouldn't invade their children's privacy, but Harold said if I think my child has a problem, it's my duty to know what's happening in my child's life. He's also the reason Sara and I are as close as we are now. There were times when I was afraid to come home because I was afraid she wouldn't be there since she threatened to run away. She was thrown off the cheer-leading squad for misconduct, was dressing in strange ways, and her grades were going way down. She was trying to be someone she wasn't—a tough teenager—which never fooled Harold, who gave us back our daughter.

"Harold always looks beyond the person. I don't think there's any teenager that has ever come through Harold's office that has thought of Harold except for who he is. They didn't see him as someone in a wheelchair. I think Sara is one of the very few people who got to ride his chair.

"We attended a wedding of one of Harold's former students. It was amazing to see him come into the room in his wheelchair and to see about six former students around his chair. One girl said, 'I don't know if you remember me, because I didn't spend as much time in your office as some of these other fools did!' They were all in their midtwenties. It was amazing how many former students talk to him when he's out in public. They all love him and it snowballs. Harold helps students become better people, and they love him for it.

"I understand there have been students from other institutions who have come to Harold for counsel, so not only has he helped students from this school, but others as well.

"I often wondered how the school would manage without

Harold, because he spent so many hours there. His car would be at the school at midnight sometimes. One time when Sara was in high school she was very worried about one of her friends who was planning to run away to New York the next morning. Sara asked me what she should do. I suggested she call Harold, which she did. The next night, Harold was counseling both the parents and that student. There are so many students who need help, and he knows how to help them. There were no limits to what he would do to help a student. He always had a method.

"At Harold's retirement dinner, he introduced Sara as his best friend. That was so remarkable. She was truly overwhelmed. He's just an honest, loving individual. Harold said we were a part of his retirement dinner because we were a good example of how parents and school personnel working together can make a difference in the life of a child, and it made us feel so proud.

"Every Christmas Harold sent a card to Sara with a precisely written personal note. I used to love when those cards came, because they were so meaningful. In fact, when his mother died, Sara was out of school, but Harold called her just to talk to her. Her friendship meant so much to him and I thank God for that. The most special gift given to Sara was the picture of Jesus Christ that was painted with Harold's eyes showing his concern for Sara.

"I have thought that if Harold wouldn't have made the decision to live when he was in the hospital two years ago, he would never have seen Sara's darling little boy, and that would have been a shame, because it brings so much joy to him and to Sara."

Sara tells her story:

"I initially met Harold at the beginning of seventh grade. In 1980, when I was a problem student, he helped me so much with my relationship with my parents. The rebellious type problems I was having in school were a direct result of the communication problems I was having with my mom. Harold dragged my parents into school, counseled them, and straightened us out. That was from the end of seventh grade and most of eighth grade. By ninth grade I was right on the road to being a good kid. In high school Harold was mainly supportive as a resource person for me on a lot of school projects.

"Harold is a strong person and doesn't easily give up a fight. He's a hard worker, refusing to give up on a troubled child. He never gave us the feeling he was going to give up on the long haul. He was there for the duration, fighting the fight until he helped us resolve things. At that age, going through puberty, when you're fourteen years old, a child doesn't generally open up and talk to authority figures and adults. Harold was so genuine and really old-fashioned; I felt what he was telling me was really true and genuine and that's why I was able to open up and learn from him. His strong family support gave him strength to be a true person, knowing who he is and where he wanted to go. He was always helping someone else with a problem.

"Harold definitely put my life on track, but who knows what would have happened to me if he hadn't kicked the rebellion out of me? I like to think I would have been fine, but who knows? There are many kids who were my friends who aren't doing nearly as well as I'm doing. I always tell Harold I wasn't that bad of a kid, but some of the things I was doing really were bad. I definitely wouldn't have been as successful as I am today if I hadn't made it through those teenage years as well as I did—and that was directly attributed to him.

"While my greatest goal was to graduate from high school with decent grades, Harold always encouraged me to go to nursing school. He loved when I worked with retarded adults in the community, and was very supportive. I learned so much during that time and it was a stepping-stone to going to nursing school. Now my biggest success is my family and my three babies, while continuing with my nursing.

"Harold contributes his positive spirit to other people. In his presence, people tend to smile more, show more genuine happiness, more thankfulness, and take on a more positive spirit. In the way he overcomes his obstacles, people learn to take on a more positive attitude. When he was in school, not only did he help students but also the teachers in dealing with students. He helped with their professional problems and growth. He has contributed in countless ways, not only from nine to five during school hours, but has helped everyone with whom he has come in contact.

"Some students who didn't know him very well focused on his disability. When I first knew him, he was walking, but by the end of my time in his school he was riding on his motorized cart. That's how they knew him—Mr. Zook, the assistant principal who is handicapped. The students who did interact with him got past his disability. They confided in him about school or personal problems or counseling in general. There were also the rebellious types that I hung out with for a while. They dreaded talking to him because he was tough, making them talk about what they had done and making them accountable for their actions. Some of the teachers would look the other way, saying, 'That kid's just a bad kid who needs to be suspended,' or whatever. Harold didn't give up on any student. Those kids just dreaded being called out of class by Mr. Zook. We would miss one, two, or three classes because Mr. Zook was counseling us. I think it would have been easier if he had given us detention. Detention would have been easier than sitting in the office every day. That was the worst! Sitting in that chair in his office was tough. By the end of their year, every one of those kids had a newfound respect for him and they all looked past his disability. Mr. Zook was our friend. We came to school dances all dressed up in our gowns and high heels and would be riding the halls on Mr. Zook's scooter. He was truly our friend and we appreciated him.

"I haven't been around him when he had tough times; at least he didn't share them with me. He doesn't want to burden others with his problems. He would not want to let me know when he was having a hard time, because he wouldn't want to bring me down. One of the saddest things he told me about was when he broke up with his girlfriend because he didn't want to bring children into this world with the possibility of passing on his disability to a child and he knew she would never be happy without her own children. How much more selfless can that be? I don't know where he would have gotten the strength to do that, because I know people who don't have the strength to break up unhealthy relationships for their own sake.

"We always kept in touch through correspondence, but one Christmas I didn't hear anything and didn't know why until I heard he had been in the hospital. I immediately called the house and asked what happened to him and was told about his hospitalization and tracheotomy. He was in no condition to be calling people.

"Harold's strong faith is partially why he was able to connect with people. It gave him a sense of accomplishment, finding joy in other people's joy. He never focused on himself or used his disability as a crutch. He knew what he wanted to do, what would make him happy in life, and that was helping others. He was never that self-centered to realize that his disability could be a big obstacle. He didn't allow his disability to take control over his life. He took control.

"We're great friends, ever since I got back on track. I want to go on record by saying I don't like to think I was that bad! He has been such a big support over the years. He's one of those friends in life who share all the ups and downs. I have never given much thought to his disability; I just looked past it. I did make my house handicap-accessible so any of my friends can visit me. I wouldn't dream of him not being able to visit me. Last summer I packed up my two kids and we had a barbecue at his home. My daughter went through his closets and was playing with the contents, and he didn't care at all. He wasn't ill at ease at all with my kids in his house. He's just wonderful.

"Last summer when Harold also came to my house for dinner, my eighteen-month-old daughter began playing with Harold's wheelchair gadgets and ventilator tube. Harold didn't make a big deal of it, suggesting in a nonchalant manner, 'We'll just put this back here.' He knew my daughter was interested in the novelty of his chair and equipment, but he didn't draw attention to the differences in his needs. He felt that if he made a big deal of it, she would grow up being more aware of the differences. This is an example of how Harold handled his disability with his family and friends. His disability was not an obstacle; it was a part of him. As he was leaving, my four-year-old reached across his wheelchair to hug and kiss him. Even at age four, when a child would be somewhat intimidated by all the medical equipment and someone she meets infrequently, my daughter bonded with him in a short time. She felt very comfortable with him and enjoyed checking out his handicap-accessible van with no hesitation. I told my husband later I was so proud of her, because that's how I've always felt about Harold. My four-year-old daughter recognized him to be a genuine person."

Jennifer

In her senior year of high school, Jennifer came to me with a serious problem. She wanted to expose the star football player. Several years before, she and a girlfriend with their boyfriends had gone to Jennifer's home. The one couple and Jennifer's boyfriend had set up a plan so when her mother left the house to go shopping her boyfriend raped her. This incident was tearing away at her all through high school. Although Jennifer and I had stayed in touch since she left junior high school, I had no idea of the rape. One day she spilled her feelings, telling me she needed to do something for healing. My reaction was that the only way she would find healing from the incident was to talk about it. I helped her to very professionally write the story of what happened for publication in the school newspaper. Eventually, everyone figured out who had raped her.

Jennifer on her wedding day

A tremendous storm erupted with some students feeling she shouldn't have exposed a star athlete, while other students praised her for her courage. The sponsor of the school newspaper came to me asking if I was certain this story should be printed. We discussed it at length, and although it was risky, the story was printed. I was deeply concerned for Jennifer's mental health. Eventually, the boy was forced by his conscience to apologize to her, which was really what Jennifer needed to put the incident behind her. She was not a difficult student and was a great inspiration to me.

Jennifer wanted me to take her down the aisle on her wedding day, but I talked her out of it because I couldn't conceive of driving my Amigo beside her in a wedding gown. She did, however, insist that I be at the back of the church to see her off as she began her march down the aisle. Her wedding was the last student wedding I attended just two months prior to my hospitalization in September of 1999.

Jennifer tells her story:

The first time I saw Harold at the beginning of my first year at Indian Valley Middle School, he was walking using a walker. I was in awe that someone could rise above his disability. I began talking to him about one of my girlfriend's boyfriends because of drug and alcohol use. Harold made me feel so comfortable and that it was a good thing to be concerned about others. I would often get very upset when other students were made fun of in any way, and Harold always understood everything I talked about. He was constantly sending me note cards when my name would be in the newspaper for any reason; he sent cards on my birthday, at Christmas and Easter, with words of encouragement. The cards have holes where I hung them in my bedroom. He was such an inspiration to me. I have known him almost twenty years, and anytime I would stop by to see him he would drop everything he was doing and just talk to me. Now that I've been a teacher for nine years, I realize how extraordinary that was. I hope I have the capacity to take that kind of time for my students.

"I firmly believe Harold saved my life. I didn't have a good relationship with my father. My parents divorced when I was very young, and I resented the loss of my father. When he remarried and had three other children, it cut very deeply that he had no time for me. I now realize I was seeking a father figure, and I found that in Harold. He made an effort to give me encouragement, telling me I was a special young lady. When I graduated from high school, he wrote a note saying if there was any young lady he would like to have for a daughter, it would be me. That meant so much to me I cried when I read it. He was there for me in so many ways.

"While in high school, I was date-raped, which I didn't understand at the time. I began sleeping with two other guys until my mother discovered what was happening. The first person she called was Harold. When I learned Harold was on the phone, I was crushed. I was so fearful that he would now consider me to be a horrible person and I would lose his friendship. But he was a wonderful source of strength. He didn't tell me I was a slut, or a bad person. My mother's reaction was horrible since she was at her wits' end, and I didn't want to go on living. Harold helped my mother understand my situation and I really believe he saved my life. He gave my mother and me his home phone number, telling us we should call him if we needed anything, and we called.

"I am a very empathetic person, and I'm sure he knew there were jokes about his toupee and his not being able to walk, but he took everything in stride. He never showed that anything bothered him. For him to rise above all those difficult things, like the fact that he never married or had children, made such an impression on me. He never allowed any difficulties to get him down. He knew who he was and looked for the good in other people; he celebrated life. He exemplified a true human spirit with high ideals, looking for the best in others. His character is unbelievable to me. He is very willing to show his vulnerability, which takes a very brave person. He painstakingly chooses appropriate cards and writes a note to go with them showing how much he cares for the recipient.

"Harold's students were a challenge to him. Middle school students wear everything on their sleeves, are very honest, and really want to know how to become better persons. Harold would find a few good things about a student, focus on them, and then challenge the student to become a better person. Harold could look past all the external stuff and see the real person underneath.

"For thirty-two years Harold presented his special award to a graduating high school senior. He chose me for the award when I graduated from high school. It was a money envelope containing a new hundred-dollar bill with this special message to me:

" '*Dear Jennifer, for the past twenty-four years I have been selecting a senior to be the recipient of my own special award. Each year it has become my* **personal** *way of privately paying tribute to that senior who over the years has in my judgment been: first, a young lady or gentleman; then, a leader who demonstrates kindness, patience, love, and understanding; also, a person who is capable of maintaining his/her own individuality without conforming or compromising his/her ideals; and finally, a citizen who has been a positive influence within his/her school, community, church, and family.*

" '*Please accept this monetary gift as a small token of my appreciation to* **you** *for being that special young lady you are—a person whose smile and outgoing personality have been a real inspiration to me and many others. As a graduating senior, Jennifer,* **you** *have so beautifully met the criteria for my special award. Now, may you be blessed as you continue to be a genuine ambassador for God and your fellowmen.*

" '*In sincere appreciation, Mr. Zook.*'

"When I read this, I was so amazed that he saw all those things in me, which helped me to want to be more of those qualities. Next year I will have my first students graduating from high school and I want to do something similar for them. This was a very powerful thing and I would like to carry on this tradition that he started.

"When students sat down to talk to someone like Harold who had overcome so very much—a condition that only a few people in the whole United States have—they can't think their world is so terrible. He helped so many students solve problems in their lives, problems with drugs, poor grades, or mouthing off to a teacher. Students were automatically enthralled with him because he took life and made it successful. He didn't look down on himself—at least not that we ever noticed. Students see that and can't help but be better people because of it. It's pretty amazing that someone with Harold's physical disabilities could keep his fingers on the pulse of the school. He always knew everything that was going on. He also accepted everyone, in spite of our backgrounds or differences. This school was a wonderful place because of him. He was the embodiment of a true human being dedicated to helping children; no one can deny him that—ever! It seems it was never meant for him to be married, because now he has a huge family.

"Harold had a very calming influence on my mother. He also helped my mother with my sister. When Harold talks to you, he focuses entirely on you. In his office, Harold had Andrew Wyeth's *Christina,* a painting of a disabled girl lying in a field, and I later bought one for myself. It had such a calming effect on me, and I often wondered if it had a calming effect on Harold.

"Harold's amazing family has been a tremendous source of encouragement for him. They are very close and he knows they are always there for him. He is also a big part of the lives of his nieces and nephews even though he is in constant pain. He rarely talks about it, but we know he suffers a lot of pain. God is a very big part of Harold's life. He never preaches to anyone, but his life shows that God is very real to him. Children also kept him going and kept him upbeat. I was worried that when he retired he wouldn't have children to keep him going, but he searches out what he needs.

"Since he had the tracheotomy, the coping skills he learned

all through his life have kept him going. He will conquer anything he confronts. Maybe it is because he has lived with difficulties his entire life and has had so much support that he has the ability to see past other people's transgressions. Others then looked past his disabilities and saw a whole person.

"When I first saw him, I saw only his disability, but as I got to know him, I didn't realize he was disabled. I am so blessed that he has been in my life. I feel that because of him, I am this incredible woman, this teacher, and without him, I don't know where I would be."

Jennifer's mother shares her feelings about Harold:

"Harold and I shared many concerns about my daughter during her school years. Harold was always very quiet and unassuming, but he knew how to get things done. Jennifer reminds me that when she was an eighth-grader she and a group of other students got into trouble and the story became rather distorted about their activities. Harold took the time to listen to their story and to learn exactly what had happened. Jennifer learned she had a confidant in Harold. Because of family circumstances, Jennifer felt she had no father figure, but she found it in Harold, who became the father she never had. He always took the time to visit and talk with her. When she went on to high school, she got into some pretty serious boyfriend trouble. I felt that when she talked to Harold he would respond in a very confidential and respectful manner—as though he were the parent. I frequently came to talk to him, and he always had time to talk to me. When she was hanging out with the wrong kids, he helped get her back on track by sending beautifully handwritten little notes and keeping in contact. I knew whatever he said would make her feel good about herself, give her hope for the future and confidence in what she did. He continued this all through college.

"While Jennifer needed Harold the most, Harold also showed concern for Jennifer's sister, sending her letters of encouragement when she needed them. He always knew when those letters were important to her.

"During their college years, Jennifer and some of her friends adopted Harold, bringing him food he could eat and having a party for him. I know it must be hard for him not having his own family; but if he had, there would have been tension between his own family and the family he developed at school. No one could replace who he was and the help he gave to students and parents. I received as much from him as my daughter did. To show my gratitude, I asked a local florist to send a series of little arrangements of flowers for his desk, accompanied by a poem I had written. Each week for about six weeks, the poem gave a hint as to the sender or a little information we knew about Harold. It gave me great joy to learn how he tried so hard to determine who had sent those flowers. We knew how much he loved flowers, and we were so happy to be able to pull one over on him. We finally had to tell him who sent them.

"Harold is very sensitive, a good listener who cares about each person, courteous, always a gentleman who does not let his handicap hold him back. He never concentrates on how long it takes him to get somewhere or the effort it takes him to do things. He is always interested in others, wanting to make a difference in their lives. He saw a lot of needs among young children and was determined to do all he could to make a difference. I believe he felt a lot of love from his family. He set goals for himself, determining to go beyond the job description to do the very best he could do. When he retired, he said he finally would have time to learn to use the computer.

"When Jennifer graduated from high school, we invited him to our house for a party. We made certain there were strong young men to help get his chair up the bumpy path to our house. We often don't realize the preparation and planning necessary for Harold to make such an outing. He had to be careful what he ate and drank because he couldn't get into our house to use the bathroom. We take things like that for granted, but he can't. However, he never allowed these handicaps to hold him back from his life's work. He never took the easy way out.

"Harold attended Jennifer's wedding. She would have loved to have had him walk her down the aisle. It meant so much to her to have him there. He kept in touch with her on all her important occasions. He's a special, special man who means a lot to my girls and to me."

To redeem one person is to redeem the world. (*The Jewish Mystical Doctrine of Tikkan*)

2

Growing Up

My parents became concerned when I was about a year old because I wasn't walking. Otherwise there didn't seem to be any problems. I had a natural birth without apparent complications. I was the second oldest, with a sister older than me. When I wasn't walking, my parents began looking for specialists and physicians, who discovered I had some kind of muscular problem. It has never been determined what that problem is. My internal medicine doctor today, Dr. Pew, has looked at all my records and charts, concluding it is something doctors have never seen. They don't know if it's neurological or muscular or a combination of a neuromuscular situation. When I had my major operations after graduation from college, they discovered only three people in the United States who had any similar problems and they were all different, so the doctors have never been able to put a label on it.

My parents then began taking me to clinics, including the Elks Clinic in Reading, where Dr. Davis from Philadelphia was one of the specialists at that time, back in the late 1930s. I was born June 2, 1937. In about 1938, when my parents took me to the Elks Clinic the doctors and specialists from Philadelphia and elsewhere would look at patients who were brought in. Everything was guesswork. When I eventually began walking at about twenty-one months, they began seeing there was a need for treatment such as therapy and exercise. But I always walked with a different gait; I never walked normally. My parents noticed that if I fell I couldn't get up unless I crawled to a tree trunk or a fence and shimmied my way up. I've never been able to get up off the floor if I fell. That was very hard for my mom. I would fall, then I would cry, and my mom would come running, pick me up, and I would go again.

My dad was a very astute man for his time, because then they didn't know much about disabilities. If an individual had a disability, he or she was sent to a special school, never to public schools. My dad wanted me to grow up in the real world; he had an instinctive sense about that. I remember, as a child, falling when he was around. He would chide my mother for picking me up. I remember vividly how he would say I had to learn to do this because my mother wouldn't be around all the time and what would I do then? When I would fall, he would intercede, saying, "Harold, you think about this. You need something to get hold of." He would suggest, "Look around you." Maybe I was in the middle of the lawn. I could roll; I could crawl. He'd say, "What do you have? There's the yard fence, and there's a tree, and there's the porch post or porch bench. Get yourself there." Then he taught me to grab hold and pull myself up, one hand over the other, until I was in a standing position. I could walk, but I couldn't get myself up into a standing position without something to hold on to.

I remember those things very distinctly. I recall my parents having tremendous concern about me. They did everything they knew. They were farmers. I remember my mom taking me to Mount Gretna, about a two-hour drive from our home, every week to see a doctor for therapy and exercises. They would take me to Philadelphia, to Allentown, to Reading. They'd take me any place where someone would say, "Try this. Try that." They spent an enormous amount of money just for my well-being. That's why I always felt a tremendous obligation to my mom and dad. I'm so thankful I was able to care for both of them until their deaths. My mom died in my home the first year we were in it. My dad died a year ago. I was able to keep them both in my home, which pleased me a lot.

Growing up, I remember being loved. There was never a question about my place in the family. I never even thought about it until my adult years. My sister, Ruth, and I were extremely close all our lives, even to this day. There were good times at Christmas. The greatest treat at Christmas was when my dad went to Reading to buy a large crate of oranges and a box of Fifth Avenue candy bars. That was a highlight at Christmastime and sometimes we received a few toys. We didn't have much. Most of the money was spent on medical care.

I don't think my siblings ever felt like they were less than I was. They didn't seem to ever feel resentful because a lot of money was being spent on my care. I recall when my brother Mervin was a science teacher in my school and a seventh-grader asked Mervin what happened to me or why I had a disability. Mervin said it shocked him. He had to think about it. He replied, "Gee, I never thought about him having a disability." Growing up, we all did what we could do. I did chores. As the oldest son I took the lead in a lot of things, and we all just grew up together. Mervin said it never occurred to him that his brother had a disability. I thought that was rather interesting. We never talked about it. It just never came up.

When I was about five years old, my legs got worse because my heels began coming up from the ground. My medical condition—and this is the puzzling part about it—was such that my body wanted to grow normally, but my tendons and ligaments didn't grow to the same proportion with the rest of my body. By the time I was ten years old, my arms kept contracting, too. I couldn't straighten them out and I still can't. When I stopped growing, my tendons and ligaments stopped contracting. However, while I was still growing, they would contract more each year. My heels would come off the ground a little more each year. By the time I was ten, my heels were totally off the ground, causing a balance problem, resulting in a lot of falls. When I would fall, I couldn't get back up on my feet. I would hurt myself, crack my elbows, and have gashes on my head.

There was never any discussion or resentment on the part of my siblings concerning the amount of money being spent for my medical attention. My parents did what they felt was necessary. We had a lot of fun growing up together as siblings. My parents never treated me differently. If I needed to do something, and I couldn't do it, my dad helped me figure out a way to accomplish the task. When I got to be nine or ten years old, I couldn't get on the tractor, so Dad would make things to help me pull myself up onto the tractor. I could hardly reach the pedals when I was doing tractor work. When I was ten or twelve, he wanted me to get involved in milking the cows, but we had stanchions and I couldn't stoop to milk the cows, so Dad remodeled the whole barn to make a free-stall barn. With his own hands he made a milking parlor, and trained the cows to come up a ramp into the parlor. I could now stand in a pit and have the cows come in at my level. The milking machines hung right there, so I didn't have to carry them. Dad also built a new milk house up against the barn and then had a pipeline going from the barn to the milk house. This was one of the first milking parlors in the area and I remember farmers coming to look at this new invention.

At haymaking time, it was hard for me to get on and off the tractor to make necessary adjustments on the baler. My dad made a lever to go all the way from the baler up to the tractor seat for me to use to adjust the tension on the baler without getting off the tractor. He was a very creative man. Even with my casts on following a leg operation, Dad would carry me to the tractor, put me on, get me started, and I would do what needed to be done.

When I was ten years old, a visiting nurse came to our house, telling us it was just terrible that my parents didn't send me to a special school. She thought I should be sent to a school near Philadelphia specifically designed for handicapped children. My dad was arguing with this nurse; she seemed to be trying to give my parents a guilt complex, saying that I could attend school easier because everything was ramped, et cetera. This discussion was going on in the living room while I was in the kitchen. My dad called me to the living room and asked, "Harold, do you want to grow up in the real world or do you want to grow up in an artificial world?"

"I want to be in the real world," I answered.

My dad turned to the nurse and said, "There's your answer. He's going to continue in public school." That was the wisdom of my dad, far ahead of his time. It didn't make sense to him to baby me or have me grow up in a world where I wouldn't learn to do things like other people.

I had my first leg operation when I was ten years old. I took it as just a part of life. As I remember, I wasn't in much pain, because I healed very quickly and I could walk in casts. Dr. Davis, one of the doctors from Philadelphia who was at the Elks Clinic in Reading, was a specialist in orthopedics and thought that if he cut steps in the tendons going up the back of my leg and stretched them, my heels would go back down to the floor. My legs were in casts for several months and I walked so much that I wore out the bottoms of my casts because I didn't like sitting in a wheelchair. That operation worked for several years.

I had a teacher in sixth grade who took a special interest in me and would work with me during my physical education classes, giving me exercises going upstairs by pulling myself up with the aid of handrails. I managed to do that at the risk of losing my balance. He was so fascinated by my being in a public school that he took a special interest in my progress and me as a person with a disability.

I remember hitting my thumb with a hammer when I was about thirteen years old. I started to cry. My dad said, "Stop that! You're a man." I remember things like that, and while it may not have been the best way, he wanted me to be steeled for life. Pity was never a part of life and I never got pity. I also remember him instilling pride in me.

When I was about twelve or thirteen years old, I was cultivating tomatoes (one of my primary jobs) when the field men from Campbell's Soup Company came out to inspect the tomato fields. They were always extremely pleased with Dad's cultivation and irrigation procedures. For a number of years he received recognition for having the best-quality tomato of the Campbell's Soup Company suppliers. In fact, in the wintertime Dad would go to Campbell's Soup Company seminars to teach farmers in New Jersey and Pennsylvania irrigation procedures he had developed that were economical and at the same time productive. On this particular visit, these men asked my dad a question about something dealing with cultivation. He said, "Well, I think I'd better have Harold answer that question. He's the expert on that." I remember getting to the end of the row when Dad said, "Mr. Staggerwalt has a question about something and I think you know better than I do what the answer is, so why don't you tell him?" I remember how great I felt being a part of something that was so important. In my dad's eyes, I wasn't disabled. I was smart and intelligent in his eyes, and he valued that.

By the time I was seventeen years old and a junior in high school, my heels were off the floor again. The surgery was repeated, but this time it didn't bring the desired results and it was extremely painful. This surgery took place during the summer right after my junior year in high school, with the expectation that I could walk again in time to begin my senior year, but it didn't happen. When the casts were removed, I could hardly bear the pain in my legs, since the tendons contracted again. The doctors wanted me to walk and I tried, but I just couldn't bear the pain. I became discouraged because the end result wasn't what the doctors had said it would be. They said I would be walking in nine weeks. At nine weeks I wasn't even standing but was bedridden, with lots of pain in my legs. I couldn't even bear to put weight on my feet. I don't remember much more than just enduring the pain, and being surrounded by family and friends, with them helping me do what I could do. I just existed, dealt with it, and eventually got on my feet again two months into my senior year.

For my senior year I went to Lancaster Mennonite High School, a boarding school, where I received tutoring for the first two months. My father sent me to this school because he wanted me to have some dormitory experience in preparation for college, even though I had no interest in going to college. People on the campus were trained to give me aid as I very slowly began walking. During that time I was wearing braces for more stability, and the doctors thought the braces would keep my feet flatter and give me more muscle, thus strengthening my legs. Those braces were heavy, made of iron instead of aluminum as they are now.

I often think about the lessons my dad taught me as I was growing up. When I was in high school, I would get up at 5:00 in the morning. Since Dad grew seed stock tomatoes for Campbell's Soup Company, we had to have weedless fields consisting of about forty acres. About four men from the company would come several times during the summer and walk the fields, pulling up any stray stalks. My dad made me responsible for the cultivation procedures. If I cultivated a tomato plant over with ground, I had a stick with a fork on the end so I could lean back and uncover that plant. I would get up in the morning while he was milking the cows to go to the fields to cultivate or hand-hoe tomatoes.

One morning, about six o'clock, I fell while hand-hoeing in the middle of a forty-acre field. I wasn't expected back to the house until around 9:30 or 10:00 A.M. Here I was in the middle of the field where no one would see me for hours. How was I going to get up? I lay there thinking and thinking. Then I remembered my dad telling me how I needed to look around for something to help me. I learned early in life not to panic. I gathered my thoughts and analyzed what I had. I had a hoe, ground, a mound around the tomato plants. I theorized that if I scratched a gully, put my feet in that, and worked my knees up on top of the ridge, then put the hoe on the other side of me, perhaps I could shimmy up the hoe. I tried several times and failed, but I just dug a little deeper and made the mound a little higher so I could get my feet in a little deeper. Eventually, when I shimmied my way up I found myself flat on my feet. Since I would fall to the side, I had to figure out a way to steady myself. Rather than panic when I got tired, I rested a little bit. Finally, I worked it so that by taking it real slow, I eventually got up. That is just an example of how such perseverance and deliberation paid off. These were examples of how my dad taught me to make decisions. He would say, "At this point in your life, Harold, it's time for you to make this decision." He had shown confidence in me, knowing that I could make these decisions.

When I was in tenth grade, I was beginning to take advantage of my disability. I was getting other fellows involved, because they were carrying my books and were getting late to class with me. The teachers were becoming concerned. They had never experienced a disabled student in their classes, and they were concerned about putting pressure on me to get to class on time. The lateness became more and more pronounced. Two other guys and I were always horsing around somewhere just making a game of this thing. Teachers never said anything to me but would ask my buddies where they were. They would answer, "We were helping Harold at the lavatory," or give some similar excuse.

The principal finally called my dad, expressing some concern about the problem and asking what they should do about it. My dad told him he would be at school in the morning. During chores in the barn that morning, my dad said, "Harold, I'm going to be taking you to school this morning." When I inquired as to the reason, he replied, "I need to check something out."

I was still perplexed, but he just told me to get my chores done and get bathed and he would take me to school. At the school, my dad asked for a copy of my schedule. We went to the first class, which required going up a flight of stairs. I always had to take the steps from the left side because I needed to put my arm on the handrail and pull myself up one step at a time, so I would wait until the stairs were somewhat cleared before going up. We got to the first class with no problem. My dad carried my books. I don't know where my dad went between classes, since he didn't go into the class. It was pretty embarrassing, because I was a tenth-grader!

The kids asked, "What's your old man doing here?"

"Well, I'm not sure!" I replied.

The second and third classes were no problem. However, it was my fourth-period teacher who had blown the whistle on my being late. But on this particular day, we got there on time with no problem. For the fourth class I had to again go up a flight of stairs. As I got to this class, the teacher was standing outside the door. By this time, I'm hustling and sweating. My dad said, "Just take your time. Don't rush. You're getting out of wind." We were a full minute early! I stood there for a bit when my dad said to the teacher, "I've followed Harold around all morning and we haven't had any problems. I don't foresee any problems. He doesn't go to the bathroom more than anyone else, and if he does go to the bathroom he can do that just as quickly as anybody else. I see no problems. If he's late, just give me a call." I was never late again!

My dad had an instinctive sense about my wanting to be normal like everybody else. When I was a junior in high school, I was planning to go out on the town with some friends and get into some mischief. I used to get so angry with Dad because he seemed to always know when I was up to something, but I never could figure out how he knew. This particular time, one of my best friends' girlfriend left him for another guy. The guy she started dating irritated this friend of mine, so three of us decided we were going to "take care" of this fellow. We were planning to first go to a store in the town of Reading where there was a booth with a camera in which we could insert a quarter to get our pictures taken for the yearbook. I told Dad I needed the car so two buddies and I could get our pictures taken. When he asked where we needed to go and I told him, he said, "Oh! Well, I need to do some things in town also. Do you mind if I go along?"

I was in a quandary, so I said, "I don't know, Dad. You don't want to be along when we get our pictures taken, do you?"

"I don't mind that," he replied. "I can pick up what I need right next door to where you're going."

Well, I knew if I balked he would get suspicious. So that evening while doing the chores, I whistled and tried to act happy and natural as could be. I thought maybe he'd lay off, but I felt that he sensed something wasn't right. He rode in the backseat, and when I picked up my buddies everyone was speechless. The entire ride to town was quiet. Nobody said a word. When we got to the store on Penn Street, the parking spaces were all taken. We could double-park, but someone had to stay in the car. Dad said, "I'll stay with the car. You guys go on in and do your business."

When we got away from the car, my friends exclaimed, "What in the hell is your dad doing in the car!"

I said, "Look, guys! You're making it tough for me. We've got to go in and get our pictures taken; then we're going out in the car and we're going to talk, and you're going to be nice to my dad. He'll never let me go with you again if he senses anything wrong with you guys or if we're up to any monkey business. We're going home just as if this is all that we were planning to do."

However, what we really had planned was to throw several sledgehammers in the trunk of my car. We knew the girlfriend's new beau would be at her house and we knew from previous "scoutings" he always parked his car beside a corn shed. While he was in the house we were going to bash in his windows and bang up his car. We were not smart enough to keep quiet about this at school, so someone leaked our plans to this girl, who told her father. Her father called the state police, who were parked inside the corn shed waiting for us, but we never showed. When we got to school the next morning, everyone was asking what happened, why we didn't show. I was so embarrassed at the time because I had to admit that my dad was along and we could not do anything. I found out later about the state trooper stationed there waiting for us. We felt pretty lucky having escaped being arrested, and I never mentioned the incident to my dad.

By the time I was in my senior year at college, my dad and I had reached a pretty good father-son relationship—something we didn't have in my earlier years, mostly because he was always on my case about something. I felt he knew too much about me. During a weekend visit home, my dad and I were reminiscing around the kitchen table when he said, "Harold, do you remember back when you were a junior in high school when I went with you guys to get your picture taken?"

"Yeah," I replied cautiously. "What about it?"

He said, "That's bothered me all these years because I mistrusted you."

I looked at him and said, "Dad, I owe you a big thank-you for that. I want you to know you saved not only your son but two of his best friends from criminal charges." I never saw such relief on my dad's face. I gave him a hug and thanked him.

He had always felt bad about that incident because he hadn't trusted me. It was during a time when he was trying to develop a trust in me. It was hard for him and he was very strict. I was only the second child, and as more children came along he became less strict. He gave me my freedom, but he had an instinctive feeling, something I call a gut feeling. What I call my gut feeling is what guided me during my career. Students would say to me, "How do you know this? How do you figure this out?" I would say, "Well, it's my gut that tells me. That's what I grew up with. That's what my dad was to me, and now I'm being that to you. I'm just letting my gut do the talking."

When did I recognize my strong inner direction rather than following outside influences? I would say it happened during my junior year in high school. I graduated from high school in 1955. Those were the days when smoking was so common, almost everybody did it. At that time, there was no knowledge that cancer would come along as a result of it. It was just something everybody did. I was only one of three in my entire class who didn't smoke. One was a Mennonite girl; another was a boy who wanted to become a doctor.

One night when I was out with my buddies driving down Route 73 toward Boyertown—I remember it as distinctly as I sit here today—my buddies were hassling me, saying, "Get with it, Zookie. Why don't you smoke? Get with it." I had always put up with the hassling. For some reason, I just didn't want to smoke. I don't know why. Something just told me it wasn't good. It wasn't that I was afraid of it. I had tried half a cigarette. I found a cigarette butt on the road one time, lit it, and tried smoking it. I didn't like the taste of it. I had tried a bite of chewing tobacco, but I didn't like that, either. Very early in life, if I didn't like something, I just didn't do it, regardless.

My buddies were really pressuring me and I became angry. I pulled the car off to the side of the road and turned around to face them. I said, "Guys, I'm not going to smoke. I don't care how much you pressure me. I'm not going to smoke because I don't like the taste of it and I don't see the sense of it. Furthermore, I don't have the money to buy the cigarettes. If you keep pressing me on this issue, I'm going to turn around right now and drop each one of you off and that will be the end of our friendship. Either you accept me as I am or go home." I was very angry about it and that was the last we ever discussed it. They smoked; I didn't. Taking a stand against smoking was very unusual for a teenager, and I can't tell you why, but that's the way it was.

At our twenty-fifth class reunion, I was sitting with my two best high school friends and their wives. One friend was by now dependent on an oxygen tank because of severe emphysema. My other friend's wife had become very large, and I learned later that she was bloated from the medication she was taking because of lung cancer. My friend said, "My wife has lung cancer." He laid his head on the table and started to cry. He said, "Harold, why didn't you kick us in the butt years ago? There you sit, healthy.

There's our friend with emphysema and my wife's going to die with lung cancer. So far I've escaped, but I quit cold turkey when I learned my wife had lung cancer. Harold, why didn't you stop us?"

I replied, "You know, I would have liked to, but it wouldn't have worked because you weren't willing to listen."

He cried like a child. When students were brought to me for smoking in the lavs at school, I would relate this story and other stories about friends who had died of cancer to them. This was the first time I recall following my gut feelings about an issue. Maybe it's because the experience is so vivid.

I was quite timid growing up and I just kind of went with the tide. I remember coming home crying a lot of times because kids were making fun of my braces and high-top shoes, which were very unfashionable at that time. To kids, they were farmers' shoes. I clunked along in my heavy shoes and braces up to my knees. I was crying about this one evening at the dinner table, and after we finished eating, my dad took me into the living room and said, "Harold, you have to figure a way out of this. You're always going to have this disability. There's nothing you can do about it. It's not your fault. It's nobody's fault. It's how God saw to make you and you're going to have to live with that and deal with it. You can either cry about it or be a man about it. I'm going to give you some ideas of how you can handle this. You can either take my suggestions or leave them. It's your choice."

I just sat and listened. "These children," he continued, "who are doing this probably have no idea what they're doing. They probably don't even mean to hurt you, but you're allowing it to hurt you. The next time somebody does that, why don't you just stop and say, 'Look! I want to talk to you about this. I wish you wouldn't do this. There's nothing I can do to change this. My parents are doing everything they can to make life easy for me. How would you like to be in my shoes? How would it feel to you if you were me and I were you and I did to you what you just did to me?

I'd like to know how it would feel to you.' " He was telling me to explain to my tormentor how it felt to be teased.

I finally got brave enough to follow his advice one day and I was immensely shocked at the reaction. This boy said, "Gee, I'm sorry. I never thought about it. I won't do it again." That was the procedure I used from then on and it made all the difference in the world. That was exactly the strategy I used with my students in my school. I could speak from the heart and somehow kids seemed to grasp the message because I wasn't just talking about some vague idea—I had experienced it.

Harold's brother Donald describes what was expected of a person growing up in their home, which helps to explain Harold's development of character and persistence in his struggle:

"To provide some insight into how we were raised, let me tell you a story that happened to me. On our farm we raised tomatoes and carrots. The tomatoes were harvested in the late summer, and the carrots were put into storage. Christmastime was when we began taking the carrots out of storage to prepare them for the supermarkets. I hated spending Christmas vacation working with those carrots. There was one day when school was not in session, I didn't feel well; in fact, I was sick. My dad took me to the carrot shed anyway and put up a seat by the conveyor belt so I could sit down to do the job instead of standing. I felt so lousy I just passed out on the job. I was carried to the house and given the rest of the day off. It was family practice that if we had a head cold or headache, we still had to go to the barn and do our work. We surely didn't want to stay home from school, because school was more fun than staying home to work. There was no slack cut for any kind of sickness or disabilities. The attitude was, 'You feel lousy! So what! You're not falling over, so get to work!' It sounds harsh. However, as siblings, if someone was feeling under the weather, we would say, 'What's wrong with you? Are you lazy?'

"If one understands the Amish culture, which is basically the culture in which we grew up, it's easy to understand our family. You don't want to be a liar, dishonest, unreliable with your words, and you don't want to be lazy. When you work, you compete with each other. If someone can't keep up, he's laughed at. While putting hay on the elevator, the fellow putting it on the elevator would put it on as fast as he could to see if he could make the guys stacking it in the mow holler for mercy. If they couldn't keep up, they'd be ridiculed. The hay stackers might yell to the fellow at the bottom of the elevator, 'Is that all the faster you can get them up here?' In this culture of hard work, one never exhibits fatigue or weakness.

"Since Harold couldn't get onto the tractor himself, we would hoist him on so he could go to work. If he needed to get off, he would get onto the wheel and slide to the ground. Today they say kids aren't supposed to drive a tractor until they can drive a car. Well, it's a different world! I was driving a tractor when I was five years old."

Another brother, Lloyd, who at nineteen lost his hand in a farm accident, provides more insight:

"As a child, Harold was crippled, having a hard time getting around, but he had the determination to do whatever he could. I don't think my father was cruel, but rather than having a pity party, he would help us realize we can do something. I recall when Harold fell in the yard and couldn't get up. My dad taught him to crawl to a tree or fence post or something to work his way up to his feet. We all treated him as a normal person who had to learn to fend for himself. In our family, normal operations called for doing whatever work needed doing. I was always glad I was the healthy one so I could do my own thing. We always had to walk to the bus from the farm. Harold couldn't walk as fast, so to make sure he wouldn't be late, he had to start out in plenty of time. On rare occasions when Harold was a little late, the bus driver would come down the lane, pick him up, and carry him to the bus. I think we had a normal family.

"I don't know if other children teased him. I'm sure there was some teasing, but I never observed it. He was ahead of me in school. I think that most of the time his friends looked out for him, especially when he got to high school.

"Harold was always a very precise person. Caring for bees was one of his projects. He kept precise records of cost and how much money he earned. Another project was chickens and again he kept very precise records. He was a perfectionist.

"I knew there were expenses caring for Harold. Somehow my parents managed to come up with the money to pay those expenses. It never occurred to me they were spending a lot of money on him that might have been spent on the rest of the family. The thought never crossed my mind.

"I think Harold's strength of will helped him get through his operations; he was determined to survive it all. It goes back to how our dad taught him. We were raised not to tease or make fun of someone who had problems. We learned to look out for that person, to help when he needed help. Our mother was a very loving person and I think she helped us stick together. I always felt Harold had a normal childhood. While he couldn't play ball, he was involved in things he could do. He was a very social, active person, and an asset to our family. We sang together as a family and still enjoy singing."

Harold's younger brother Mervin comments, "A favorite remembrance of mine is the authority Harold exuded. It's the same authority he had with students at school. If he told me to crawl, I crawled! I didn't ask any questions. I don't think students hated him, except at the moment when he had to discipline them, but they strongly disliked him. However, they respected him highly. I never knew Harold had a disability until I was old enough to know what a disability is. In my mind, he wasn't disabled, because he could tell me to do what he couldn't do and I had to do it! It was kind of a unique thing. I knew he couldn't catch me and I knew he couldn't make me do something if I didn't want to, but when he told me to do something I just knew I had to do it. His disability surely didn't affect his mind. He was just Harold. He's probably the center of the family. Most everything we do revolves around him.

"There's a picture of Harold and me when I was about ten or twelve. He was much larger than me. If he fell, there was only one way to get him up and that was to pick him up. It didn't matter how long it took: if there was no one else around to help, I did it myself. That was the type of relationship we had. If he needed help, we gave it to him. There was no excuse. You couldn't give an excuse not to help him.

"One of the most vital ways his life has affected mine is in developing sensitivity to those who are handicapped. I see myself as a very compassionate person, and I think much of that comes from seeing what Harold has been through in his life, realizing that if someone doesn't help him he's not going to make it. It's that way with others that I see, even in teaching—kids can be cruel. I just could not tolerate kids picking on fellow students who may be helpless or weaker than they are. That's the kind of spirit I developed through our relationship. For example, I never saw him run and he seldom went barefoot. One day he wanted to go barefoot and to walk across the gravel lane. There was no way he could walk across those stones until we figured out that if we laid a carpet down, he could walk barefoot across the lane! And that's what we did—just so he could experience going barefoot. That's the kind of sensitivity I developed from living with him.

"There was never a thought about the expenses incurred with Harold's medical care. My dad never would have said, 'We must pay for Harold's medical expenses, therefore we don't have money for other things.' It would never happen. When Lloyd lost his arm in a farm accident, Dad bought him a farm with his workman's compensation money. Now, that's an investment! Dad did what was needed for each of us. There was never a question of whether one got more than another.

"I think Harold developed strength to withstand all his surgeries because our dad never treated him differently because of his disability. Dad never protected him. He realized from a very early time that he had to stand on his own. Our mother also had a great influence on him, since she was disabled as well, suffering with multiple sclerosis. We saw her fighting to maintain a normal life. He seemed to realize from a very early age that if he didn't do everything he could to delay deterioration, it would come much faster. One memory I had was at school when he was in his administrative years and he refused to ride his wheelchair until he absolutely could not walk. He would ride to his office on his cart, then get out of his cart and sit on his desk chair. I have watched him get up out of his desk chair and it would take him a full minute just to stand up. Watching him made me think that if I were in his place, I would say, 'It's not worth it.' I felt I didn't have his determination. I asked him why he didn't stay in his cart. He said he thought the students would make fun of him. I told him people don't make fun of people who can't walk. I think it was his way of saying, 'I'm not giving up until I have no other choice.' Where he got that strength I don't know, unless it's what Dad taught him—that if you don't do it for yourself, no one's going to do it for you."

Harold's older sister Ruth shares her impressions:

"I never thought of Harold as being any different from any of my other siblings. He was handicapped, but he was treated no differently from the rest of us. We were all expected to pull our fair share. I am fifteen months older than Harold, and there are four years between Harold and the next brother, so Harold and I were like two peas in a pod. I remember as a toddler when he fell I would just pick him up, but to me he was never handicapped. Sometimes other children would make fun of him and my defensive ire would come up strong. It's still a pet peeve of mine to see a person with a handicap being mistreated. As a school bus driver, if I ever saw a child making fun of any other child for any reason, I would intervene, telling them about my brother and my relationship to him. I felt very protective of Harold when we were children.

"I remember after earlier surgeries when he came home from the hospital in casts up to his hips with only his toes sticking out. It was very painful because his ligaments and tendons were cut and being stretched in the backs of his legs. Periodically these would be stretched more and more. We could hear him moaning at night when we were trying to sleep. Those years were awful. But Harold was determined to live as normally as anyone else, which made it easier for us, too, because we never gave it a thought that he was disabled. He was no different from us. We just accepted him as part of our family. It was difficult at times growing up, especially when we were playing softball or football. However, since he couldn't run, he would keep score. He would participate however he could.

"While growing up, each of us children was encouraged to have a faith; there was a special purpose for each one of us. There was a very strong circle of family activities and my dad had high expectations for each of us. The combination of a strong faith, a sense of purpose, and high expectations instilled in Harold a positive attitude. Harold was born with a strong spirit to succeed and make his fair contribution to his family and to society. His faith had a lot to do with his self-motivation. We never used the word *handicap* in our family; we didn't know the meaning of the word.

"We had a quarter-mile lane to walk to the bus. Many times Harold would fall before getting to the end of the lane, so we would pick him up and get him on his feet again. We had the very best bus driver there ever was, because many times he would get off the bus, come down the lane to meet us, put Harold on his back, and take him the rest of the way. When Harold got too heavy to carry, the driver made a little footstool to make it easier for Harold to get on the bus.

"We never dared use the word *bored*. Being lazy wasn't part of our lifestyle, either. We learned we didn't play 'hooky,' because our parents soon learned we weren't really sick and we were put to work. We eventually learned it was easier to go to school than to stay at home and work hard. There was never a bottle of aspirin in the house. If we were sick, we were told to go to bed and sleep it off. We went to bed and stayed there until we felt better. Even when we were sick and stayed home, we had to work, so we would often go to school even though we were sick. I feel that as I have been a sister to Harold he has been an inspiration to me and to our whole family. I just thank the Lord for this privilege."

Harold's favorite cousin, Grant, has great memories of their childhood:

"I always felt like we were brothers. For the first four or five years we lived in two apartments in the same building; then we lived on the same farm for a few years. We've been together all our lives, working and playing together. We never treated him as a handicapped person; we always included him in everything we did. Even when we played baseball we gave him the bat to hit the ball; then we pushed him around the bases on his wheelchair. He was one of us like everyone else. His disability probably brought us closer together. When he fell or needed help, I was there to help him. Both Harold and I recall times when he would fall and I would try to pick him up. We would have our bellies against each other, and since Harold was a little taller than I was, I had to struggle to get him up. We would get a laughing fit and would both fall down. We would say, 'We have to get serious now.' But the more we tried, the more we would laugh. I would almost get Harold up when one of us would pass gas or something, so we would laugh and fall over again and need to wait until we got serious enough to finally get him up.

"One time we were catching sheep by lassoing them with a rope. When the rope got so tight it almost strangled the sheep, we were really scared until we finally managed to get the rope loose enough to get it off the sheep. There was this one certain place in the lawn where there was muddy water and green fungus, and his mother had just put some freshly washed sheets on the line to dry. We decided we were going to do mud art. The sheets looked so beautiful with the green fungus and brown mud. I don't know from where his mother came, but she must have been wearing a three-foot yardstick like a soldier wears a sword. I learned to know what a yardstick was—three things: it had three feet, exactly thirty-six inches, which we never forgot, and it had something in common with the Ten Commandments—they were both broken.

"Another time, we wanted to be so kind and helpful to my dad. He had just bought a 1937 Chevrolet business coupe, one of those with the long trunk and just one seat inside. My dad was so proud of the '37 Chevy. He had just polished it and it looked just beautiful. Harold and I got the notion that we were going to make it look pretty, too. So, just like my dad, we got this can and rags. You have to remember this was back in about '43, so we were about five or six years old, and since we were short guys, to get the roof we had to climb on the car. We polished the whole car, including the windows. When my dad saw this 'beautiful' job, he was just furious. Harold and I had used axle grease! We thought we were doing a good deed.

"Once we decided to make baked potatoes. We built a little fireplace using eight-inch concrete blocks with a screen over it, then wondered how to light the fire. I said I knew how to light it since I had seen my dad using gasoline to light fires. I got a quart of gasoline and dumped the whole quart on the leaves and wood. We were lucky enough to be lying on our bellies. The explosion blew the screen about twenty feet up into a walnut tree. We were a little on the naughty side. We never told our parents about that. These are only a few of the episodes we got into. I just saw him as my cousin—one of us. One of the things that has made him stronger is that we always treated him no differently from anyone else. In his mind he didn't have a handicap. He felt like one of the guys.

"All his life, Harold was determined to do things. It gave me determination also. He contributed a positive and upbeat attitude to us as a family. He also helped a lot of people in the school where he taught and worked. To this day on construction sites when people hear my name is Zook, they ask if I'm related to Mr. Zook who was at Indian Valley Middle School. When I tell them I am, they relate how he helped them with many problems.

"When times were difficult, Harold had help from everyone. He had a lot of motivation because he is a Christian. Also, he learned from his dad that he wasn't going to get more help than he absolutely needed but would have to learn how to help himself. He could understand what was happening to the children at school. He sometimes used his handicapped body to show people what they might be if they continued on the wrong way."

Some of the comments by fellow students at the close of Harold's senior year of high school indicate who he was becoming:

Enjoys a good joke.
Your smile will always help you. Thanks for the asset.
I certainly admire your cheerfulness and optimistic view of life.
You've been a great asset to our class.
Your cheerfulness has been an inspiration.
You're a capable public speaker.
You've been a great challenge to the whole school.

Harold's experience growing up shaped his character, outlook on life, and his response to his disability. It greatly influenced the remainder of his life.

3

A Caring Family

Harold's five brothers and two sisters and their children mean much to him. All of his siblings except his sister Ruth live within a forty-minute drive from his home. His nieces and nephews were the nearest he came to having children of his own. On the corner of his father's farm, he built a house with a finished basement that accommodates family gatherings. He was able to provide a home for his mother and father during their final years. His parents' wish was to die at home and Harold made certain their desire was granted.

His older sister Ruth says, "I always thought of Harold as being very optimistic, very courageous, and one who loved life. He's a good, good brother—my soul mate and a good role model for me. I thought of him as having wisdom. My three children were his children. There were times when they would call him for advice. Sometimes they felt more comfortable talking to him than to either their father or me. We were always comfortable with that because we felt he was a good role model for them. Our kids always had a lot of admiration for Harold. Our one daughter who isn't married said she never wanted to be a parent, but she wants to be a special aunt to the children of her siblings just like Harold was a special uncle to her.

"Harold was always willing to do whatever he could physically do for anyone in the community. They always appreciated his selflessness. He has a good reputation in the community and church. He refurbished the little chapel at Saint Michael's Evangelical Lutheran Church. It's a beautiful little chapel with one of the paintings dedicated to Mother and Daddy.

"Harold is a man of integrity, optimistic, grateful, and a perfectionist. I understand his perfectionism because I'm one, too. There's only one way of doing it. Let's do it right. What gave him the strength to persevere is the faith he had in himself and his love for Mother and Daddy. He never wanted to disappoint them. They made possible his education and he never took that for granted, repaying them in many, many ways. We never doubted Harold would be a success. Even though Mother had a disability, she never gave up. She had a lot of self-motivation and was also a perfectionist. We're all pretty much go-getters.

"Harold never thought of himself; he thought of others, which was very evident by the many people who attended his retirement dinner. I remember the administrators saying they wouldn't let him retire but would bring him back on a stretcher. There were many students with problems whose lives he touched. At his retirement he handed out a card with the poem 'Others' by which he lived. [See the beginning of chapter 5.] None of us had ever seen that poem until his retirement dinner. Everyone who knows him knows that's how he lived."

A brother, Kenneth, remarks, "Harold's not the only one in the family who is handicapped. My brother Lloyd lost his left arm in a corn picker when he was nineteen years of age. At that time our dad helped him buy a farm across the road from our home farm and now he owns four farms—about five hundred acres in all. He does everything anyone else does, except button his shirt sleeves. He uses that arm, cut off just below his elbow, to do about everything. He even steers the tractor with it. He has a prosthesis that he wears for dress. He had a hook for a while, but he says it gets in his way. He used to load tomatoes. If there was any way he could do it, he would. That's just the way it was. Dad wasn't cruel, but he didn't give any pity. We were much better off for it.

"Harold is a brother just like the rest of us. We have great times together. We stick together. He's just one of us. We've taken several trips to Indiana together—just the six brothers. This last time, we took his van so we could take his wheelchair. I know he's handicapped, but I don't think of him as such. To me he's a whole person. He's never a burden to any of us. It's pretty neat, actually. Sometimes at night when his nurse doesn't show up, I'll put him to bed and spend the night with him because he can't be left alone. He's very much a part of our family. We're all together at holidays—Easter, Thanksgiving, and Christmas. We gather at his house because it's easier for him. This house was built for that when Mom and Dad were still living. There are about thirty or thirty-five of us, so the large room in his basement accommodates all of us. It's wonderful to have such a large family."

One of Harold's nieces, Elizabeth, writes:

Uncle Harold is what I have always called you because of our blood relation, but there are so many things that you have been to me throughout my life. You have been a mentor and a special friend. On Sweetest Day you are my sweetheart. On Valentine's Day you are my valentine. You are my knight in shining armor. You are my prince. To me you have always portrayed what every man should be.

Having been fortunate enough to have you in my life, I carry with me many fond memories of our times spent together. I'll never forget how special you made my sixteenth birthday, my high school graduation, and all those quiet weekends we spent together. I smile when I think of us sitting at the kitchen counter quietly reading or talking about the places we would like to have traveled together, like Africa, to go on an African safari. Instead, we would curl up together on your lowboy chair and watch hours of *National Geographic* specials. To this day, I still recall all those hours spent with you when we did nothing more than enjoy each other's company.

Of the earthly possessions I have acquired over the years, two of my most treasured gifts have been from you. The first is *The*

Prophet. The second is *The Snow Goose.* Both books will always have a special meaning to me. Of all the gifts from you, the best is, you have given of yourself to me. I will forever carry you with me in my thoughts and heart.

Love always, Elizabeth

Harold's sister Ruth comments, "Today as I was thinking of you, Harold, I was and am again reminded of the beauty of your life. Your quiet ways, your gentleness and concern when you sense a need in others, your ability to stand by someone, giving support and encouragement. The blessing you are and have been to all of us and especially what a very special uncle you've been to Gene, Beth, and Tricia. How special and fun you made their sixteenth birthdays, their graduation from high school and college, and all the other times you have been a special part of us!"

Cousin Grant and his wife Lorraine write:

What an accomplishment you have achieved. . . . The contribution you have made to Indian Valley Middle School is phenomenal by helping to educate young people and encourage them to follow their dream—even those who had no dream. You helped to give them one. It was a pleasure and an honor to be able to gather all the testimonies and memories of the many lives you have touched so deeply. It was a blessing to us to hear so many people react so positively to any one person. However, it breaks our hearts to see you physically struggle as you do, but you have turned these hardships into a powerful tool to help others, especially me. What an unselfish gift.

In spite of everything, you have maintained a sense of humor which obviously strengthens a relationship. Grant loves to reminisce about the "good old days" when the two of you were young and naughty. We wish for your retirement to be filled with experiences in new and exciting territory that you never had time to explore before. We hope to always remain part of your life. You are our "hero!"

All our love and admiration,
Grant & Lorraine

Harold remembers: When I was ten years old we had an old wheelchair with a cane seat. My cousin Grant would push the chair to the top of the barn hill. I would sit in the seat, and with Grant standing on a little platform on the back of the chair we would go flying down the hill for a big thrill. Once when we hit a bump, I fell off and broke my casts, so my mother had to take me back to the doctor to have them repaired.

Niece, Trish, Ruth's youngest daughter, writes: "Uncle Boo, there are things we are given in this life which can only be described as unmerited gifts from God—a relationship with you is one such blessing. . . ."

Harold has a keen sense of humor, which shows as he describes how he came to be called Uncle Boo.

There's a story about "Uncle Boo." I had a habit of scaring people. I think I did it to every one of my nurses one way or another. Trish had gone to the bathroom and when she came out I was by the door, so I said, "Boo!"

Trish said, "Uncle Harold, sometime I am going to get you. I guarantee it!"

During another visit, when I heard her coming to my bedroom, I pretended to be asleep. I could hear her say to her boyfriend, Chad, "I'm going to tiptoe to his bed and give a bloodcurdling scream." She came tiptoeing to my bedside and gave the loudest scream, but I didn't even flinch. I lay there quietly. She did it again, but I still didn't flinch. Since my back was turned, she said to Chad, "Something is wrong with him. Go around and check."

"No, you go," he said.

They both came around cautiously, thinking I must be dead. There wasn't much space between the bed and the wall, so they had to get very close. I held my breath, pretending I wasn't breathing.

Trish was very concerned. "He's not breathing, Chad. Something's wrong. Touch him to see if he's cold."

"No, you do!" said Chad. "Trish, you've got to check. Something's wrong."

As she touched my hand, I said, "Boo!"

And they hit the wall, knocking the picture down. "You will be Uncle Boo from now on!" declared Trish. Now all the nieces and nephews and their children call me Uncle Boo!

On another occasion, Trish and her now-fiancé Chad, a graduate of the Naval Academy, were coming for a visit. Chad wasn't a Christian, but Trish kept taking him to church and now he's a church elder and they are very happily married. During their first visit after they became engaged, I stretched a big banner across the driveway that said, "CONGRATULATIONS" in big letters.

The reason they came to visit me was because Chad knew I was very possessive of my nieces and I had talked to them a lot about life, character, and womanhood. Trish and Chad were high school sweethearts and he was afraid I wouldn't approve of him. He knew I wanted the perfect guy for Trish. One day they called to say they wanted to visit me. I took them out to a real nice restaurant, and during dinner Chad said, "Uncle Harold, I know how much you love Trish. I love her too, and I really want to marry her, but I don't think it's right to do so until I have your approval." He continued to say he would always love her; would never mistreat her, and would never leave her. He assured me he would be a top-notch husband. Then he asked me if I would give my endorsement to the marriage, which I did, and it's a great marriage today.

Their little boy was a miracle. When Trish was pregnant with him, the doctors wanted her to abort him. They said there was a big spot on his head, he would have Down's Syndrome, and his life wouldn't be very long. Before Trish was married, we had spent hours talking about why I didn't get married. She couldn't understand why a woman wouldn't accept me with my disability, and I would explain to her that I wouldn't want to be responsible for bringing a handicapped child into the world. This was her second pregnancy and the baby wasn't developing normally.

She and Chad were devastated. She said she didn't believe in abortions, but she didn't know what to do. The doctors kept telling her the spot was growing on the brain. After a struggle, she and Chad decided they would have this baby regardless of what happened. They would love this baby even if the baby lived only a short time. There were prayer chains all over Pennsylvania and Indiana, anywhere there was a friend. A month later Trish was examined again and the spot was gone. Their son, now in fourth grade, is perfectly normal, with no defects at all—a bright young man.

Trish's sister and Harold's oldest niece Elizabeth describes her uncle and their relationship, "As he never had children of his own, Uncle Harold's nieces and nephews were his children. I always felt really special, as though Uncle Harold was my surrogate dad. I could always tell him things that I couldn't even tell my own parents. He wasn't my dad, so he didn't judge me like my own dad may have. He was always available and there was nothing I couldn't tell him that would make him love me less. That was pretty special and it continues to be that way. When I was in high school, he paid for my air ticket to come to visit him for our own special weekend. We enjoyed being together even though we weren't always talking, although when we did talk, it was always something special. I felt he was my prince in shining armor, ready to come to my rescue if necessary. When my siblings came along, our relationship changed a little, but when I was in high school, we corresponded every week. I had an uncle who was my pen pal, and I still have him.

"Because of his disability, he never wanted to burden anyone by getting married. He didn't want to limit anybody. Because of that, I felt like I was incredibly special to Uncle Harold, and I still am. I feel I'm as close to his having a child as possible. Many of his students at school felt the same way.

"As an adult, I see Harold as having given so much to his

family, his school, and his community. He was willing to do anything to make things better for people and he still does. He has taught me a lot of things, including that we all make mistakes, but it's how we handle those mistakes that shows one's true character. He has taught that to a lot of people. He also taught me the love for books. He gave me *The Prophet* when I graduated from high school. *The Snow Goose* also made a great impression on me because the story is very relevant to Harold's life. It's a story of a little girl who went to the home of a disfigured man who had a bird sanctuary. The little girl learned there was much more to the man, because he cared for injured birds until they were ready to be released. Harold related to the man's disfigurement because he felt that people's first impression of him would be his physical appearance, but when they learned to know him they would realize there was so much more to him. Just as the man healed the birds, that's what Harold did with many students. They came to him crippled emotionally, and he took them in, healed them, and then released them into the world. He has done incredible things for me and for others. I see him as someone who looks for other people that have bigger disabilities than he has, not on the outside, but on the inside.

"Harold has contributed so much to my family. For several Christmases we convinced him to fly to Florida to spend Christmas with our family. He couldn't go on the sand very much, but we played cards, laughed, and had wonderful fun. He watched the sunset from the veranda every night. Harold has been a significant part of the lives of all his nieces and nephews. My brother, Gene, spent a summer with him before he went to Europe. Harold and my mother, Ruth, have a very special relationship. I can't imagine our life without Uncle Harold. He is unique, one of a kind, and the most giving person I've ever known. I don't think the school system or anybody's life he's ever touched will be the same because of him. To know him is to love him.

"The love and support of his family helped him when he was younger. He has a strong will to achieve and to make a difference in the world, which I believe has helped him overcome all his difficulties. There were people in his life who encouraged him. Probably his strong will—his Amish will—never allowed him to quit. The people with whom he has surrounded himself have made a great difference to Harold. All the love he has given returns to him."

Harold's brother Kenneth comments on their growing-up years, "Harold didn't do quite everything the rest of us did, but he did more than most people would have done with his disability. In our family, everybody carried his or her own weight. I remember when we were just six or seven years old we were out in the tomato fields pulling weeds. Harold seldom did that because he couldn't walk in the fields. He would drive the tractors and haul the tomatoes to Philadelphia and Camden, New Jersey. We'd hoist him in the truck or onto the tractor and he would do everything he was capable of doing. He couldn't get on the tractor himself. Whoever was around would just get under him and hoist him up and off he'd go. When he needed to get off, we'd help him. He wasn't nearly as disabled then as he is now. I don't think he could ever run and he couldn't climb very well, but he could walk.

"I don't remember playing games. I think all of our games were work. We didn't have much time to play around. Sometimes we would run down to the creek and go for a swim, but I can't recall Harold ever swimming. We would play baseball on the lawn, but he wasn't able to do that. We usually worked from sunup to sundown.

"I have no idea how much money was spent on Harold's medical care. It was never an issue. It wasn't even a concern. My parents did what was necessary as they would have done for any of us children. He went off to college when I was pretty young. I remember the surgeries he had to try to correct the problems in his feet. He went through a lot of aggravation and pain to try to better himself, but it didn't help too much.

"When I was a teenager, I did exercises with him on an exercise table, which was rather strenuous for him. It was a stretching exercise to stretch his muscles to try to make them extend more. He never complained when we would push hard. He still does exercises to keep himself loosened up. What would be a small movement for us we can't even get from him. We would push his arms and legs really hard. I don't know if it was painful for him, but he never complained, even when we pushed as hard as we could. He had a lot of resilience. Pain didn't seem to stop him; it didn't matter if it hurt; that's the way we were brought up—you did what you had to do. His muscles didn't extend very far, maybe about one-fourth of what a normal person's muscles would do. He couldn't get his hand to the top of his head. Over the years his ligaments and tendons kept getting tighter and tighter.

"I'm sure when driving a truck or tractor he compensated. He drove a car until a few years ago. He had a hoist in the garage to help him get out of the car. He operated that hoist himself until recent years. There were no adaptations in the car. It had to be his car, though. The car had to be big enough for him to get in and out of—such as his Lincoln Continentals. I don't think he could have turned quickly, such as to try to avoid an accident. He always compensated by giving himself plenty of time. I don't believe he ever had an accident.

"I don't know the details of this, but one time when he was driving out west to visit our sister he leaned over to get something on the seat and fell over. He had his car on cruise control. Before he righted himself, the car was down in the center of the grass medial strip. He just drove right back onto the road and kept going. He didn't know what was going to happen, but he kept his cool and got himself out of the predicament.

"I don't know how he managed to drive those tomato trucks to Camden, New Jersey. He must not have gotten out of the truck there. Maybe they knew him and waited for him down there and helped him; I don't know. He took lots and lots of tomatoes down there all by himself. That was before Route Four-twenty-two was built. He drove down Route Seventy-three, through Skippack, through Philadelphia, right across the Ben Franklin Bridge, right into Camden, New Jersey. That was great. He couldn't help load here at the farm, so he was the hauler. He made one trip right after another, often three trips a day. As soon as he got back, we'd load him up again and off he'd go. We did that a lot of times. These weren't tractor-trailer trucks, but they were large, holding about three to four hundred baskets of tomatoes—tons of them! I don't know how he managed, but he was well taken care of wherever he went. People knew him and looked out for him. He could move around much better then than he can now. He moved his legs with his whole body. Over the years he kept getting more and more handicapped because of the degeneration of his muscles. When Harold was very young his bedroom was upstairs, but his bedroom was later moved downstairs because he could no longer walk up and down the stairs.

"In thinking of his last operation, we know that death will happen sooner or later. We're amazed he's still here. All that would need to happen would be for him to get sick; he could die in a day. That ventilator is so precarious. If he would choke, he'd be finished just like that unless someone would know what to do and do it quickly. We're aware of that. I guess the hardest part for me, since I am his legal power of attorney, is that he had signed a living will. When he was in the hospital, we had to decide whether he would be put on a ventilator or die. Fortunately for me, he was able to make the decision. He had to have a tracheotomy then. As a family, we encouraged him to go for it—to live, even though his living will specified not using life support. We saw right away how much better he was when he got oxygen. He should probably have experienced some brain damage, because he was so near dead. It is unbelievable that he is alive. His carbon dioxide level in his blood was up high enough to kill him. He was rescued in the nick of time, and when he received oxygen, he recovered rather quickly. He's in much better shape now than before he was placed on a ventilator. He was simply running out of air. He was unable to breathe well. It happened so gradually we didn't notice. He was becoming delirious because he was running out of oxygen. That's when we took him to the hospital.

"After receiving oxygen, he was able to think, to reason and make decisions. The decision to live was tough for him since he knew the restrictions he would be on. Twenty-four-hour care is extremely costly, but my feeling—and I think the rest of the family feels the same way—is that in a large family, the older generation contributes a great deal without knowing it.

"I don't think our children realize how privileged they are to be in a family that's so large. We can do anything. We can play a full game of basketball, softball—anything—because there are enough of us. We sing and do all kinds of things. I look at it that it's worth having him around for what he contributes to our children—his nieces and nephews. It is doing our daughter, Julie, a tremendous amount of good to be here as one of his caregivers. She is growing and maturing so much because of her experience taking care of him.

"There is so much potential for infection; even with all this technology, there are so many things that could go wrong, but he's very astute, very precise and particular. He's very regimented, doing everything every day that has to be done. He keeps a log on all his statistics, the oxygen level in his blood, his blood pressure, et cetera. He does everything right! I think that's his specialty. Even as an administrator, he was very detailed in all his work. That's why he's here in such good shape.

"One of the problems he had at first was with sores from sitting all the time. These sores can bring real difficulties if they're not treated. He worked at that until he got it figured out so it wasn't a problem anymore, but it took a lot of nursing care and a lot of detail and precise following through. That was very important for him since he's in that chair or in the bed twenty-four hours a day.

He's truly amazing and it's great for the rest of the family to experience this.

"Harold does the neatest things, such as when the kids go off to college he sends care packages, like a big can of popcorn, cards, and remembers their birthdays. They really appreciate that. It's not that they appreciate the rest of us less for not doing it. We're his family, so he takes care of all the grandchildren, and they love it. They stop in at his home to see him. We would have missed a lot if we had made a quick judgment about him living or dying. Sometimes we are too quick to make a decision without understanding the ramifications of the decision. The Lord's been good to us. I live on the home farm, which is such a privilege. As far as I know, there's no sibling rivalry. There are no secrets, no hard feelings that I know of. Everyone can come around anytime, do whatever they want—it's a great thing."

Harold's cousin John's wife Priscilla says: "Harold's disability made me stronger." *His cousin John says:* "I was impressed with how Harold's dad helped him in so many ways—or how he didn't help him. Harold was taught to do as much for himself as possible. His dad had a lot of influence, but so did his mother. Harold was very close to his mother. My family visited his family a lot. His mother was always very considerate and kind and Harold learned from her. It seemed like Harold was able to deal with a lot of pain. I think the support of his parents helped him learn to handle the pain. When he was down, the whole family supported him. The time he was in the hospital with bone surgery following graduation from college, I couldn't believe anyone could take that kind of pain. I was always scared of pain, but that helped me learn to conquer my fear.

"Harold has a very strong constitution. I don't think I've ever seen anyone in a wheelchair with as much ambition and courage as he has. That gives me courage. He has a very kind heart that extends out to a lot of people. His faith in God and his family give him great courage. While there have been heartaches in the family, they always pulled together. I've never seen Harold really down, except when he was doped up in the hospital. He was the kind of person to whom I was always drawn, and we were very good friends for many years. He and I were both very serious and there wasn't much joking. I always pitied him, although I shouldn't have. I built the house in which he now lives. Harold always liked helping with whatever I was doing. Harold has a lot of influence on all the people he meets. I've always appreciated Harold."

Harold's brother Mervin says, "Because of Harold's disability, even at this point, what I treasure most is our close family ties. We get together periodically throughout the year, usually at his home. Harold always enjoys singing. When Mother was ill and two or three of us were together, we would sing for Mother. When our father died, that stopped. Harold mentioned that he missed our gatherings, so we began doing it again, and it is so valuable to us. Harold has pulled us together, probably because he can't get around as well as the rest of us can. It binds us together. When Mother was ill, I came periodically to care for her. When Harold needs help, I care for him. If the time should come that his money runs out and he needs help, we will all help him. I think this has influenced me to go into nursing at this time in my life."

Harold's younger brother Omar tells about his relationship with Harold:

"I don't have many memories of Harold growing up since he was gone by the time I came along. There is thirteen years' difference in our ages. My earliest memory of Harold was being on the porch with him and using an unacceptable word. He told my mother, who took me to the bathroom, where she washed my mouth out with Lava soap. We learned that life was pretty harsh when we stepped out of line.

"Harold took a special interest in me. I recall him taking me around every week to deliver the newspaper, the *Grit*, to about twenty-five or thirty customers. He helped me to initially develop the route by going door-to-door to get customers for my route. The paper route gave me an opportunity to earn money and learn how to take care of it. When we had fund-raisers at school, such as a candy sale, Harold took the time to take me door-to-door to sell candy, even though he was very busy with chores around the farm. This helped develop a very special relationship with him. If his disability made any difference, it may have been that he had more time to spend with me. I don't think his disability made any real difference in our family relationship. I saw him as a caring sibling, someone to whom I looked up. I appreciated the interest he showed in me.

"Harold was somewhat of a father figure to us younger siblings. He always had a caring heart, willing to invest extra time in us, much like my sister Ruth, the oldest in the family, was like a second mother. My mother was ill much of my life. By the time I was a teenager, I remember helping her in the garden to relieve some of her work. By the time I was in high school, she had to work in the garden on her hands and knees. Later she needed something to help her balance when she tried to walk. My mother's dealing with multiple sclerosis made a great impact on our family. I believe that's where Harold gets some of his determination and sensitivity.

"I know Harold invested a tremendous amount of time, energy, and his heart in his career. There's where his handicap made a big impact on a lot of people. He gave a lot of effort in bringing resolution to a lot of problems. He made a tremendous contribution to the school and through the school to the community. He pulled in community resources such as police to help fulfill his responsibility to the school.

"Harold's character is strong, resolved, straightforward; he doesn't pull any punches—what you see is what you get. He has a strong emotional commitment and fortitude, with a great strength of the inner person. He's resolute, directed, and self-initiated, with a clear sense of purpose and sense of mission. I think the family has had a large impact on giving him strength to persevere. He credits his parents in helping him not to use his handicap to get by but to overcome it. When he went to college, he was very overwhelmed and wanted to return home, but Dad wouldn't allow it. That illustrates how Dad responded, and it resulted in Harold internalizing the determination and strength. The same principle was instilled in all of us from childhood. Harold's faith was a very strong component, and by the time he became a young adult, his faith was something that was very deep, very personal, and very strong. I think that helped him derive a sense of higher purpose and mission in life.

"Harold had the ability to make friends. He always had a special close friend or two or three from whom he derived a lot of support, strength, and encouragement. He had a special relationship with his cousin Grant, with whom he did many things. Harold was very active in our Mennonite Youth Fellowship, at one time serving as president of the organization. I believe Harold's faith guided him. Helping people energized him. Even when I was a young boy, he was helping his younger siblings. Later that translated into helping students and others in his professional career.

"Harold lived to serve God by serving others. That in a nutshell explains how Harold lived. Harold told me once he was very concerned about me and that I might have some serious problems. He thought I might need psychiatric help. It's rather ironic, because that's the profession into which I've gone. I grew up much like Harold, with a passion to help other people. It was in my college days that I developed a clear sense of calling to help others."

Harold talks about his niece Julie, who helps with his care: Before I went to Saint Joseph's Hospital two years ago, my legs had become so swollen I could hardly walk with crutches anymore, so I asked a therapist to come to my home to assess the situation. She immediately was frightened by what she saw, immediately asking me to go to the Reading Rehabilitation Center for hospitalization to learn how to deal with my legs. I said, "I can't do that because I am helping take care of my father." Several days later, I went for a week to the hospital, where a very skilled therapist knew a technique she had learned in Germany that involved wrapping my legs. I also needed range-of-motion therapy, which Julie learned as well as the leg wraps. Julie learned all this when she was only fifteen years old and has continued helping me for five years.

The therapists were amazed at Julie's skills and abilities. She became a perfectionist and is now training my nurses to do the leg wraps and range-of-motion exercises. She has been a very important part of my life.

Julie comments, "It's hard to put into words how I feel about Harold. I'm so proud of him because I remember how much he parallels the main character in the movie *Mr. Holland's Opus*. I would tell my friends that my Uncle Harold is handicapped, but I always made sure they knew he wasn't handicapped mentally. He's probably the most generous person I know. He's always kind and thoughtful, doing such things as sending a mug with flowers to his nurses on Nurse's Day.

"I feel I've learned to know him more by working with him. He's very much a perfectionist, which gets on my nerves sometimes, but other times I think he's so healthy because he is so organized. He gets a lot of things done and he's right most of the time, probably more often than I would like to admit. He really loves and appreciates his family. I know that because the reason he chose to live was his nieces and nephews, to whom he gives a lot. It's easy to see how proud he is of me even though I feel he overestimates my abilities sometimes.

"He lives a very normal life; like the other day we went to a volleyball game. He had two of his nurses drive him six hours to attend my brother's wedding. As a boss he is very generous, and as an uncle he cares about me and my future. I have been considering taking some missionary trips about which I am very fearful. He asked me what was keeping me from doing it. He told me if I chose to go and money was stopping me from going, he would pay for the trip. He always believes in me and my abilities. He thinks I would be a great nurse. He has made a definite impression on my life. From Uncle Harold I have learned a lot of patience, among many other things. A lot of my interactions the last few years have been because I work for him.

"My uncle's resources are our resources; for example, several days ago I needed an encyclopedia, so I used his. If I need a computer, his is available to me. He is a very special uncle to me because of the time and energy he puts into me. He invited my brother and his wife to his house for a chicken barbecue. He taught me how to garden and cook since I started to work for him."

Harold says: After I retired, I spent time writing to my nieces and nephews. I felt I had neglected them in the latter part of my career. I made some contacts with them, mostly through letters. That went on as usual with the family. I don't recall that I did that much. We felt it was important as siblings for us to get together once a year in an effort to bond. The first time we got together it was such a tremendously valuable experience for all of us. We cried together, we reminisced together, we fellowshiped together—we did all those things. It was especially meaningful to my sister Ruth because we went to Indiana; she had less contact with us than we did with those who live close by. I can't recall doing very much other than taking care of my father.

Harold's cousin's wife Lorraine comments, "I first learned to know Harold through my husband Grant when we started dating forty-two and a half years ago. I was always so touched and impressed with Harold's attitude and felt so challenged by him. He never seemed to consider himself disabled. That was a testimony to me. His determination was something that meant a lot to me. I suffered from migraine headaches and I looked to him as a role model in perseverance. I saw him as a very strong, happy person, never feeling sorry for himself. He had more strength and character than most people who don't have to fight the many challenges he had. In my challenge with pain, he contributed a very positive attitude; a real inspiration to me. I have never seen a family that worked so closely together with his best interests at heart. They have stuck together and were so supportive, with Harold being the strength of the family."

Georganne, the nurse who worked with him and his father prior to and following his last hospitalization, describes Harold's larger family, possibly his third family, after his blood family and his school family:

"I took care of Harold's father for four years and have taken care of Harold for two years. Harold has a very strong, stable character. He has a way of being steadfast, yet he is laid back, listens to everything, thus getting the whole picture. He is such a unique human being, very religious, caring, understanding, and always wants to put the other person first.

"Harold's relationship with his caretakers is one of gratefulness. We didn't realize how sick he was. When he was at death's door, he let go and went with it. At some point in the hospital, he realized he was alive and made the conscious decision of 'I'm alive and if I'm alive after all I just went through, I'm going to go with it to the end.' He persevered through everything that had to be done for him to breathe and to maintain life. When all the caregivers came into the picture, it was amazing how much training took place in the home. Harold retained all that knowledge and communicated it to his caregivers. He was always so grateful and happy to get his care under control.

"Harold had this steadfast way of making me feel so cared for in his presence. He was able to teach me how to care for him, which made me feel really great, to know exactly what to do. I had worked in an intensive-care unit, but I had forgotten some of my skills regarding respiratory care and I was a little nervous to take care of Harold. He reassured me that he trusted me, that I had the capability required for his care. He was so patient and kind, which brought back my self-confidence. Harold cares for my family and what is going on in my family. Many, many times my family comes to his home and it's amazing how with a normal conversation he can solve a problem. My family has become part of his family.

"I feel Harold's family has helped him persevere. At one point when he felt death was an option, he made a conscious decision to live for members of his family. He has been conquering his disabilities for a long, long time. I think he felt he was just going to make the best of things. He learned that if he could go into a room with a positive attitude and a smile on his face, the disability disappeared and people related to him as a normal person with so much to offer. There are many nurses caring for Harold who have a personal problem, and when they come to work Harold has this way of being so dependable that he cares for them as much as they care for him. I don't know if he is aware of it, but he must know that his positive attitude comes back to him. I think he knows that living this way is the best. He says people give him a great attitude, but it's really he who gives others the great attitude. It's a great circle of love.

"I believe God has given him the strength to accomplish the things he did. At all times Harold goes back to his faith. He thinks of things in a godly manner. He never, ever preaches; he doesn't have to. His faith is just there reflected in all aspects of his life. He never acts in a 'holier than thou' manner; he just lives it.

"Harold cared for both his parents during their final years. The last years of Omar's life, Harold's father, were difficult. Omar suffered from some form of dementia. Harold was raised in a very strict, religious home, and it was very difficult for Harold to see his father using inappropriate language. Harold would say, 'Dad, what would God think right now?' Then his father would be very quiet for a few minutes and change his behavior. Even then, Harold drew on his faith. He was wonderful to his father. Omar always knew Harold would take care of him.

"One time Omar could not be found. They looked outside to find him lying on the road. He had gone to get the mail and had fallen. He could never be left alone at all. We had lots of people in the house then. There was someone to clean, someone to cook, a caregiver for Harold, and I would care for Omar. There was lots of food and a lot of fun. There were times when Omar would reminisce and Harold would get tears in his eyes. Omar loved his wife dearly and would talk about her, bringing up things from Harold's childhood and the times when they were younger. There were lots of fond memories.

"Possibly from working with middle school children for so many years, Harold has developed the quality to listen to the entire story. He never prejudges anyone.

"It has been such a pleasure to be part of this family, to have taken care of Harold's father and to get to know Harold. Harold has brought so much peace and joy into my life. He has picnics and gatherings for his nurses at his house, which has developed a great camaraderie with all of us. Usually when caring for someone in the home we don't meet the other nurses. But with Harold we learn about the other nurses through him and we all want to meet each other. We go to ball games and have such a great time together. He has touched our lives and brought us together in a most unique way. It has been a godsend to have Harold in our lives. We all know he knows negative things about all of us, but he never shares those—only the positive ones. Being a nurse for twenty-five years, I know some patients can be cranky at times and often like to complain about their caregivers, but with Harold it's not like that. It's the best situation one can ever have. At one time there were twenty-eight caregivers, and there was never any discord.

"When I was in my twenties, I was into belly dancing. Some of the nurses thought it would be fun for me to belly-dance for Harold. We had our picnic at a pavilion in the township park where I didn't think any other people would be noticing my belly dance. Two girls happened to come by who were friends of my son and were surprised to see me belly dancing. Several days later the mother of one of the girls called to ask if I would belly-dance for her daughter's twelfth birthday, which I did. I had a wonderful time talking to the girls about various aspects of belly dancing. Later, I was asked to perform for two Girl Scout troops. Because of Harold, I have a little side hobby that I enjoy.

"Harold had T-shirts made up with HAROLD'S ANGELS written on them for the female nurses and HAROLD'S KNIGHTS for the male nurses. Everyone loves to wear those T-shirts. We had such fun having a party for him.

"Another loving, caring way of Harold was when my mother came to live with me because of a brain tumor; Harold said it was fine for me to bring my mother to work with me. Most of the time I brought her when Harold wanted to visit someone and we all went along. He was always taking cakes, pretzels, and jams to people he was visiting.

"Harold's father, Omar, was born into an Amish family but later became a Mennonite. Harold's Amish Uncle Mike, the last of the family, is still living, and Harold makes a point of visiting Uncle Mike—always taking his favorite pretzels and candy. Uncle Mike's face would light up when Harold went to visit. During those visits I would bring my mother, and it touched my heart so much to have my mother included in such activities rather than leave her home alone. My mother got her own HAROLD'S ANGELS T-shirt; she was invited to our parties, and toward the end of my own mother's life, I was able to bring her to join in our fun. Her last and most enjoyable function was a Christmas party at Wegman's Restaurant. Even since his acute illness, Harold continues his social activities. He continues to live for other people. The love that comes around is a life-giving, healing thing."

4

Maturing Years

After I graduated from high school in 1955, my father sent me to Eastern Mennonite College—much to my displeasure. I wanted to be a farmer. I loved everything about the farm—milking cows, cultivating and growing crops—and I could do it quite well at that time. However, my father would say, "Harold, there will come a time when you won't be able to do these things." At that time, there weren't the modern conveniences we have today. Now the machine throws the hay bales onto the wagon without their being handled by a person. Tractors with power steering weren't in use then.

At the end of his career Harold stated: I wanted to be a farmer, but my father had the sense to know I wouldn't be able to survive. Back then, I didn't know that physically there would be things I couldn't do. So, I went off to college. I went into education because I didn't know what else to do. I fell in love with the teaching profession later.

At the beginning of my college freshman year, during the week of testing, I purposely tried to fail the tests. I think my dad may have spoken to my counselor, telling him I might want to try to come home, because my counselor called me to his office, saying, "Harold, I know you can do better than this. Your high school records show that. I understand you are homesick and you don't want to be in college." He talked to me very sensibly for about an hour, explaining my dad's concerns about that time when I might not be physically able to handle the demands of the farm.

With that inspirational talk from the guidance counselor, seeing a little deeper into my dad and having enough respect for his judgment I decided to give college my best shot. I had no idea what I wanted to do, but I decided since I could speak English, maybe I could become an English teacher. I remained in college and made the best of the situation, making average or a little above average grades.

My initial goal was just to get through college. I felt I was in college because my dad made me go. I was biding my time just to get through. It wasn't until I got into my teaching career and started to love my career that I developed goals. After college I wanted to have successful foot operations and get back on my feet.

Those were difficult years for me. They were such an adjustment because I wanted to be an adult, but I had a lot of subconscious fears about being disabled. I wanted to be normal. At college, there were many steps on the outside of our dorm as well as steps on the inside. I would take the long way around to those inside steps, which were hardly ever used, just so no one would see me awkwardly going up steps. I plagued myself during those freshman and sophomore years. As I reflected on what I was doing, I realized no one ever spoke to me about my disability, so I began to think that maybe I was the stupid person about this. I asked myself why I wasn't accepting my disability for what it was. During my junior year, I began feeling more at ease about myself, saying, "This is crazy. Why don't I take the shortest route to wherever I am going? Why not take the outside steps?" I had enough strength in my upper body at that time to lean against the side cement wall and push myself up. It just took longer. As I felt more at ease about my disability, I began having more fun, realizing it wasn't a burden anymore.

When my previous operation at the age of seventeen was completed, the doctors could give me no guarantees about my future prospects. I was also concerned that I might pass this condition to my offspring, but the doctors couldn't give me any guarantees about that. The only thing they theorized was that there would be a deterioration of my condition and that eventually—they had no idea how soon—I might be wheelchair-confined. That was simply a wild guess; but as I went through college, my condition began deteriorating more rapidly. My walking became more difficult, and by the time I was a college junior my roommate came to my podiatrist to learn how to pad my shoes, exercise my feet, trim my calluses, and generally care for my feet. By the time I was a senior, I was bearing my weight on just a small portion of each foot—about the size of a half-dollar on the outside of my foot behind my little toe. The calluses were so deep, blood blisters began to form in them, and the doctors could no longer cut out the blood blisters. This caused intense pain for me. A lot of the time I wouldn't even go to the dining room because it took too much effort to walk down all those stairs and back to my dormitory room. Sometimes guys would pick me up and carry me down, making a joke out of it, which eased my concern a bit.

By the time I was a college senior, our geology class took a field trip to Jones' Wharf to work with fossils, specimens, et cetera. I told my professor I couldn't go with them since I couldn't walk on sand. Hearing about this, several college friends got together to make a seat complete with a padded cushion and side handles. They brought it to my room, telling me they had something for me to try. When they told me to sit on it, asking how it felt, I said, "I don't know what you guys are doing, but it feels fine."

They picked up the chair and started carrying me all around the campus. They had shifts of guys taking turns carrying me for about twenty minutes each. My reaction was, "Guys, cut it out. You're being ridiculous! What's this all about?" They were having so much fun running all around, up and down the steps! Finally, they said, "You're going with us to Jones' Wharf on our field trip next week!" I couldn't believe it. I'll never forget those guys. Most of them are doctors today. That kind of caring gave me an immense self-confidence, just to say, "It's OK to be who you are."

College really helped prepare me for the real world, because I then went into teaching. Without college, it would have been very difficult for me to leave the shelter of the farm. In my growing-up years, I had been pretty confined to the farm. My senior year of high school at Lancaster Mennonite School did a lot for me, too, because I got out and experienced dorm life. I made a whole new set of friends. College also helped me mature. I learned how to fend for myself without family. My mother taught me how to do my own laundry, to iron my shirts, and to sew. I could take care of myself pretty well during my college years. It also helped me to lose my self-consciousness about my disability. Before that I could deal with it privately, but in college I had to deal with it publicly and it took me several years before I realized people were not making fun of me and looking at me as being totally unusual. College also taught me a lot of discipline in my studying. I discovered I loved to do research after I got involved in it.

I remember a time when my college friends played a joke on me called snipe hunting. A group of guys convinced me that snipes were a valuable game bird very pleasing to the palate and most easily caught on a foggy night. So one foggy night they got me to sit on a chair on the walkway that circles the center of campus—in plain view of the girls' dorm—holding a large laundry bag into which they were going to chase the snipes. After holding the bag for half an hour with no catch, I finally got wise to their trick—especially after hearing snickers and looking over to the girls' dorm to find every window packed with girls watching me in my vain efforts at catching a snipe. That's OK. I went out the next day and bought two very small chickens, had the cooks prepare them for me, and enjoyed eating them at dinner that evening with a few buddies—only to convince other envious and naïve onlookers that there most certainly are snipes. And so the "game" of snipe hunting continued at college.

Those years when I entered adulthood were hard at times. At that time, people didn't deal with disabilities very well. I remember being made fun of by adults, which was very difficult for me. I recall being in a neighboring town walking to the bank when two adult men in a pickup truck went by. One of the men yelled out the window, "What's wrong with you? Do you have a hard-on?" That was extremely difficult for me. It really set me back in my self-confidence. He was making fun of the way I walked. That happened several times. I attributed it to there not being many people with difficulties out in the public at that time. My dad never allowed me to be sheltered from the public.

At the close of Harold's freshman year in college, students wrote these comments in his yearbook:

Your cheerful attitude is greatly appreciated.
I like your cheerfulness and sense of humor.
Your life has challenged many with your continuous pushing forward and always being cheerful.
Your optimism is very impressive. You have a warm personality.
You certainly were a cheerful help to our campus.
It was inspiring to learn to know you this year. It was a real help to discuss problems and common interests with you. Keep that smile and you'll always be a "hit."

Some of the comments from college students at his graduation were:

Continue to have that nice personality and to give those you meet in the future that smile of yours.
It's been good having you on campus. You have helped to cheer it.
I've really appreciated your fine Christian testimony and character and your friendly ways.

Your constant Christian testimony and cheerfulness has been a challenge to me.
A real fine Christian friend who has been a constant challenge to me these four years.

Comments from the high school students Harold student-taught during his college senior year indicate the person he was to become:

Best of luck to a good student teacher.
Best wishes to a swell Lit teacher.
Best of wishes to a very good English teacher.
For a good teacher.
I'm glad you were our teacher this semester.
I really enjoyed having you for Spanish.
You are really a good teacher. Glad to have you for English and Spanish.
I enjoyed being in your class. You are a swell teacher.
Best wishes to a swell English teacher. I'm glad I had you this year for Lit.
I've really enjoyed having you for Spanish and English. You're making a great teacher.
Best of luck to a swell teacher. Some kids are really going to get a good English teacher.
It was nice to have you teach us in literature. Sure enjoyed it.
Good luck to a swell Spanish and English teacher.
Thanks for being a wonderful teacher.
You are a swell teacher. Appreciated your Christian testimony.

By the third major operation, the one after college at the age of twenty-two, I had developed a great deal of maturity. I had begun to find myself and accept my disability without too many questions. I began losing my embarrassment and sensitivity to my disability, but I had so much pain by the time I graduated from college that I was exempted from some of my classes. At that time, chapel services were mandatory, but I was allowed to listen to them on the radio instead of attending in person, so I could get as much rest as possible. I don't even understand how I made it through my senior year. There were so many concessions made to accommodate my weakness and my disability. My goal was just to make it through college.

By the time I was a junior in college, my podiatrist had become an orthopedic surgeon at the University of Pennsylvania Hospital. He began talking to me about more surgeries, but I said, "No way am I about to go through any more operations like I went through at seventeen years of age. I won't go through being cut again." But he kept talking to me and very gradually convinced me there was help. It seems that all through my life, God opened one door after another, bringing all the people into my life who nudged me through this door, through that door, when I didn't see anywhere to go.

Every month when I would visit my podiatrist, Dr. Pritchard, to have my calluses trimmed, he would keep talking. Gradually he showed me diagrams of how he envisioned this cut or that cut would be made and how it would affect my feet. Podiatry was making so much progress in bone surgery about 1958–60. He also showed me X rays of my feet and what he envisioned would work. It would be a very serious operation, but he had a feeling it would work. It would also be my decision. By the time I graduated from college, I was in so much pain I was willing to do almost anything, no matter what. On one of my visits to Dr. Pritchard, I said, "Let's get serious about this. I need you to be my guide, to tell me what to do and where to go."

We decided the surgery would be done at the University of Pennsylvania Hospital with Dr. Grice, who was the main orthopedic surgeon at the University of Pennsylvania Hospital and also at Boston Children's Hospital. Dr. Grice was designated to have his team be my doctors—a team of about seven doctors, including a resident who was being trained to do very specific surgery. I remember them looking at X rays while discussing how they would cut this bone off, cut this one out, make a V in this one, and then lay this structure together to heal. There were about fifty X rays on screens around my bed. Dr. Grice wanted me to hear this discussion so there would be no surprises, because I would need to make the final decision.

This operation would be very unique in many ways. The team again came to me the evening before the surgery, right before I was to be scrubbed down in preparation. The doctors all discussed the operation procedures together, while all I did was listen. They would ask one another, "Do you have any ideas about this? What do you think about that? Do you think there's a better way?" This was quite a novel operation, since they had never seen a foot quite like mine.

After the discussion was all over, Dr. Grice stepped up to my bed and said, "Harold, I think this can work, but it's going to be a toss-up—fifty-fifty. It might be successful or it might not be to the point we may have to amputate your foot."

I asked, "Well, what do you envision if it is successful? How much more will I have that I don't have now?"

His reply was, "If it is successful, you'll be able to stand flat on your foot. However, you'll lose some of your side-to-side motion, because we're going to fuse most of the bones in your foot."

The surgery involved cutting Vs in all the major bones in the foot so the foot would lie flat, which was a gamble itself. Dr. Grice continued, "We think if this is successful, you'll be able to walk without pain, because your foot will be flat on the floor."

"How long will this take?" I asked.

"You'll be in a cast for as long as three months. Then there will be therapy. We'll have to make a decision about how soon to get you on your feet after the surgery. There are a lot of unknowns about this which we'll have to take week by week."

After about a half hour of my asking them questions, I called Dr. Pritchard to my bed. I thanked him for getting me this far and for putting confidence in me, saying, "I just graduated from col-

lege with a teaching degree. I want to make something of my life."
I thanked him for getting me there and said that I would put my
faith in these doctors, trusting God to take care of the rest. I had no
idea how religious these doctors might be, but I felt such a burden
about the risk that I asked if I could pray for them. I asked Dr. Pritchard to take my right hand and asked all the doctors to join hands.
Another doctor walked around my bed and took my left hand. I
prayed a simple prayer, something like this: "Lord, you know
what's in store. I believe you know me and you know right now
what the success of this operation is going to be. I put my life in
your hands and I pray for each of the doctors. Would you guide Dr.
Grice in his leading of this team?" I prayed for each doctor by
name and then said, "Gentlemen, I feel at ease. Let's go for it."

I couldn't believe the reaction of the doctors. Everything was
very quiet when they all left. The scrub team came in to shave my
legs and do all they needed to do to prepare me for the surgery. The
next morning, just before they administered the anesthesia, I saw
the team in the operating room. I was a bit groggy at this time. Dr.
Grice, a very humanitarian doctor, walked to me, putting his hand
on my shoulder. He asked, "Harold, can you hear me?"

I said, "Yes."

He said, "Do you mind if we pray one more time?"

I remember mumbling something; then he took over. He took
hold of my shoulder— and I can still feel that squeeze today—saying, "Lord, this is a man of faith. May Thy will be done," and went
off to operate.

Because of the long surgery and being under anesthesia so
long, I went into a coma for nearly a week. The surgery was on
Monday and I didn't come out of the coma until the following Friday afternoon. I can tell you that I firmly believe people in comas
have acute hearing and an acute sense of what is going on. I remember nurses slapping my face, yelling at me, trying to get me to
respond. I wanted to say, "I can hear you. Don't talk so loud." It
was almost irritating. I could hear everything that was going on

around me, but I couldn't respond. I couldn't even blink my eyes. My eyes were shut. Finally, on Friday, I opened my eyes and turned my head a little bit. Everyone ran, calling for the doctors to come. I came out of it very peacefully, very gradually. I felt pain in my foot where they had operated, but I felt at ease. I wasn't afraid. I was eventually moved out of intensive care to a room where the nurses' station was right at the foot of my bed.

The next morning when I was getting my shots, I told the head nurse I didn't feel quite right. I had a pain in my chest. She never said a word. She dropped the medication, heading right for the phone, and did a Stat 9. I wondered what the emergency was when just like that four doctors were around my bed with stethoscopes. I had developed a serious case of pneumonia because I had been flat on my back for so long following the operation. They feared that this might happen. Getting the fluid out from around my lungs would present another real problem, because I was flat on my back with my leg in traction, up in a sling with just the right amount of elevation. The reason they thought the operation might not be successful was because they had to destroy many of the blood vessels in my foot and the risk was whether those vessels would find new routing and grow back again. If they didn't, then there wouldn't be enough blood circulation and the foot would have to be removed. They thought my health was good enough so that my blood vessels would reroute. My health had always been extremely good since I had lived a very healthy life, never having smoked or drunk or abused my body in any way. Again, I think this is why God told me in eleventh grade along Route 73 to say, "Guys, I'm not going to smoke."

To get rid of the fluid, the doctors had to get me off my back. One doctor held the sling with my leg and rotated me very carefully. Another doctor held my other leg that hadn't been operated on, while another doctor held my hand. When I had to cough, I would squeeze his hand and he would say, "Out!" to the doctor who had a needle in my back through which fluid was being drawn from around my lungs. When he heard: "Out!" he would take out the needle to avoid puncturing my lung when I coughed. There was a lot of fluid drawn from around my lungs. It was touch-and-go for about another week.

I had been told before the operation that they wanted me to understand that this would be the most serious and painful operation any human being could ever bear in terms of bone surgery. Cutting blood vessels is extremely painful, more painful than the bone surgery. We got through all that.

Dr. Grice was magnificent. He would fly to and from Boston. One morning when he was making his rounds along with about five interns and the head nurse, I was in extreme pain. I had steeled myself for the pain and hadn't said anything about it.

Dr. Grice said, "Harold, you must have pain."

I responded that I did.

"This isn't necessary," he said. He called the head nurse to his side, saying, "I want you to watch this one more time. This is a human being. He's not an animal. He's a person with a college education. He has feelings. Right now his leg is hurting him pretty badly. Don't ever let me come into this room again and see this leg not in the position it should be." I felt embarrassed for the nurse.

Dr. Grice took my foot in the sling, doing so little I couldn't even measure what he did, but within five minutes I could feel the pain subsiding from my foot. The throbbing began to cease. He stayed with me for about ten minutes. By the time he left, I felt almost no pain. He didn't belittle the nurse but thanked her for paying attention, assuming she had. I can tell you one thing, she was extremely careful every time after that.

About four weeks after the surgery, they were trying to get me up on crutches using my foot that hadn't been operated on. I had a therapist who was rather crude, with a very poor bedside manner, saying things like, "Come on. I know you can do this. Get with it. Stop being a baby." That kind of tough talk was supposed to spur me on, but for me it did just the opposite. When Dr. Grice asked me how it was going, I told him, "I really want to make progress, but I can't." When he asked what was wrong, I said, "I just don't have the willpower to do it." I explained to him the actions of the therapist.

"Enough said," Dr. Grice responded, and immediately got me a new therapist, a little blond girl, just about five feet high, with a Boston accent and a wonderful personality. I literally worked my butt off for her. Even if I only wiggled my foot, she would say, "Wow! That's great!" I worked so hard for her, and that's when I started to make progress. I tell every one of my nurses that how they work with their patients makes such a difference in that patient's progress. There's a tremendous amount of healing, mentally and physically, that goes on with the proper care.

After I had been in the hospital for about three months, Dr. Grice got me into more advanced therapy. I could hardly walk on crutches, because I didn't have the strength of a normal person due to my disability. It was always a risky kind of thing and also very painful. I eventually did get home, but I was so drugged with medication—shots every four hours for weeks and months, causing both arms to be black and blue from my elbows to my shoulders. My stomach and both my bottom cheeks were black and blue from all the shots given to try to ease the pain. The sleeping pills had lost their effectiveness. I couldn't get to sleep anymore.

When I got home, my parents cut out the pain medication almost immediately. I was convinced I had become a drug addict. I couldn't sleep for three days and nights. We didn't know about drug addiction back then as we know it today. My parents were told that I should be able to progress, and so they just cut out the drugs cold turkey. I begged for medication, but my dad said, "No, you're well enough now. You should be able to do this," and he wouldn't get me any medication.

I suffered immensely for the next six months. I just begged for the medication, trying to explain, "I just can't do this!" My pain really wasn't that great anymore. It was an addiction. Later in my career, when I was being trained in drug addiction for my school experience, I realized I had experienced a lot of the same kind of reactions I studied.

Eight months later I was walking flat on my foot. I still had pain, but it was bearable. I went back for the operation on my other foot. In the meantime, I lost Dr. Grice, who was killed in a plane crash leaving Boston when starlings were sucked up into the engines and the plane went down at the end of the runway. He was on his way back to Philadelphia. That was a great loss to me.

The rest of the team of doctors brought Dr. Zochall, a well-known bone surgeon from Johns Hopkins Hospital in Baltimore, to Philadelphia to perform this second surgery. The surgeon was a small lady with only three fingers on one hand, who had to stand on a stool to reach the operating table. I went through the process of learning to know a new surgeon. I recounted my experience of coming out of anesthesia—of course, she had that all on my records. I told her about my horrible experience getting off the medications, telling her it was so painful I didn't want to go through that again. In the meantime, the team had decided they could give me spinal anesthesia, meaning I would be paralyzed from my waist to my feet during the operation.

Getting the spinal anesthesia was an experience in itself. I couldn't bend. Because of my unique medical condition, the last five vertebrae in my back were almost fused. The anesthesiologist had to insert a needle between my vertebrae to put the anesthesia in my spinal cord. That was another risk. As I was lying in fetal position, one doctor got his long arms around my neck and under my knees, squeezing as hard as he could. This way, the anesthesiologist was able to get through to my spinal cord, giving me the necessary injection. I was awake during the entire operation, but I couldn't feel anything.

Two nurses, one on either side, kept me occupied in conversation during the operation. I recall one time Dr. Zochall was pounding with a mallet and chisel—cutting the bones on my left foot. At the time, construction was going on outside the hospital, building another wing onto the hospital. They were hammering steel pins into the structure; a lot of hammering was going on. I had no problem with that, since I knew which was construction hammering outside and which was hammering on my foot. I heard the surgeon say, "This is ridiculous. I don't want Mr. Zook to be put through this." She told one of the bystanders to go out to find the chief of the construction crew and tell him to cease all construction until she gave them the go-ahead to resume. About fifteen minutes later, all construction stopped.

This shows the kind of people who have been in my life. It's something I haven't thought about for years until now. She was another great doctor, taking the place of Dr. Grice, whom we all loved.

The recovery from this operation was much better than the one on my right foot. The second day after this surgery, I ate a chicken dinner. I had a good appetite and my chest felt normal. There was no problem with my lungs this time. However, feeling gradually began returning to my feet and legs. The pain started coming more and more and more, until all the medication given me during the surgery had worn off.

That's when I learned to pray intensely and seriously. Even though I thought I was spiritual before because of my upbringing, I feel that was the time I got really serious about my prayer life. There was no other way to get through this. The doctors and nurses couldn't believe I could get through this without pain medication. I told them that I firmly believed you can convince yourself to do whatever needs to be done. They agreed to let me try, but wanted me to be aware there was medication available if I needed it. It would take me half an hour just to turn a little bit. I didn't want to aggravate the surgery. I got through it. I had great nurses. One nurse would sit by my bedside during the night hours while she did her charting to talk and occupy my time. I eventually dated her for about a year after I was released from the hospital.

Had I not had my disability, I would in all likelihood have been married and would have made that commitment paramount in my life. Since I believe in family life, I believe my greatest goal would have been to build a successful and compatible marriage. Some of my nieces have talked to me on occasion, telling me it would have been nice if I had married. This is a very personal part of my life that I've shared with very few people, but maybe it's important for people to know about it. Marriage is the one thing in life I will never have experienced, and I will always wonder if I would have been successful at it. I believe I would have because of the way I feel about marriage and its commitment. I would have enjoyed doing the niceties for a life mate.

I very consciously decided against marriage after this last operation on my feet. There were too many unknowns about my situation. I only knew I had so much pain at that time. After the operations were successful, I called my doctors together, asking them to give me their honest opinion concerning the genetics about my condition, wondering if there would be a possibility of my passing this on to my offspring. The reason I was concerned about this was because of a developing relationship with the nurse I had met in the hospital. We fell in love and we dated for about a year after I was released from the hospital. I was very concerned about the possibility of passing my condition on. After much deliberation, the doctors couldn't give me any guarantees because there was no benchmark to go by.

As the nurse and I became more serious, the question of marriage arose. During our courtship, I did some things out of love—small tokens of appreciation, et cetera—which led this lady to believe I was getting serious about a firm relationship. I brought up the subject of children, telling her I didn't want to take the risk of being responsible for bringing a child into the world with disabilities like I had. I felt very strongly about it. We discussed it at length several times. She said we could adopt children, but I felt strongly that every woman would want to have the experience of having her own child. I wasn't convinced adoption was something I wanted to become involved in. We eventually broke off our relationship, which was very difficult for both of us.

To this day I often wonder about this friend. I realize that I could find her. I know she has four children of her own, which really rivets in my mind that she would have had the desire to have her own. It was very difficult in my young life to make that decision, but I have never wavered from it. Perhaps it's in God's plan, too, because I would never have had the experiences in my career had I not made this decision. She was a wonderful, warm person. That's one regret that I have in life. Since my most recent surgery and having had a tracheotomy procedure done, I've been glad I never married because I would never want to put a wife through this kind of experience with all my limitations.

Nurses in nursing school and doctors in residency at the University of Pennsylvania made numerous visits to do studies on how, through mental discipline, one could push pain out of one's life. You really don't push it out, but you deal with it. I remembered reading about the Civil War days, when soldiers would have their limbs cut off and then the remnant would be put into a bucket of hot tar to seal the wound. I thought that if they could take that, I could do this. I made myself believe I could do this. I kept thanking God for the first success while praying for the second success to occur.

The second operation was much shorter, since they knew more about what they were doing. In fact, Dr. Zochall's assistant was the same resident whom Dr. Grice had trained and who had actually helped do some of the previous operation. He talked Dr. Zochall through some of the steps of this second operation. Again, I believe it was God's leading that he was there, since they needed him due to his experience with the first operation. I could hear Dr. Zochall working with this resident, with them talking together and working as a team. At one point, I could see my reflection in the lights above the operating table and I was watching them cutting on my foot. I was engrossed in the process until they saw I was watching and then moved the lights so I could no longer see my reflection. The nurses who were to keep me occupied ran out of things to talk about after several hours. This operation went very smoothly, with no complications, no pneumonia. As soon as the surgery was over, I was given an incentive spirometer to increase the strength of my respiration, thereby decreasing the possibility of pneumonia.

After a month or so, I was out of the hospital and home. That was a more successful operation, because my left foot was even flatter than the right foot. These operations allowed me to walk for a number of years, until I began experiencing greater deterioration.

My parents were very fortunate during these operations. Since the doctors were so interested in my unique disability, they performed the surgeries at no cost to me or my parents, who were still supporting me. A social worker was assigned to work exclusively with me, working through the state system that got me some state funds. I understand that Dr. Grice took no money from the state as well as none from my family. He was happy for the privilege of having the experience. My stay at the University of Pennsylvania Hospital and all my medications were paid for by the state. When some years later I asked to see my charts, I learned the operation itself cost over $70,000. In 1959 that was big money. I couldn't believe the operation could cost that much.

The medical people stayed in touch with me, sending visiting nurses to my home to check on my progress. When I was well enough to ride in a car, I went back to Philadelphia every several days for physical therapy and so they could keep checking on me.

After getting my feet straightened, I began having pain in the lower vertebrae of my back. I felt it was important never to show pain in my career as a teacher. However, I began developing more pain later. I was beginning to become hunchbacked because of this lower back pain. Sometimes if I picked up something the wrong way, pain would fly into my back so severely it almost knocked me onto the floor. I went back to the University of Pennsylvania Hospital to ask if there was an operation they could do that would relieve my back pain. X rays were taken of my back and studied thoroughly. They could see how my body was deteriorating—pulling my spine together and pinching my spinal cord. I wasn't sure what was happening.

After a team of four doctors studied the X rays for quite a while, I was called into a conference room to learn why it would be insane to operate. My vertebrae were so tight and everything was so stretched they couldn't operate without damage to my spinal cord, probably making me a paraplegic. I learned they wouldn't take the risk. That was a hard time for me. I almost lost it, because in my heart I thought doctors could do anything. If they could work miracles on my feet, why couldn't they work a miracle on my back? I couldn't find a doctor who would even consider it.

Fortunately, I no longer have the intense pain I had during those earlier years. I'm never without pain, but it's bearable. I don't know if I'm just getting accustomed to it, but I do think it's better. I attribute that to prayer also.

At the time of the last operation, I became very depressed. I just wanted to die. I didn't have the nerve to commit suicide. I prayed that I would be in an automobile accident sometime. I recall driving by a quarry wishing I'd lose control and go down over the bank where nobody would ever find me; nobody would ever know what happened. I was really at my wits' end. I was at the bottom. I wouldn't even get out of bed.

It was my friend Eleanor, a school nurse, who got me through that. She came to see me one Sunday, but I would not leave my bed. She came to my room and sat on my bed, telling me I needed to get up, to get my life back. I told her, "I have no desire to get up." She tried to point out my successes in teaching, but that didn't mean anything to me.

I lay there for several hours with her staying right there by my side. Finally, she said, "Harold, please get up."

"Why?" I asked.

"You need to do this for me," she replied. "I need you."

Nobody had ever said that to me before, and it hit me like a bolt of lightning. I loved this nurse. I loved her as a human being; I loved her for her skills in nursing; I loved her for what she did in the school as a nurse. I finally got up. "Eleanor," I said, "I'm going to give it my best shot."

I went back to work, deciding I would just do the best I could. As I look back over my life, I feel there was the leading of the Lord in all of this.

I was coming home from work one cold, rainy October day. In the driving rain, I saw a person hitchhiking along the road. I later learned he was a nineteen-year-old boy. I had been told never to pick up hitchhikers. My dad would pick up servicemen but never anyone else. However, I pitied this fellow, so I stopped, telling him to get in. I asked him where he was going and he answered that he was going about twenty minutes beyond where I lived.

We talked as we drove along, and by the time I reached where I would normally turn off to my home he said, "This is where you need to drop me off."

I countered by saying, "No, I don't care how far away you live; I'll take you there."

After reaching his home, we stayed in the car talking for another half hour. He spilled the problems he was having, why he was hitchhiking, how his home life was so bad. We confided in each other. I prayed with him, then took his hand and said, "I just want you to know I care about you and I'm glad I had the opportunity to pick you up." I left him, never to see him again. I came on home with such a euphoric feeling of accomplishment and self-worth because I could help this young boy to look at his problems. I vowed when I got home that night that I would do a good deed, something out of the ordinary, each day from that day on. I made a concerted effort to do that, which is what drew me out of my depression—that euphoric feeling of having done a good deed that wasn't expected, that was above and beyond the call of duty. I did a lot of that for students who had bad home lives. I would take them somewhere—to a ball game, to McDonald's. That's what developed my credibility with kids.

When I was teaching, I had a room in my parents' home. My mother always waited up for me until I got home. She got a bit lonesome during the day and I was the only child living at home anymore. My mother had multiple sclerosis and couldn't do the dishes anymore but would have to wait for someone to come in to wash them. Sometimes when I got home from school I remembered I hadn't done my good deed for the day, so I would wash the dishes for my mother or stay up and read to her for half an hour or just chat with her for a bit. I knew it meant a lot to her.

What I had discovered by accident—doing unexpected deeds for others—made me what I am. I began encouraging this kind of action with students. I would ride around the cafeteria on my Amigo saying to students, "Hey, Johnny! Did you do your good deed for today yet?"

"What do you mean?" would be the perplexed reply.

"Well, did you do something that wasn't expected of you today yet?" Then I'd say, "There's a piece of paper [or a piece of food] on the floor. Would you mind picking that up for me, because I can't stoop down to pick it up?"

The student would eagerly do as I asked, saying, "No, I don't mind!"

I used that tactic every time I had a student with drug problems, depression, who was suicidal, or anything. I'm telling you it works. When I began instilling within students the "do a good deed" idea, they would see me coming down the hall and look around for something special to do—just so they could show me that they had done their good deed for that day.

5

Philosophy by Which to Live

Harold's Amish-Mennonite farm background forged his philosophy and beliefs. It taught that work is a virtue, that actions have consequences, and that one must take responsibility for choices made. Compassion and forgiveness is a core tenet, since all persons are frail and tend toward poor choices. People from this background view all persons as children of God. Our role in life is service to others and maintaining a community wherein each person can thrive and realize his or her potential. As a man of faith, Harold was motivated by the culture in which he had grown and matured. This society did not question God but accepted what life gave as God's will and gift.

As we examine what Harold has done with his life, we must ask what motivated him and gave him the strength to go on in the face of great odds, pain, and suffering. He says that early in my teaching career, I came across a poetic prayer titled "Others," which I eventually accepted as a personal motto. During my thirty-six-year career as a teacher and administrator, I pondered on its meaning often and found it to be my guiding light.

Others

Lord, help me live from day to day
In such a self-forgetful way,
That even when I kneel to pray,
My prayer shall be for "Others."

Help me in all the work I do
To ever be sincere and true,
And know, that all I do for You
Must needs be done for "Others."

And when my work on earth is done,
And my new work in Heaven's begun,
May I forget the crown I've won,
While thinking still of "Others."

"Others," Lord, yes, "Others!"
Let this my motto be.
Help me to live for others
That I may live for Thee.

An example of Harold's philosophy in action is illustrated in Harold's sending flowers to various persons for various reasons. He says:

I was in my early career, only teaching about five or ten years, when Eleanor, a dear friend of mine, the lady who saved me from having a nervous breakdown, lost her ninety-year-old Polish grandmother. It was a devastating blow to the Hillegas family and to me. I wanted to give something during a time of bereavement to the Hillegas family that I felt was appropriate, but I didn't know what it would be. All I could think of was flowers. I wanted my emotions to speak through flowers. I went to a flower shop in Reading just three minutes before closing time, and in spite of my offer to pay double, they insisted they couldn't make my arrangement. When I asked if they knew of another shop where I might go, they directed me to the newly opened shop of Nancy Hoy. Nancy was so happy to have a customer. She invited me into her shop, giving me a stool to sit on.

For the next half hour I explained my deep inner feelings and what I was trying to do for the Hillegas family. Nancy began with a vase and some purple carnations with a white fringe. I watched as she carefully added other touches until she stepped back, asking what I thought. "Oh, Nancy," I said, "it's perfect." That was the beginning of a great business relationship. I kept returning to her shop, and she has been my official florist for the past thirty years. Eventually we began socializing together, going out to dinner, going to shows, as well as my having Nancy and her husband as guests in my home. We never talked price; I just talked to her about the person to whom the flowers were going, why I was sending them, and my feelings associated with the gift. Sometimes she would ask about the price range, but I would say, "Just do it and we'll talk about that later." She has never disappointed me.

Nancy converses about her relationship with Harold: "In the nineteen seventies I had just opened my store when Harold first came to see me. It seemed that I always knew the kind of flowers he wanted and the design he wanted. From then on I was his florist. Over the years my husband and I became very good friends with Harold. We started going to shows at a theater after having dinner together. There were always six of us, plus Harold. Harold loved to eat at the very best restaurants.

"I see Harold as a very courageous person who is smart, very interesting, and always thinking about something. He's always very upbeat, enjoying everything to the fullest. His faith in the Lord gave him the strength to persevere, as well as a deep belief in himself and a love for other people. He just can't meet enough people.

"He has supported me like no other. When we went out with him socially, he treated everyone with respect. He is the nicest person and it was always a pleasure to be around him. He surrounded himself with really good, honest people since he knew how to find good people. He loves to send flowers and to make people happy. He always wants top quality. He knew the people very well to whom he sent the flowers, especially liking petite arrangements containing such things as tiny rosebuds.

"It was definitely his faith and his family that helped keep him going. His whole family was a very good, close family. Harold is one of a kind. He can look into a person's eyes and reach their heart and soul.

"We attended the funeral service for Harold's father and met the family. Harold had asked me to fill several vases but hadn't told me what flowers to use. When I got to the funeral, Harold was overcome with appreciation, praising my work. All the sons got together and built the casket, and the daughters did the lining, which expressed a great love for their father. It brought tears to my eyes when the brothers got up to sing. It was a beautiful tribute to a strong family."

Harold discusses his philosophy: My philosophy of life is that for some reason we're here in whatever way or capacity, normal, disabled, whatever—there's some reason we're here. It should behoove us to be the best that we can be under all circumstances—to love, to be kind, to inspire—that's what I believe. And I believe if we do anything less than that, we're disappointing our Creator and Maker. I've never had a temptation to be less than I could be with what I had. I never questioned it. Maybe that's why I turned down smoking, why I turned down alcohol, and I'm thankful about that. I would tell youngsters that once you ruin your life, you can't bring it back—it's gone. I talked about marijuana and how it destroys brain cells, the damage of which can't fully be recovered.

I don't know why anybody would want to be less than he/she can be. That's what creates the joy of life. When you do that, it radiates to other people. The hardest thing about these terrorists is why would somebody want to torment people? They have souls like I have. Why can't somebody get through to them? They're human beings. How can somebody torture somebody? How can somebody go to war and kill and maim? I don't understand that.

My philosophy is to be the best that one can be. Enjoy life. Enjoy what God has given us—the beauty of our surroundings, the beauty of our environment, the beauty of family if it's functional as it should be. Why destroy that? Why not build on it? Why not enhance it?

Richard and Virginia Close are fellow teachers and parents of two daughters who went through Indian Valley. Dick was a science teacher and department head and Ginny was for many years a substitute teacher. They engage in a conversation about Harold:

Dick: The key word that comes to mind in describing Harold is integrity. He was a man of his word and a man of compassion. One of his gifts was working with kids who had struggles, having the capacity to see through the surface problems to find and focus on the bright spots in a student. He was a man of excellence. Anything he did had to be excellent. That's what made him stand out. While most men are satisfied with eighty percent, for Harold his work had to be one hundred and ten percent. Because that was his character, it spilled over into the lives of the staff which is what made our school outstanding.

Ginny: Harold worked hard at his craft and it showed. The faculty would sometimes chuckle about his super-detailed organization, how he had different-colored forms for different-colored needs, but the faculty always knew exactly where they were supposed to be at any given time. I recall when Dick came back to school late at night with students from a science fair Harold would be at school. He was always there.

Dick: I taught at Indian Valley almost thirty years during which time we had many science competitions. Harold said whatever we needed by way of equipment, et cetera, he would support us; we knew this was significant to him, not just to me. I took great pleasure in reporting our successes to him. Of the twenty-one years, we won the county championship about eighteen times, much of which we attribute to Harold's encouragement. When we won, his smile with, "You've done a good job," said it all. That's what teachers need to hear and feel. Harold knew how to give praise and words of encouragement.

Ginny: Since 1981, I spent quite a lot of time at Indian Valley. I always felt a calm in the building that I felt was because of Harold. If a problem was referred to Harold, I knew it would be dealt with, and that's very important to a substitute teacher.

Dick: Harold sees worth in himself as well as in others. That's why he survived his most recent ordeal; he felt there were still things he had to do—and he is doing them. It's amazing, while in his situation, he is still able to encourage and challenge others. A year ago our daughter was married. She was his "hugger." He wrote her a wonderful letter when she was married. One of his gifts is being a wonderful writer. For many of us, there are a lot of "should haves," things we think of doing but don't. For Harold, there were no "should haves"; he carried through.

I think God puts a peace in his heart. He asked about the prayer breakfast we now have for the teachers and was very interested in it. When a pastor came to pray with him, he knew God's hand was upon him. There's a spiritual aspect to Harold that is very significant.

Ginny: I don't know much about his background except that he was raised on a farm, and was taught to work and persevere. When one is raised with that kind of stock, it keeps one going during the hard times.

Dick: He made me the teacher that I am. I had some general ideas about teaching, but because of Harold's model of excellence, it made me push myself to be excellent with my students. He brought me a lot further than I ever thought I would be in my career.

Ginny: In addition to the excellent students, there were a large number of students with problems. Harold entrusted you with those students, knowing the two of you together could really help experience success in their lives.

Dick: The great thing about working with Harold was that although I didn't send kids to the office often, I knew that when I did, Harold would sort out the problem. I took care of my own discipline problems as much as possible, but some students were beyond my capabilities, and those students I would send to Harold.

Ginny: Harold would work long and hard, regularly and consistently, with those problem students to help them be better, and to work through their problems.

Dick: I saw Harold give a lot of encouragement to other staff members. They knew if they worked hard, Harold would support them in any way he could. If we were willing to step out and try things, he made sure we succeeded. He was married to the school. Sometimes when I went home after a department meeting and drove by the school at eleven o'clock at night, there was still a light in his office and his car was still outside. I was exhausted and wondered how he ever kept going. I was amazed at his stamina. When you realize your leader is putting in that kind of effort, if you have any character at all you're going to do your best, too. Harold went the extra mile for us, laying the foundation for the teachers to go the extra mile for the kids and for the school. It's because of Harold that the school won the National Blue Ribbon Award.

One of the greatest things I saw Harold do was to organize a Walk-a-Thon for a family that was having a very hard time. The school raised eighteen thousand and two hundred dollars for a single mother who had two elementary-age boys, each severely afflicted with Duchenne's muscular dystrophy. The idea continued year after year, with other deserving families being identified and assisted. He could get students so enthused with the project. One eighth-grade student got so enthused she gave up her lunch period for nearly two weeks to call various businesses in the area seeking donations.

Harold used his disability as a motivator. At times when he was still walking, I would walk behind him thinking he was absolutely amazing. While it was painful to watch, it was truly amazing. When he began riding in his Amigo, I thought he would slow down, but it began a whole new era for him. I love the picture in the hallway that was put up when Harold was retiring, showing a sign with the words: "I brake for fundraisers!" Harold never did those projects for himself; he always did them for other people, for helping out students. It seems that because he had such a difficult time in his own life, he had a great, compassionate heart for others with difficulties. That spurred him on to inspire the student body to help families in need.

There's a story in the Bible about a man who was blind. They felt that if something was wrong with a person, it was because of sin in someone's life. When the Pharisees brought the man to Jesus, asking who sinned, this man or his parents, Jesus responded, "Neither this man nor his parents. This man was made blind so God's glory could be revealed," and with that Jesus healed him. People were absolutely amazed. In Harold's situation, I can't help but believe Harold's life has glorified God.

Ginny: I know how special Harold was in the life of our daughter. She would pop in at his office, and she said how kind he was to her. He would always buy magazines from her and she won a gumball machine because she was the top magazine salesperson that year.

We recall his inviting our daughter and us to his house for dinner when he cooked a wonderful meal for us. Our daughter brought him an angel food cake, which became a tradition. When she graduated from high school, he wrote a very special letter to her recalling the good times they had together, a letter she continues to treasure. He truly is special to us. It means so much to the heart of a parent to see your child valued in that way. It's very precious and the person who extends that value becomes very precious, too.

Dick: I saw a lot of kidding and laughter around Harold. Our principal, R. Brooke Moyer, loved Harold like a brother. Harold could take a joke. There were times when teachers would tease him, but when the joke was over, they knew Harold meant business. The annual field day was an example of his super organization. Sometimes we would have a stack of sixteen or seventeen pages of directions about who was scheduled to do what at a certain time. We moved minute by minute, but at the end of the day everything had gone like clockwork.

Harold had a good relationship with everyone in the school—the custodians, the ladies who come in at night to clean, the cafeteria workers, and superintendents. Everyone looked up to him. He always put other people's needs ahead of his. He viewed the school and education in general as an opportunity to impact people. A lot of people were challenged to a higher level of excellence. They probably wouldn't have achieved as much without his leadership.

Harold saw students as people who were maturing, always thinking the best of them. He felt they could accomplish things as well. One special needs student was a "pain in the neck" for many teachers; he was volatile, and didn't take directions well. Harold saw some qualities in him, working with him throughout his time at Indian Valley. As an adult, he is now functioning well as a truck driver.

Harold is able to look for the best in people and to bring it out and make it better. That is an outstanding quality in his life's philosophy of putting others before himself and making them better. That's what his life has done. At the end of his career, he is able to look back and say, "That's what I was supposed to do and I'm satisfied with it."

I believe Harold kept going because he thought in the back of his mind that there is still more to do. Harold has the unique ability to see that he will always be able to challenge people no matter what his physical condition. To see him come back from his most recent hospitalization, and to see how far he has come, is amazing. He has an internal drive, a sense of purpose for his life, and an understanding that he can continue to impact other people. His life story can be a challenge to many people who feel their life hasn't worked out for them as they thought, either physically or emotionally. Because of his view of people, Harold is able to continue to impact people, and with that feeling, he can fight through the tough times just as he has done his entire life.

Ginny: Harold has invested his life in people, and when that's done, there's a very strong sense of mission that has kept him going through the tough times.

Dick: Probably Harold's strongest motivation was to see parents and students being the best they could be. In spite of the different kinds of families they came from, Harold challenged kids to be all they could be. He did that same kind of thing with teachers. He demonstrated how to be a great teacher. I talk to people who were in his classes thirty some years ago who still remember his exactness and commitment. One person who is now director of admissions in a college in the Midwest remembers a trip Harold took to New England, how he taught them manners at dinnertime, taught them how to approach people and how to function appropriately in the world.

Harold not only taught students book knowledge, but he taught them life skills—how to live in the world. He taught them by example and by verbal teaching. He poured his life into his students. Someday we're all going to die and the question is, "Into whom did you pour your life?" Harold is a guy who walks the talk. It's one thing to say the students are the most important, but it's another to act like they are the most important. I count it a great privilege to have been a part of Harold's life.

Ginny: Many junior high students have feelings of inferiority and uncertainty about themselves. For them to observe Harold work with a visible and great disability, and to see how he conducted himself just as any other administrator would, how he handled his job and responsibility, was a great demonstration to kids at this juncture of their lives when they're facing a lot of uncertainty about who they are and how they relate to other people. Harold showed them how he conducted his life in spite of a disability.

Dick: It was a great privilege to have Harold as a great friend and a mentor. I hope I'm able to view life as he has, not as a hundred-yard dash but as a marathon.

Harold comments: I'm still human. I still have fears that crop up. Occasionally I wonder what happens when I run out of money to pay for all this care. I made it very clear to my doctors and nurses that I don't want to go through this again. Next time, I want to go on to greater things and a better place. I don't regret that I made the choice to live, as difficult as it was. I'm reaping the benefits of that now when I see I can help a nurse through a difficult time, when I can help a niece through a hard time, when I can work with a nephew, when I can work with a brother, a friend, an acquaintance; those are my rewards now. And they're big enough to sustain me. But I do have fears—I sometimes feel that medical science is making me so well now that my life will go on forever—for a long time. I'm not sure that's something I want. But then I go back to my prayer life. I just have to recall that God has promised not to tempt us beyond that which we are able to bear. That sustains me. I can honestly say that God has been faithful because he has not given me more than I can bear.

Bob Steenlage, drug and alcohol motivational speaker from Wisconsin, says of Harold: "I have traveled all over the United States giving drug and alcohol motivational speeches to schools and other organizations. Because of the high quality and truly professional man Harold is, he spent a whole year checking me out before engaging me as a speaker in his school. During that time, Harold and I became very close friends over the telephone. In my eyes, he's such a great man, I can hardly talk about him without getting choked up because of the quality of person he is. Talking to him is very strengthening because of his character. We bonded as strong as anyone can bond because we have similar strong spiritual beliefs.

"In true Harold fashion, he not only asked me to talk to his school; he lined up a whole week of talks that included many schools in the area. He wanted to make the trip worthwhile for me. When I was finally introduced to Harold, I was taken aback, although I tried my best not to show it. Since our contact was only by phone, I did not know Harold was handicapped. He never told me, nor was his attitude such that I discovered it. There was no reason for him to tell me and there was no reason for me to suspect. It was never a hindrance to him. I said, 'Harold, I had no idea you were handicapped.' Harold nodded his head and we kept on going.

"As I walked down the hall by his side in his Amigo, Harold saw a piece of paper wadded up on the floor. Before his hand came up very far from his lap, about three people made a dive to pick up that piece of paper. I had been in schools where I was assigned a bodyguard, and here was an administrator who commanded such respect. It showed me what kind of school Harold was running.

"Harold grew up in a strict family environment where they didn't just talk about God—they lived it. All of his siblings are wonderful people, but Harold's handicap has contributed a lot to his character, which is above reproach. Much of it has to do with his commitment to God, which gives him a great heart for other people and a faith that is real, causing Harold to touch so many lives.

"There are many contributions he has made to me personally. He became my family away from home and inspired my faith. Because of my work, I deal with a lot of negative situations, leaving me like coming out of a desert feeling very thirsty and very dry. Visiting with Harold would be spiritually and physically refreshing.

"As a totally unselfish person, Harold has rescued many

young people from very difficult situations. The foundation of Harold's philosophy is giving, not in a proud way but in a humble way. He was always in a giving mode, which motivated him. He needed to make it another day, because someone needed him. He knew deep in his heart he was a vessel to help others. No matter what the obstacles were, he found a way to overcome them. In many ways his thinking influenced Harold. His thoughts were never like a runaway train, because of how he was raised in a stable, loving home. As a result, his life is like a beautiful flower, a part of the universe, which fulfilled his purpose on earth. He truly is an important part of the universe.

"I loved Harold's cooking—his famous barbecue—and it was wonderful being in his beautiful home. It was a great blessing to be around Harold. I have shared his precious friendship with many, many people. I keep a picture of him in my billfold, and whenever someone feels sorry for themselves I bring out Harold's picture and show them what he deals with on a daily basis."

Harold's philosophy concerning children reveals his sensitivity and concern. He does not believe there are bad youths, only that they make wrong choices. When a student turns around his or her life, Harold does not believe the past has any relevance, but it should be forgotten. Harold indicated how the high school principal or his assistant would come to him with the yearbook and ask that potentially problem students be pointed out:

I said I wouldn't do that. I never did that with students coming to me from the elementary school. In fact, if anybody from the elementary school told me, "We're getting a bad bunch of kids," I thrived on that. It was a joy to me because it gave me another reason to be where I was. I kept track of every student's misconduct—the infraction and what I did about it. These running logs on four-by-six cards would for some become very thick. When these students were leaving Indian Valley, I'd call those fellows to my office, telling them, "Guys, I appreciate the changes you've made.

I'm going to destroy your records." I didn't believe in passing these on.

The students would often say, "Do you really mean that?"

"Yes. Would you like to destroy your own disciplinary record?" We would then take the record to the boiler room, throw it into the furnace, and watch it go up in smoke.

I can't tell you how many students—mostly boys—came back to me in their sophomore year saying, "Mr. Zook, I want to thank you for destroying my disciplinary record. I haven't been in trouble one time these first two months of school."

I would say, "You mean nobody hassled you?" One student even went to the guidance counselor asking to see his record because he was sure there would be something in there about his past behavior. Sure, he had seen me destroy his pack, but he was sure there would be some notation about his behavior. He noted that he couldn't find a single reference to his past record.

I asked, "How do you feel about that?"

"It feels good!" he replied. "I feel like a man!"

"That's what it's all about." I smiled.

He continued, "I'll come to see you again when I graduate to prove that I won't get into trouble again." And that's exactly what he did. He's a great guy, a great man!

Now you know why I like the Conflict Transformation Program. It has all the right elements. You find out what's causing the problems; then you solve them. You do something about it that helps people reform. You see how thousands of kids have been impacted with proper treatment and then find yourself asking, "What has each of these done because of what was done for them?" It gets transferred to their kids. They're learning how to be good parents, how to give a youngster who makes bad choices a break and learn from the mistakes. Those are my joys; those are my accomplishments. After my first year of teaching, I can't remember a single day when I didn't want to go to work, that I didn't long to go to work. What a joy! Sometimes my nieces and nephews indicate they want to please me. I tell them, "I don't care what you do, even if you're a ditchdigger, as long as you do your job well and love every day you go to work, along with being a good influence to the other ditchdiggers around you, that's what it's all about. It's not whether you graduate from college or whatever—that's fine, that's great, but that's not where it's at."

Harold believed that rules were to be followed or revised, as the following account indicates:

I always believed in the work ethic that my dad instilled in me when he said, "Work makes a man." I believed in work detail. During my first twelve years as an administrator, I had no after-school detentions. I didn't believe in detention. That had been the normal procedure previously, and I always hated it when twice a year I had to take my turn monitoring the detention hall. As a teacher, I never put my students in there. I hated the procedure: students had to sit on backless chairs, fold their hands in front of them, sit erect with feet flat on the floor, and remain totally quiet. Those were the rules, but I would go by and see those rules being violated all the time. Students would be talking to one another while the teacher sat in the back doing some work. As long as there was a margin of order, everything was considered OK.

I am a man who happens to believe that rules are to be obeyed. As a teacher, I always received tremendous respect, because when there were discipline problems I dealt with them in my own way. So when it was my turn to take detention, I would say, "Students, we're in this thing together. I don't know why you're here and I don't care why you're here. I don't need to know. All I know is that we're going to get through this hour and a quarter together. I'm going to be your model and you model after me. Here are the rules. You know them and I know them. If you don't make it with me now, you'll have work detail with me personally after school this week. Are you ready?

"The rules say you're to sit up straight, you're all to have your feet flat on the floor, so that's something we're all going to do.

You're all going to have your shoulders straight; we're not going to talk, either I to you or you to me. Is there anyone who has to go to the bathroom? OK, go now. Is there anyone else who has any other needs that will keep you from getting through these exercises? If not, let's go. If I talk, you may talk. If I look at the clock, you may look at the clock. If I shrug my shoulders, you may shrug your shoulders. If I move my feet, you may move your feet. You will do exactly as I do. Remember, I'm your model."

I'd suggest anyone try that for an hour and a quarter! There is nobody who knows how foolish that is or how hard that is unless you try it. I would get to the place where I would begin having a muscle pain, so I would move a bit. When I did, the students would do the same. I could sense when it was nearly time to stop, so I would look at the clock, and as I did, I would say, "Well, it's almost time to go."

A cheer would erupt, "Yea!"

Then I told them it was time to get down to business again, so we'd be quiet until time to dismiss. When the time was up, we'd all say, "We made it!"

My procedure for carrying out detention got around, and all the students wanted to know when it would be my turn to monitor detention so they could be sure not to get in there! That's what convinced me that if I ever got into a position to change the detention procedure I certainly would.

Harold did not believe in punishment per se, but he was a firm believer that a person must accept responsibility for choices made and that those choices had consequences. A student must accept the consequences. Firm but loving, Harold did not accept excuses but sought to transform situations so excuses were not needed.

Harold says: Kids don't do bad things; kids make mistakes. I tell them it's not that they've made mistakes that is important—it's what they learn from them. Youngsters need to make restitution for what they've done so they can get it behind them.

I'm a firm believer that you have to close the chapter, and once it is closed it doesn't get opened again unless the student does something to initiate it.

Harold did not believe in forced apologies. He says, Sometimes students would ask, "Do you want me to go back and apologize?' I would answer, 'That's for you to decide.' I told them I disliked very much when a principal forced a student to come to me and apologize for something he had done. Forced apologies are no good. I would tell them, 'Yes, I would be very pleased if you did that and it would tell me a lot about your character. It would tell me you're a young lady or a young man; but do it only if you're sincere about the apology."

Harold spent many hours helping students work through difficult situations by listening to them, disciplining them, and running interference with parents and police if needed. Harold says, "I can put a very heavy hand on some kids, but it is not my first choice." He had students draw up "action plans" and answer written questions designed to make them think through their behavior. There was always a lot of talking and listening.

Some of his methods may be controversial. He believed in having students work off their misbehavior, with tasks such as scrubbing floors, but always followed by a talk with him. School personnel tend to attempt to control students, to tell them what to do, to treat them as elements in a system. The health of the system rather than the health of the individual students becomes the chief concern. Forgotten is the fact that the health of any system is dependent upon the health of its parts. Harold understood this. His philosophy went against that of many school personnel. He believed students were responsible and could learn to make good choices.

Students could learn from bad choices so that in the future better choices could be made. In doing so, he rejected the model of controlling students, replacing it with one in which he helped students take charge of their actions. He helped students diagnose their own problems and determine how to correct them. Only when students accepted ownership did they gain insight into their problems. Students gained knowledge not through a disciplinarian telling them but because he helped them see themselves and their experiences in a new light. This gave students wisdom to deal with their problems and to create for themselves a new and better life.

Richard Hawkins, a teacher and athletic director who worked with Harold during Harold's entire experience at Indian Valley, testifies: "Harold and I worked together for nearly forty years. As I was the adviser to the student council, there were a multitude of student activities we planned with student leaders. Many of these activities required approval of the administration. Harold always had time to hear any request, no matter how busy he was. He gave me the feeling he felt these activities were worthwhile and worthy of his consideration, always giving his honest opinion. He tried to give student leaders as much responsibility as he could, even when it was difficult at times. He was very enthusiastically supportive of the activities.

"Every year we had a fundraiser to benefit Easter Seals which was a basketball event with students finding sponsors. As the event drew to a close, Harold would ask me how many students were delinquent in bringing in their pledges. After Harold called those students into his office, they somehow came up with the money they had pledged. For me as an adviser, Harold's support was invaluable. That illustrates the kind of support he gave to us teachers. As administrators, Harold and Mr. Moyer made the school what it was. Harold had a unique ability to lead a group to work together.

"As athletic director and football coach, I worked closely with Harold. As a coach, if I had any problems with student behavior I could count on the fact that Harold would have time to talk to the player and help work out the problem. Harold always was interested in what was best for the student, not necessarily what was best for the coach or anyone else. Uniforms and equipment were always an issue. Harold always focused on the safety of a player. Although bound by the budgeted amount for athletics, Harold worked within the school guidelines to meet the needs of students.

"Harold is without a doubt a very sincere individual, and in all my dealings with him I saw his sincerity and honesty. Considering his disability and all he has accomplished, it's obvious he has a lot of courage. I often wondered if I were in his situation would I have that determination. Someone said that some winners are ordinary people who have extraordinary determination. He certainly had the extraordinary determination. He was very thorough in everything he did, including figures and comparisons. When he was chief negotiator for the faculty, he had all kinds of information that he gained from hours of research. He was truly a diligent person. When disciplining students, he could be very stern, but he was also compassionate. He could read into a situation what was needed, knowing when to be stern and when to be compassionate.

"The following story gives an example of Harold's philosophy with students: A man came home from work after a tough day, wanting only to relax with a newspaper. His son asked him to shoot baskets in the driveway with him, but he didn't want to. His son asked him to do several more things, when finally the man took a picture of the world from his newspaper, cut it into pieces, and gave it to his son with the instructions to put it back together. In a very short time his son returned with the completed picture. 'How did you do that so quickly?' the father asked. The boy replied, 'You see, Dad, there's a picture of a boy on the other side and when the boy was all together, the world was put together, too.' Harold felt if he got one student straightened out, the class, the school, and the community would be a lot better off.

"The following poem, 'The Art of Giving,' represents what Harold has given to the school:

" 'We give of ourselves

110

When we give gifts of the heart;
Love, kindness, joy, understanding, sympathy,
forgiveness.
We give of ourselves
When we give gifts of the mind;
Ideas, dreams, principles, projects, poetry, plans.
We give of ourselves
When we give the gift of time;
Patience, attention, consideration, perseverance.
We give of ourselves
When we give gifts of the spirit;
Beauty, inspiration, prayer, and faith.
We give of ourselves
When we give the gift of words;
Encouragement, guidance, motivation, inspiration.
The finest gift a man can give to his age and time
Is the gift of a constructive and creative life.' (Author
Unknown)

"Harold was a great inspiration to me. He viewed his disability not as a handicap but as 'This is what God gave me; this is what I have to work with,' and he did the very best with what he had. That spurred him to greater determination. I never saw him feeling sorry for himself. I told my wife, that if I ever complained about anything she should remind me of Harold. I visited Harold in the rehabilitation hospital and saw all the tubes, et cetera, when he couldn't talk. I thought it would be a short visit. He had a legal pad on which he wrote about seven pages as we held a wonderful conversation. He told me of his goal to get out of the hospital, and he reached it, although I was doubtful he would make it.

"Harold treated all students alike, regardless of their academic standing or home background. He looked for ways to help every student. He taught me that a lot can be accomplished collectively if one is willing to work with others. Not every parent agreed with his methods of discipline, but most of them were grateful for what he did for their children. When a student transgressed, Harold didn't simply punish the student, but he tried to help the student experience what he had done. He often had the student perform some service to the school.

"Students discovered the benefits of being valued, loved, of belonging, and of feeling worthy. In doing so, they found their place in the world, not just their place in the school. Harold believed in them, their individual worth, thus giving them hope. His strength of character helped students develop their own character. Instead of denigrating students in trouble, he treated them as worthy individuals, giving them value and worth."

Harold believed in helping those in need, as revealed by the remarks of Marvin Godshall, former head custodian and building engineer at Indian Valley:

"I worked at Indian Valley for twenty-one years. I met Harold in 1965 and we have been very good friends ever since. I have two grandsons diagnosed with Duchennes' muscular dystrophy. I had retired due to my health problems and was no longer working at the school. The student council decided to sponsor a Walk-a-Thon to benefit my grandsons. Harold allowed the students to use the school phones during their lunch periods to call local businesses soliciting their support for the Walk-a-Thon that was very successful, earning eighteen thousand and two hundred dollars. He was the motivator behind the Walk-a-Thon. My daughter, mother of the grandsons, was reluctant to let the public know about her sons' problems. I convinced my daughter to come to the assembly to receive the funds, and she was so pleased. The entire faculty and students made her feel so important. That was the first of many Walk-a-Thons to benefit other deserving families. Harold was a great motivator, telling students that if he could get up and walk, he certainly would do that.

"We have remained great friends. When I think I'm going to cheer him up, he cheers me up. He's a great help when I'm down.

Harold's strength comes from God and his family and he likes to be as independent as possible. He chooses to help others. I remember his desk at school was covered with glass under which he had many pictures of students he had helped.

"Harold was able to bring people together in support of all the school activities. He even helped finance an elevator to accommodate handicapped students. For a person like Harold, who had no children of his own, he understood children in trouble and turned them around. He even brought families together.

"In my previous job, I worked with only adults, so coming to work in a school with adolescents was new for me. Harold helped me learn how to understand the students and teachers, going the extra mile to help me feel comfortable here. He was a wonderful guy for whom to work, and a tremendous friend.

"Occasionally, when I came to work in the morning there would be a note on my desk; 'I'm sleeping in the nurse's room. Please wake me up.' He had worked so late he was too tired to drive home. He was so dedicated to do everything just right. He kept me on my toes, too, reminding me of little things that I had missed."

Harold's faith kept him humble, without either a low or high opinion of himself. Believing that God would empower him for whatever task God gave him, he operated from an internal rather than an external motivation. While he was not driven to protect a "reputation," he achieved an outstanding reputation because he was authentic. Harold says:

I think every public school should have a person hired who does nothing but work with dissident children—counseling if needed, disciplining if needed—just working with children who are suicidal, who are misused by parents or other relatives, students who are just not making wise choices in life. I think it would pay for itself in the matter of human resources. My philosophy has always been that for every child you save at a junior or senior high school level that's one less adult you have to deal with in the criminal world or in some expensive health situation or whatever.

Somehow people think there's no money for those kinds of things, but it's always disturbed me because we have money for sports, bleachers and stadiums that sit half the year without being used. That's one thing that has always bothered me in my career—that we don't have that kind of person in a school. If you can get the right person who is trained properly in that field, it would be a tremendous benefit to parents, families, siblings, schools, and society in general. That would have been my real love.

Harold's brother Mervin, who taught at Indian Valley, says; "His strength as a teacher and administrator was his belief in his own judgment. He was not afraid to go against the tide. If he had to, he would stand alone for a student, not backing down. The students seemed to realize that even with his disability, he was on their side. He would do everything he could to help them develop and accept responsibility for their actions. He didn't slack off in punishment, yet if he saw a student was making an honest effort, he would encourage that effort.

"After I quit teaching, I worked at carpentry for a while. One of the guys I worked with had been a troublemaker at the school where Harold was an administrator. He told me this story. 'After I straightened out my life, Harold told me he would throw my records away and he did. I watched him.' It made such a positive impression on that student. Harold had a tremendous amount of integrity with the students, because if he said something, he followed through; if it was punishment, he followed through; if it was forgiveness, he followed through. That was a real strength he had with students.

"This was also true with teachers. If he had a hunch about something, he would not back down; even if all the other teachers were against what he said, he would not back down. He had a great respect from the entire staff. In addition to being a teacher, he was also the chief negotiator for the teachers' contract. He had the respect of the entire school community. Even other school districts learned about his way for negotiating teachers' contracts. His tactics were not conventional; they were unique. He wasn't afraid to go out on a limb when he had a hunch about something. It's a very hard job, but he had the respect of all the teachers, administration, and school board members."

Harold had probably never heard this statement by Confucius: "If my own heart tells me that I am right, I shall go forward even against thousands and ten thousands."

6

Growing in a Career

Harold's career began in 1960, at the Indian Valley Middle School, Harleysville, Pennsylvania, at a time when disabled people weren't easily hired. "I know the question will come up; this man is going to have difficulty with discipline," said the superintendent who did the hiring. But Mr. Warner, the principal in need of a teacher, insisted that Harold be hired. Years later, a letter from the principal's widow informed Harold that her husband, William Warner, felt Harold had a human quality that he wanted to see rub off on kids. Harold exhibited honesty, integrity, the ability to listen to kids, and the ability to understand kids. Harold says:

My first year of teaching was horrendous. I thought children would eat out of my hand, but I didn't realize that I would have to earn that respect. I was ready to quit. I had already looked into becoming a used car salesman; that's what I was interviewing for because I had discipline problems that were just unreal. I also had difficult classes—classes that nobody else wanted. Students in one seventh-grade class couldn't read above a third-grade level, and there were no reading materials back then to help these students. At that time, if one didn't teach straight grammar, he/she wasn't teaching correctly. There was very little writing or vocabulary in the curriculum. I was determined I would not come back a second year.

The teacher assigned to me as a "big brother" was also the English Department head. He tried to help me get through the year. Midway through the year, the principal had to have surgery, so this department head was asked to fill in for him. The first day when working as principal, he stepped into the room and everything got quiet. He was a very quiet man, a smart man who was rather austere. He said to my students, "I'm Mr. Evans. I'm going to be the principal here for the next six weeks. As you know, this is Mr. Zook, your teacher. I expect you to treat him politely and with respect. There are seven rules: Number one: You don't leave that seat. [I had trouble with students getting out of their seats during class.] You don't leave that seat unless Mr. Zook asks you to. Number two: You don't speak unless Mr. Zook recognizes you and asks you to speak." He went down the line, telling them they were expected to walk into class, take their seats, open their books, and prepare for class. There were seven rules of order and discipline. After giving them these rules, he left the room. For the next six weeks, I had total peace and I said to myself, *How can a man do that? How does he have so much power with so little effort? Why can't I do that?* That's just the way Mr. Evans was.

We had to sign yearly contracts back then, but I didn't sign my contract for the second year. The superintendent asked Mr. Evans, department chair, to talk to me about it. My comment was, "This is not for me. I'm not cut out for this job. I can't stand children not learning under my supervision."

He said, "Harold, you are coming back next year. If you don't sign this contract, I will forge your name on it. I'll guarantee that you'll have less difficult classes," explaining how my classes would be assigned. Out of respect for him, I signed my contract. From the first day, I loved that second year, and I never had a problem after that. It was a great experience because when I became English Department head, I made certain new teachers were not put in the position I was. I made sure they could communicate with me when they were having problems so I could help them. During my first year, I wouldn't even go into the faculty room because I

117

felt so embarrassed and unqualified. My self-esteem was simply gone.

That second year, I taught and tried to be myself. In college courses, I learned certain ways to do things; but I discovered I wasn't teaching to my personality. Now I decided I would do it my way. I started teaching what I felt was important. One day the superintendent of schools came into my class to observe my teaching. Instead of teaching grammar, I was teaching a lesson on writing. After the observation, the superintendent asked, "Don't you teach any grammar?"

I replied, "Yes."

He said, "These kids need hard core grammar; you should teach them diagraming, et cetera."

"I can't," I said. "These students aren't even reading on a third-grade reading level."

The next year the state of Pennsylvania mandated a reading course requirement for seventh-graders. The superintendent sent us an old high school literature book that was supposed to be our reading text. I don't know where I got my wisdom, but I felt this wasn't the way it should be.

Students were failing their college entrance exams, so I did some research on that. I asked the high school guidance counselor to give me a set of five years of information about these tests. I discovered the biggest drawback was that many high school seniors were failing the vocabulary section of the test. They didn't know how to do analogies, opposites, et cetera. They didn't have a vocabulary background and there was a whole section on vocabulary, so most of them would fail. Based on that research, I started a vocabulary program in my classes. By the time my students got through high school, they were no longer failing the vocabulary section of the test. I also started a strong writing program, which was brought into the state curriculum about five or six years later. Mr. Evans also felt vocabulary and writing were very important. He was ahead of his time, so I had good support in what I taught.

The word was around that I was fair, that I understood, and that I cared. Those three things the students respected. Students tried to get me as their English teacher and they told their younger brothers and sisters to try to get me as their English teacher. I did things with students. If we studied *The Yearling* as a novel, I would take the students to Philadelphia to see a pre-Broadway show based on that novel. If there was something we needed to do, we did it.

My number-one objective was to teach students respect. I taught them about our school mascot, the Eagle, and all the attributes of the eagle—its prowess, its strength, its vigor, its sight, and why we chose that as our mascot.

At his retirement Harold prepared and contributed a plaque to the school as a reminder and distributed a handout about the "Spirit of the Eagle." (See Foreword.)

I would also do a lesson on the significance of the American flag, which we saluted every day—what it stands for, the meaning of its colors, why there are stars and what they stand for, why there are thirteen stripes, et cetera. I felt if we were by law going to salute the flag every day, students should know what it means and why it's important as our national emblem. There were no tests on these topics, just general understanding. I taught proper respect for the flag, how it is to be flown, how it's never to touch the ground, and the honor it would be to fly that flag every day. Each year, there were always more than a dozen students from my classes who would go to the office to ask for the privilege to raise the flag every day. I gained a lot of respect from students for that because they knew I loved my country and my flag. I was disappointed when we could no longer pray the Lord's Prayer and have Bible reading, which we used to have in our public schools.

At that time, my disability still allowed me to stand to teach. I would walk throughout the classroom as I taught, and I would touch my students. I always arrived at least an hour early to school every day. I knew where each student's seat was, so I would focus on one to three students that morning, and it was usually students who were having difficulty or for some reason needed something special. I would focus on those students and say a prayer for them. Nobody ever knew I did that; in fact, this is the first time I'm sharing this information. That is part of my hesitancy in telling my story—there are many things I have never shared with anyone. Even my family doesn't know about this. I don't know how I could have taught and been a principal without the love of God or without that inner spiritual strength, because there were times when I would be at my wits' end, not knowing what to do.

One such time was when a seventh-grade girl tried to commit suicide—a lovely girl. I was so disturbed by the thought of this that I felt the need for someone else to pray with me. There was a church friend who was a very religious man; in fact, many people made fun of him because he was so ultrareligious. He wasn't afraid of his religion. Young people in the church would make fun of him and his children all the time. I never understood how people could make fun of this man and his family like that. When I came home from college, this church friend would always be there to ask how my college life was going, always taking an interest in me, telling me, "Harold, I'm praying for you. I know life's tough for you." Then, during my first year of teaching, he said, "Harold, if you ever need another pray-er, just call me and I'll pray with you."

I had an 800 toll-free number at my house so any parent or student could call me at any time of the day or night. When I got a call from this seventh-grade student's parents telling me their daughter, a student in my homeroom, was in the hospital because she had attempted suicide, I was so deeply upset and couldn't go to sleep. Finally, at two o'clock in the morning, I remembered what my church friend had told me, so I called him. He picked up the phone on the first ring, and I wondered how this could be. He told me, "Harold, I awakened at twelve o'clock feeling something was wrong with someone, and I've been on my knees since twelve o'clock." We prayed together over the phone, which left me with such a feeling of peace. The next day, I talked to my homeroom students about what had happened and what we needed to do about it.

There were times when I would sit in my easy chair at home wondering what had gone wrong that day, what I could have done better. The next morning I would tell my students, "You know, students, I got very upset with you yesterday. I need to talk to you about that before we start our class today." I would tell them why I got angry and upset with them. I would say, "I want you also to understand that I was angry because I felt I wasn't able to get through to you. I really want the very best for each one of you."

Everything had a goal, every class session and every unit. My goal was basically to help kids become the best they could be—not just academically but humanly. I honestly believe it paid off, because when I retired I received hundreds of letters from students all over the United States who wanted me to know what had happened to them after they left high school. I said at my retirement dinner, "You know, when Sir Edmund Hillary climbed Mount Everest, he described in his book the awesome view he witnessed when he reached the summit. I feel I've reached the peak. It's wonderful to look back over the valley without any regrets." I can honestly say I have no regrets. I challenged those in attendance to conduct their career to the best of their ability, so that someday, they, too, could look back with no regrets and see what they had accomplished during their lifetime.

During my first year of teaching, I wanted to get through it and start over again. My primary goal, then, was to be the best teacher I could be. I wanted to help students, especially those with discipline problems. I wanted to make learning fun. Students should take a serious attitude toward learning, but it should be an experience they can carry with them through life. I remember drilling students on the mechanics of the language, dealing with those troublesome things such as *there-their, to-too-two, lie-lay,*

121

and *let-leave.* I always felt that it was important they learn to speak English correctly. I was amazed how many times students came back to remind me about learning those things and remember how we made it fun. I gave students points for finding words misused in newspapers, magazines, or books. During vocabulary tests, I insisted they use the words in sentences with clues as to their meaning. For example, the sentence "I sat on a rickety chair" didn't give me any clues. How am I to know what a rickety chair is? A better sentence would be: "I sat on a rickety chair and it broke into a hundred pieces."

At a restaurant one summer, I met a former student whom I had taught ten years before and who was home from acting school in California. He was a shy young man and I couldn't believe he chose acting as a career. He asked if I remembered him, and I said his name, asking what he was doing. "I've completed acting school," he said, "and I was the only one in my class who was not required to take a remedial English course!"

"You're kidding me!" I exclaimed.

"I'm serious," he assured me. "Do you remember how you drilled us on all that vocabulary and you made us use them properly in a sentence? When I took my preliminary courses, all those little troublesome words were there. I had to know how to speak correctly." This budding actor was so appreciative that he didn't have to take the remedial English class.

I felt it was so important that students learn simple things like addressing an envelope—the return address had to be just right. Everything we did had to be just right. It's amazing how many students come to seventh grade from elementary school taking what a teacher says as gospel truth. I disliked that. I would deliberately say things incorrectly or misspell a word and then chide the students for not correcting me. I told them, "I'm a human being just like you. I make mistakes like you do." I taught them how to criticize professionally, and then I gave them points for correcting me. I taught them that we were in this learning together, not with me as

God preaching to them, but they were there to teach me things, too. It was my goal to help students be the very best they could be and I felt I had a very important role in doing that. When my homeroom students got their report cards, I always looked at them. I would either praise them or ask why they got less-than-satisfactory grades. Most of the time they didn't know why they got low grades. I told them, "You need to know that. How are you going to do better if you don't know why you did poorly?" Many of the students were afraid to question their teachers as to why they got a bad grade. I went with them to their teachers and we'd figure it out. I took one period after grades came out to talk with students about the grades they earned in my class. I said things like, "This is your grade. I'm giving you a C this time even though you really earned a D-plus." "This is what most people would call a D, but this is the first time you've been in my class and I'm giving you the benefit of the doubt for this marking period. I'm slipping you a C because you're so close. Now, I want **you** to earn that C the next time." It was amazing how many times a student would work so hard to make that happen. I didn't deflate or discourage them. A little sugar on the spoon went a long way.

I became convinced in my career that there isn't a bad student beyond repair. In my final years as a teacher, I asked for a group of homeroom students—the worst kids in the school. There were twenty-nine of them. One day a boy, Adam (not his real name), challenged a teacher in the cafeteria. The teacher told the principal about the boy refusing to do as she requested. The principal, a tall World War II veteran who wasn't afraid of anyone, went to get Adam. In the meantime, the students saw what was happening and gave the defiant student a challenge. As the principal approached Adam to take him out of the cafeteria, he stood up and winged a cupcake right into the face of the principal. The principal took off after Adam and pulled a hamstring. He was suspended for five days and no one knew what to do with him.

I asked the principal if I could have this boy in my

homeroom. He thought I was crazy, suggesting we should have Adam put away someplace. "No," I said. "Just let me have Adam in my room." Another chair was put into my room for Adam. It wasn't easy. In fact, it was tough. There were lots of times when I came home wondering why I had done this. There were days when there were fights—when students would decide they weren't going to take anything from anybody. I'd call my church friend, telling him, "I need your prayers. These students aren't being respectful and I need their respect or I can't do anything."

I would keep working with them—kind but firm. I have tried to tell teachers how to do that, but it's hard to tell someone else how to do it. Even my family, my brothers and sisters, say they don't understand where I get that ability, but it seems that it has always been a part of me. I wonder why everyone can't see that there's a better way of handling people. That's why the conflict transformation concept intrigues me so much. There's so much that can be done when we work to transform a bad situation. It's the right way.

I told the students we needed something to give us pride. We had three school drives during the year. The first one was a booster drive that involved selling pieces of paper with the athletic schedule on them for a buck a piece. The school kept track of who the high seller was and which homeroom had the most sales. I said, "Kids, let's go for it. Let's be the highest-selling homeroom in the school!" I turned their minds from fighting to a different kind of challenge. I offered very small prizes, such as a Chinese dinner, so we could have something more than any other homeroom. We won that booster drive by about six dollars! Man, those kids jumped up and down when it was announced on the intercom! It did my heart good to see that.

We kept struggling along until we got to the magazine drive about six weeks later. The students said, "Let's get this one!" They strategized about who would do what. Some students said their parents wouldn't allow them to go out to sell magazines. Those students were assigned to help with the bookkeeping and serve as cheerleaders. The drive went for ten days. Some days we would be the top sellers; other days we'd fall behind, which would discourage them. They planned who would work as teams to go out in the evenings, even outside the district, to get sales. We won that drive by a pretty good margin. The students felt really great about that.

When this class got into eighth grade, we won all three school drives. When they got into ninth grade, we won the first and second. By this time I had them eating out of my hand, so to speak. I had very few discipline problems. The final drive was a candy drive. Because our homeroom had won so many awards, everyone in the school was determined we wouldn't get the school record three years in a row! It was tough! We were losing.

This might be stupid, but I like to think God got these two guys into a fight in my homeroom on the Friday afternoon before the drive was to close on Monday morning. I walked into my room to see two guys slugging it out over some minor thing. I broke it up and said, "Guys, sit down!" Since it was the end of the day, I dismissed the other students, telling the fighters, "Guys, don't worry about the buses. I'll see that you get home." Then I asked what the problem was, how it got started, what sparked it. Who threw the first punch? Who wasn't man enough to stop the fight? I would always tell them that it takes a man not to fight. I would ask, "Who was the little guy this time?" They would tell me.

I always preached that discipline was for one reason only and that was to pay the price, get it behind you, and go on with your life, never to have it brought up again. I said, "Guys, there's a price. I'm disappointed. I thought you respected each other as classmates. I thought you respected me more than for me to walk in on something like this. There's a price that must be paid. What are we going to do?" We talked about that for a while. They asked if I wasn't going to send them to the office. I said, "We will deal with this right here unless you guys can't cooperate." I told them why I felt it was better to resolve the problem internally rather than going to the office, what I had to gain from this—my self-esteem. I told them it meant a lot to me.

After discussing the problem and shaking hands, I made a suggestion. "We're behind in this candy drive," I said. "I'll give up my Saturday. I'll pick you up at ten." During the drive, everything except peanuts had been sold. I said, "We'll load up all the peanuts my car can hold and we'll sell all those peanuts. That should maybe put our class over the top!"

I took each boy home and talked to the parents. They all agreed this was a better punishment than suspension. So, on Saturday morning I loaded my Renault with over 300 cans of peanuts. The car was so full there was hardly room for the boys to sit. Before we started, I said, "Now, let's set some ground rules. I'm giving my time and my gas as well as the wear and tear on my car. You guys are giving your legs and your energy to this and we're going to split the sales right down the middle. If one of you sells two hundred and the other sells one hundred, you'll each get credit for one hundred and fifty cans toward the drive, which could make you high sales person for the drive."

We started out, one on each side of the street. We moved on to the next town, and it got to be noontime. The guys were getting hungry, so we got a bite to eat in a fast-food place. As we walked back to the car, I heard the boys begin to argue because one had sold more than the other. I said, "Hold it, guys! Ground rules, remember?"

"Yeah, but I'm working harder!"

"Oh, no! Ground rules. We shook on that before we left the school. We're men. We don't violate our agreements."

They got their differences ironed out and went back to work. It was four o'clock by the time we got our last can of peanuts sold, and the boys were exhausted! We went in Monday morning with well over $300, which was enough to put us over the top by about $100. Otherwise, we wouldn't have made it. Those two boys became the highest salesmen for the drive. I can't begin to tell you what that did for that group of "bad" kids. The drive was in April, and when we got to the end of the year the parents of my homeroom students were 100 percent in my court. They thought I couldn't do anything wrong. They thought I must be a god of some kind to turn their "bad" children around. That was an extension of what I taught them—that they didn't do good things just for school or for me as a teacher; they did it for themselves, for their parents, and to feel good about something. I would tell them to do something good on the weekend, to surprise their parents, go out and rake the leaves or dump the trash without having to be told.

When the end of the year came, we had set a record that has never been broken—namely, winning nine straight school drives. I continued to emphasize to teachers and administration that we had accomplished that record with so-called bad kids. As far as I know, there's not one of those students who has become a "bad" adult. I have every reason to believe they may not have turned out that way had someone not intervened in their lives. I always told teachers, "Wherever there's a soul, there's a spark. All you need to do is find that spark and feed it and you'll eventually get a flame." One of those high "salesmen" is now chief of police in a neighboring town, a man who came back before I retired to ask if I had known of his accomplishment, which I hadn't. The other "salesman" became a missionary in Africa. He had come from a religious family, but he had a temper and wasn't going to be taken down by anybody. Another boy in that homeroom also became a local police officer.

Four years into his teaching career, Harold was persuaded by his principal to become head of the English Department and, then, six years later to begin preparing for an administrative role. He says: At the time each of these positions opened, I didn't think I was qualified to be either a department head or principal, but it turned out that I was very capable as well as very successful in both positions because I had some experiences that helped me.

Harold began taking graduate courses at Lehigh University.
Of his work there he says:

It's a miracle I ever made it through Lehigh University. My principal encouraged me to attend Lehigh because of its tremendous reputation, telling me about outstanding professors in both the education and administration departments. I really don't know how I did it. Lehigh University's campus is built on a hill with steep walkways, and many of its buildings incorporate many steps.

Most of my graduate courses were taken during the summer months. The main education building had about ten exterior steps without a handrail. Getting into this and other buildings always proved to be a real challenge. Carrying my books in a satchel or briefcase, I would swing the satchel back and forth a few times in order to get enough momentum to get up—one step at a time. I learned how to use the weight of my briefcase to lift my left leg, swing the briefcase forward and upward, then jerk up my right leg while keeping my body perfectly balanced. Fortunately, I never fell. At that time in my life, I still had just enough strength to negotiate hills and steps.

During one very hot summer, my class was held on the fourth floor of a building that had no elevator. I would arrive at least a half hour early in order to negotiate the four flights of stairs without others observing my awkward struggle. By the time I reached the fourth floor, I would be drenched in sweat. Arriving early also enabled me to cool off a bit and get my wind back. Going up those steps with my books in one arm and pushing against the iron rail with the other proved to be hard work, but I was focused on getting my master's degree and nothing was going to stop me.

I eventually gave up taking courses during the winter months because of potentially bad weather. During one ice storm, the sidewalks and steps became quite icy. I was struggling to keep my balance and became very fearful of falling, knowing if I were to fall I wouldn't be able to get up on my own. Eventually, another graduate student heading in my direction saw me struggling, so he took

128

my briefcase, asked me to take his arm, and assisted taking me to where I needed to go. This type of kindness was shown numerous times during my eight years of taking graduate courses at Lehigh. The university was also very considerate and gave me free parking permits so I could park as close as possible to the library and other buildings in which my classes were held. Everyone was always so helpful.

Ten years into my teaching career and midway through my efforts at attaining a master's degree, Mr. Warner again began encouraging me to prepare myself for stepping into an administrative position. Only a few years away from retirement as the principal at Indian Valley, he wanted me to become his assistant principal in time, but I loved teaching very much and wasn't really interested in becoming anything else. Finally, he persistently said, "Harold, you're the only man I want working with me as my assistant. As a teacher and English Department head you have proven your effectiveness, but you are dealing with only a few classes and one department within the school. As an administrator, you could effectively work with an entire staff and school—not to mention hundreds more students."

On that advice, I switched majors in my graduate work and earned a master's degree in secondary administration. Shortly thereafter, I accepted a position at Indian Valley Junior High School as Mr. Warner's assistant principal. I loved the new challenges associated with the job and began to understand why I was led in that direction. Mr. Warner had a great sense about knowing where each staff member's strengths lay—a keen insight he skillfully passed on to me.

As my graduate work at Lehigh drew to a close, my disability began increasing rather quickly. I would do something one evening and the next day I couldn't do it again as easily. There were spurts like that. I worked quickly to finish my education before my physical condition deteriorated to the point where I would no longer be able to attend classes at Lehigh. During one three-week period, there was such a dramatic change in my physical condition that I told the principal he should perhaps consider hiring someone to replace me. Eleanor, the school nurse, even drove me to New York City to confer with a renowned doctor and medical specialist known for his many dramatic medical successes. Fortunately, my rapid deterioration then became somewhat dormant for a while before returning years later.

In a span of eight years, I had earned a master's degree and completed an additional sixty graduate credits beyond my master's degree. Yes, it was very taxing from both a mental and a physical point of view—but very rewarding. Now, looking back on those years, I can't even begin to imagine how I did it. My strong determination to reach a particular goal always seemed to inspire others to pitch in and give helpful assistance whenever necessary as I traveled along my journey of life.

Reflecting back on my ten years as an English Department head, I was most fortunate to have Mr. Warner as my principal and mentor. Together we developed an excellent English Department by hiring highly qualified teachers, many of whom I had the privilege of interviewing and recommending for employment. Mr. Warner placed a great deal of confidence and trust in my ability to read people and come up with a winner. Sitting down with a prospective teacher, I always looked for 60 percent personality and 40 percent flexibility, gearing my interview questions in that way. What grades the applicant made in college weren't of primary interest to me; I felt if prospective teachers were smart enough to get through college, they were intelligent enough to teach junior high school students. But I also knew if a person lacked a dynamic personality or wasn't very flexible, he or she could not effectively teach no matter what his or her level of intelligence happened to be. Having some influence on what was to be taught in English classes, I stressed writing, reading, usage, and vocabulary, but I also placed a strong emphasis on the teaching of respect and responsibility. I always stood right behind my teachers. At first I observed my teachers because of school policy, but eventually I had so many invitations to visit classes that I no longer observed out of necessity. Teachers would ask me to help when they experienced a problem or when a certain unit wasn't working for them.

A former student teacher of mine who was then teaching in Connecticut found that a new program wasn't having the effect she thought it should. She asked if I would come to Connecticut for a week to observe her teaching this particular program and give her suggestions. I scripted everything she was doing in all her classes, so we could discuss at night what was happening. It finally dawned on me that students never saw the entire picture of what she was trying to teach. They were working on such minute steps that by the time they got well into the program, they had forgotten the beginning steps. There was no awareness of how the tiny steps related to the whole.

When I taught writing, I started with a paragraph and worked down to a single word, so students could understand there was a lead sentence with other supporting sentences. The mechanical portion of this teacher's program was so detailed that in studying paragraph writing the students didn't get to see the whole.

Teachers began seeing that if they had a problem, I could help them work it out. This was also true with discipline problems. Students always thought I was in a class to observe the teacher, but many times I was there to observe a particular student. I would script what the teacher did and how the class reacted to her actions. If I were zeroing in on a student, I would script what his/her reaction was in relation to the teacher or class. Frequently I would notice the teacher neglecting to interact with that student who was having a discipline problem, perhaps thinking if she calls on him, he'll give a smart answer. However, that problem student would do something else to get attention. I would help the teacher relate to that difficult student and involve him in the class.

When a student in my class misbehaved, I kept him or her after school. I helped with his or her homework enabling that student to become the best student in my class the next day. If we were working on vocabulary, I'd drill the student until he or she had it down perfect in spelling, meaning and usage. I never called that detention. I called it an after-school session to help the individual become a better student. We would also talk about the misbehavior. When that student would go back to class the next day, he or she was the first one I'd call on. Other students would look at him or her and say, "Wow! He's [She's] no dummy!" Many times students who got into trouble had difficulty learning, but by drilling and working at it they could become a star for a day. Later other students would ask me if they could stay after school so they could be stars, too.

I had charts in my classroom where I placed, for example, a gold star for a perfect score on a quiz. It always did a student good to see that he or she was progressing along with the others. The only way some students could achieve that was to get extra help, something many students didn't get at home. That's how I got so many hours in after school. I would do all my paperwork in the evenings so I could deal with children during the school day. I seldom took work home. Many times I didn't get home until 11:00 at night and then I would sit with my mom for a little time before going to bed.

I took a seventh-grade class through the New England states one August. I had been director of a summer reading program and I felt the $2,000 I received for being director was "pork barrel" money. I thought it was a bit excessive, so I decided not to spend it on myself. That year, I was in turmoil with contract negotiations. The board or superintendent would call me out of class unannounced and I would have to leave my classroom—usually the same class of students who had me for a double period.

They were a great group of average students, but I felt they were often cheated by my absence. I had to assign a student to lead the class, because the administration would sometimes forget to get coverage for me. I always designated two students to learn what the lesson was going to be, and those students would lead the class in my absence. One time I was gone for both periods and one of the students went to the principal telling him they had run out of things to do. The principal had walked by my classroom earlier and had seen the girls at the front of a very orderly class. At the end of the year, the class received recognition for being a model class learning to do things on their own. I called four girls together, telling them I had this money and I wanted to honor their class for the difficulties they had during the year.

I asked the four girls how they would feel if I spent $2,000 on a trip for all twenty-seven students. They were very enthused, so I called the parents in, explaining I would like to take their children on a three-day trip to Ausable Chasm in New York State, over the lake to Vermont, through Massachusetts, to Sturbridge Village, and back home through New York. It would only cost the students two dollars each for the trip. All the students were excited except two boys who had never been away from home overnight and were afraid of becoming homesick. I assured the parents I would take care of them. My goal was to teach the youngsters how to be ladies and gentlemen in every aspect of the trip—eating in restaurants, carrying suitcases, opening doors, being polite, keeping quiet in the hotel rooms, et cetera. Parents couldn't believe their children would have such a trip. Each student was told to bring along a nice article of clothing and some casual clothing. My school nurse accompanied us, as did several other chaperones.

I hired a bus, explaining to the company what my goals were for these students. This was a very average group of kids from average homes who had not been away from home very much and never had experiences like wealthier kids. The first stop was in New York at a small theme park. The next stop was a very nice restaurant in a sports club. En route I had been educating the students about proper etiquette. I had ordered the best meal I could get, including appetizers, steak, and dessert. I warned them that sometimes steaks are rare or too well done. I explained they would be asked how they wanted their steaks.

As we all sat around a table and the waitresses took our orders, the students were extremely polite and orderly, with no rowdiness at all. The waitresses asked how they would like their steaks done, and after they were served I walked around the table asking each child if their steaks were done to their liking. Two students found the medium steaks they had requested were too rare, but they were too timid to say anything. "That's part of why we're here," I said. "When the waitress comes around to ask how everything is, you just tell her your steaks are a little too rare for you," which is what they did. They were all so impressed when the waitress gladly returned the steaks to the kitchen and brought them back done just as the girls requested. They were accustomed to taking what they got! You just ate it! I wanted to teach these students the restaurant was there to serve them, to have happy customers.

The waitress was so impressed that she asked the proprietor to come and see this great bunch of kids. When I paid the bill, the proprietor said, "Knock ten percent off that bill. I've never seen a bunch of school kids like this."

Ausable Chasm was our next stop. It was a huge gorge a hundred fifty feet deep where one could go through the chasm in small boats—an awe-inspiring experience. We ate our breakfast there, requesting the restaurant to prepare bag lunches since we were going across Lake Champlain into Vermont to visit a marble quarry. Before going to breakfast, I told the students people were going to expect them to be a wild bunch of kids, but I asked them to prove the people wrong. I always got the most beautiful dining room available. The students quietly found their seats, exhibiting the best of manners, waiting to begin eating until I had said grace. I heard comments about their excellent behavior.

While the students went through the chasm with their chaperones, I remained behind to supervise getting our lunches. A huge expensive gift shop was on the premises and I asked the manager if the students could visit the gift shop. He exclaimed, "Gosh! If they behave like they did at breakfast, they're more than welcome. You can tell your students they can buy anything in that gift shop at forty percent off." When the students returned, I told them they had thirty minutes in the gift shop and that since the manager was so impressed with their manners at breakfast, they would be given a 40 percent discount on anything they bought. They learned that good behavior brought them positive recognition.

We took the ferry across Lake Champlain, saw how marble was quarried, and then had the experience of riding a ski lift in southern Vermont. We spent the night in Springfield, Massachusetts. Since the students loved drama, I had arranged for them to see Carla Alberghetti and Edward Everett Horton performing in *The Fantastiks* live at the Storrowton Theatre in West Springfield, Massachusetts. I chose a classy motel, with a wide staircase leading from the lobby to the second floor. "This is where we're having our dinner and then we're going to the theater," I explained to the children.

As was my usual procedure, I went to the registration desk to be certain everything was in order. I overheard two businessmen talking: "Oh, man! There's a whole busload of kids coming in here. I guess we'll not get a lot of sleep tonight."

I ignored them, telling the reservation desk attendant who we were. "You have that whole wing at the top of the stairs," he told me.

When I returned to the bus, I told the students what I had overheard. I told them, "You've been super. Let's just be super again. You have it in you now!"

By this time, the girls never picked up a piece of luggage. The boys handled all that. The boys also held the doors for the girls. The first night we had done these things, two guys said, "Well, I'm not gonna take that girl's luggage."

I responded with, "Wait a minute, guys. This isn't a matter of whose luggage you're carrying, it's a matter of being a gentleman. And you ladies, it's a matter of you being a lady. You guys will each take two pieces of luggage, your own and one belonging to a lady. You ladies will follow the gentleman who has your luggage."

Early in the trip, several guys rushed ahead to be first going through a door, but I cautioned them, "Whoa, guys! Remember to be gentlemen. You hold the doors. Ladies go in first!" By this time into our trip, the bus driver would set the luggage on the ground and the gentlemen would pick up the luggage as it came off the bus. As we walked through the double doors, the guys walked two by two with the luggage followed by the girls walking up those red-carpeted stairs. One of the businessmen I had seen earlier exclaimed, "Where the heck are those kids from?" There were no disturbances during that night.

The ladies dressed up in their best dresses and the gentlemen put on their coats and ties before going to the dining room for dinner. Each table was set for six people, with the appetizers on the table. I was talking to a lady from the theater who had arranged to meet us so she could show me the way to the theater. A waitress came to me saying, "Mr. Zook, I know you're on a tight schedule. We have the appetizers out and nobody is eating."

I said, "Oh, excuse me for a minute." I sat down with the students, said grace, and took a bite of my appetizer. The students then began eating.

With that many students, I had to buy cheap tickets that were for seats in the back rows of the theater. However, when we got to the theater, the lady who was stunned by what she had just seen in the dining room met me at the bus, saying, "Mr. Zook, we have a change of plans." Since it was a Thursday night and the theater wasn't filled, she moved us to the first two rows of seats—the most expensive seats in the house—at no extra cost. She moved a few people around so we could all sit together as a group.

I wanted the students to experience the colonial history of

Sturbridge Village. As we explored the village, I noticed a group of girls chatting with a man from a bakery truck and not paying much attention to the village. I wondered what they were doing, but I didn't say anything. That night we stopped at a very nice restaurant for our dinner, planning to drive through the night to get home. Again we had a lovely meal with all the trimmings, and the waitresses were again impressed. As the meal ended, a chaperone told me one of the students had something she'd like to say.

Three students brought out a huge cake they had bought at Sturbridge Village. Since they couldn't find any frosting, they had found pieces of different-colored rock salt with which they spelled out: "Thanks, Mr. Zook!" The waitress saw this and couldn't believe the response of the students. When I paid the bill, the owner of the restaurant took $200 from our bill. When we got home, we had $800 left because people along the way gave us a break.

One of the two boys who was reluctant to go on the trip is the actor mentioned before and the other one is a police officer. The parents of these boys attributed that trip for their losing their fear of being away from home and helping them become integrated into their class in high school. The students purchased an engraved plaque for the bus driver. With the leftover $800 we put on a catered dinner for the parents in the school cafeteria where we displayed our photos, brochures, et cetera, and showed the video of our trip. The media learned of it and we got some nice publicity. Some of these students still tell me how much that trip meant to them and the rewards they got for being good hard workers in school.

7

Compassionate Disciplinarian

The Reporter *of Lansdale, Pennsylvania, published on October 4, 1986, in the "Getting to Know Your Neighbor" column reported of Mr. Zook:*

"His [Harold Zook's], first goal as an assistant principal was to eliminate after-school detention because, he said, it wastes the teachers' and students' time. Instead, he believes in work details for students who have disciplinary problems.

Students are warned for the first offense, have a personal visit with Zook for a second, and then are disciplined the third time.

"Very few kids get to the third level," he said.

Parents find that Zook is willing to meet with them after work so they don't have to take a few hours off to discuss a child's problem.

"I think it's more effective to allow parents to come on off-hours," Zook said. "They are more relaxed and have more time without being limited."

Although he lives with pain every day from a debilitating disease that forces him to drive a cart around the school, Zook remains happy.

"I am living with pain every day, but so do a lot of other people," he said. "It is difficult to live with a disability."

The only time he is grateful to have a handicap is when one of his students is caught taking drugs. When that happens, Zook gives the student very serious advice.

"I tell the student that he/she has a beautiful body and I don't have that," he said, and continues, 'I'd give a million dollars to have what you've got.' Somehow, that seems to penetrate."

His patience and understanding seem to pay off for those students who discuss their problems. A few years ago, a girl was competing with her best friend for boyfriends, and she was beginning to turn to drugs.

Two years later, the girl returned to her junior high school in a prom dress, escorted by her boyfriend.

"She said, 'You told me that if I was able to keep myself free from drugs, I'd be able to have boyfriends and be popular. That all came true,' " Zook said. "There are never any guarantees, but I'm glad it worked out in her case."

Zook said he is content to remain as an assistant principal because he prefers to work behind the scenes.

Usually, Zook said, he takes everything a day at a time. "When some people get to be assistant principal, they use that as a stepping-stone to a principalship," he said. "But I love to deal with the kids. If I were a principal, I wouldn't be able to do that as much."

In a Reading Eagle *article titled "No Holds Barred," reporter Pam Rohland wrote:*

He says, "I can do a very heavy hand on some kids, but it's not my first choice."

The photographs (under a glass on his desk) are a gallery of his professional success, tangible proof that one caring adult can bring about a transformation.

Zook looks at the pictures with obvious fondness.

"Isn't she beautiful?" he asks rhetorically, pointing to a smiling, wholesome-looking young woman. "She used to shoplift for her friends. She was so street-wise."

During my first year as a vice principal, my car aerial was torn off several times by a clique of seven or ten guys who were hard-nosed. They tried to crash dances and do things like that just to be difficult. I would go to all ends to find out who did that, and I would discipline them very firmly, but with love. I didn't know any other way to do it. Eventually, the message got out that "you don't mess around with Mr. Zook."

However, if those same boys needed something, I would treat them like any other student. I would never treat them as though they had done something bad. One boy was determined he was going to beat up another student. This boy assured me I couldn't touch him after he was out of school, in the evenings, and on weekends. I said, "Don't try me." I had a feeling he was going to his intended victim's home to beat him up that weekend. I informed the boy's parents that their son was going to be attacked, telling them I would call the police to be on standby over the weekend. I suggested to the parents that if they saw the attacker coming on their property, they should immediately call the police. Sure enough, about ten-thirty Saturday morning the boy showed up. The parents called the police, who arrested him. I told the police to charge him to the hilt because I wanted to give him a message.

I remember sitting in court with this boy when he said to the judge, "Mr. Zook can't do that. He can't rule my life when I'm not in school." The judge responded harshly, giving him a week in juvenile hall. That gave him a very strong message. Those kinds of things gave a strong message that I was a strong disciplinarian, but at the same time I went to juvenile hall to visit the boy twice during that week. I told him that I would work to reduce his time so he could come back to school if he was willing to make amends, which he did.

There were two boys who stole about five hundred dollars' worth of fishing equipment and the state police were involved. They had all the circumstantial evidence, but the boys wouldn't confess to the crime. These were two boys in special education. Incidentally, these boys were in my school because the other junior high school couldn't handle them. They were arrogant and hard and were both learning-disabled. I looked at them as trying to compensate for their disability by being difficult, because I knew that's the way I had done. I would be something I didn't want to be just to become part of the crowd, so I wouldn't be labeled as someone stupid.

The officer came to the school and gave me all the circumstantial evidence, but he couldn't get the boys to confess. I asked how he had dealt with them. He said, "I was harsh. I even told them I would throw them in Monkey Hall," which was a juvenile center. "I threatened them, but I couldn't break them."

"Officer," I said, "that's where you're wrong. Let me talk to the boys and I'll get back to you."

I called the boys in together. The officer had talked to them separately trying to get one to squeal on the other one. I said, "Boys, I had a state trooper here about an hour ago, and I understand there is suspicion that you stole fishing equipment." I could tell by the way they looked at each other that there was something wrong. I told them, "Look, you have dealt with me for two years now. I respect you as being young men and I want you to respect me as a friend and your vice principal. We need to discuss this. The officer said this is circumstantial evidence, and I don't know if you did it. The officer doesn't know if you did it."

I talked for some time about the virtues of being honest, about being a man, and about how a man will be honest about making mistakes. After all that, I said, "Boys, you don't have to answer this question, but I really would like you to be men. If you did make this mistake, I will go to the police station with you. I will go to court with you. I will do whatever needs to be done to help save you from any undue discipline."

I looked at one boy, asking, "Were you guilty of this crime?" He looked at the other guy, who I could see giving subtle signals meaning, "Don't do it." I told him to take his time, that this was a very important decision in his life that would help make him a man or make him a child.

He waited about a minute before he said, "Yes, Mr. Zook. You respected me. I confess that I did it."

I asked the second boy, "Were you a partner in this crime?"

"Yeah," he admitted, "we did it."

I asked if they knew where the loot was and they said they did. "Are you willing to get it and give it back?" I asked.

The boys were reluctant to do that and I didn't know what the problem was, but I said, "I'll tell you what. We'll get through the rest of the day; we'll call your parents right now so you can hear what I tell them." I called the parents telling them the boys had confessed to this crime. They were most distressed, but I told them there was a good side to this because the boys had made an honest confession and were willing to go with me to retrieve the stolen goods. The parents were at work, so I told them I would take the boys to get the goods, take them out to dinner so the parents didn't have to worry about that, and we would meet at the police station at 5:30. The parents agreed.

I called the state trooper back to tell him what had happened. He was very upset and began swearing. I reminded him that I had gotten this confession, not him, and I wanted to be part of the decision for punishment. The boys and I drove to the house where they said the goods were to be found. I said, "You boys go on in and I'll wait in the car." I waited for about twenty minutes, but finally they returned with the fishing lines, tackle, and all kinds of things. They went back for the second load of stuff. Then I learned about a nineteen-year-old boy who had wanted these things and had it stashed away. The older boy didn't want to release the goods, and it took these younger boys quite a while to convince him that he needed to give them up.

I took the boys to a nice restaurant for dinner, telling them, "Fellows, this may be the only meal you'll ever get from me, so chow down!" And they did. I never saw two guys eat so much food! As we ate, we began chitchatting and the boys unloaded their lives, including all the trouble they had gotten into, how they lied to their parents. For an hour and a half they unloaded while I listened. I hardly said a word as they told me all the bad things they had done.

When they ran out of things to say, I asked, "Guys, do you feel better?"

"Yeah," they said, "but you aren't going to tell on us, are you?"

"No," I responded. "I don't need to tell. That's for you to tell. Remember, a man faces his difficulties and becomes better because of it. You guys have experiences that ninety percent of your classmates will never have. You can be ninety percent better than them because of the mistakes you have made, as long as you learn from them and don't make them again."

I proceeded to tell the boys a few of my episodes, about the time I was planning to trash a boy's car and a few of my shenanigans and how my father saved me from getting into too much trouble. They just couldn't believe I had those situations in my life. I think it made me seem more human in their eyes.

When we got to the police station, the parents were very nervous. I asked them to relax, telling them the boys had confessed and how much that should mean to them as parents. I felt that should mean far more to them than the crime that was committed. I left it to the officer who questioned the boys and they confessed to him just as they had confessed to me. The officer then "threw the book at them," giving them the maximum penalty. He was going to lock them up.

I said, "Wait a minute, Officer. Can we go to another room and discuss this?"

In the other room, the officer said, "These sons of a guns! They wouldn't confess to me. I'm angry!"

"Why are you angry?" I asked. "These boys are boys. They made a mistake. They confessed their mistake. They made it easy for you. They got the stolen goods back for you to give back to the owners. Why are you angry?"

After about fifteen minutes' discussion I said, "Officer! I won't stand for this. If you do what you said you were going to do in there, I'm going to ask the boys to recant their confession and I will recant what I've told you, which will put you right back where you were before we came here."

"What do you want?" he asked.

I had just heard about a Scared Straight Program at Rahway Prison in New Jersey. I said, "I would like these two boys to be taken to the Scared Straight Program with one of my local township officers and spend the day in Rahway Prison." The officer reluctantly agreed to that, even though he thought there should be other punishments in addition.

"Let's see what happens to the boys," I suggested. "You'll have their actions as a matter of record if they get into further trouble."

The officer and I returned to the boys and their parents, where the officer told them he had made the decision to have the boys go to Rahway Prison. This came as quite a shock to the parents until I explained the program and its purpose.

Several days later, I arranged for a local officer to take the boys to spend a day at the prison. They walked into four cement walls all painted yellow, doors clanging behind them, into the waiting room. As part of the program, a big black prisoner walked up to the boys saying, "Oh! What are you guys doing here? I know what you've done. You probably lie; you've probably lied to your parents; you probably steal; you probably do drugs!" The boys were jolted because they had done everything he mentioned.

They went through another gate that clanged shut behind them. The boys were in a corridor with twenty other juvenile offenders, all black; my boys were the only whites among them, all of whom were getting their hands stamped. As one of the tough black guys approached to have his hand stamped, he pulled away saying, "You're not going to stamp my hand!" *Bam!* The boy got a stamp right on his forehead! These boys were scared skinny! My

144

boys weren't as yet hardened criminals like the other offenders, so they were very impressionable.

They went through three more gates. By this time, the boys were feeling like they were being incarcerated! They came to a room where five prisoners—lifers—were sitting behind a table and all the other offenders plus my boys were to sit on benches in front of the table, similar to a classroom. The prisoners behind the table told what it's like to be in prison. They asked my boys to stand up. "You white guys think you're hot stuff, don't you, just because you're white? You're just honkies!" The prisoners continued to talk tough, using rough language, while the boys shook in their shoes. The officer was sitting in the back of the class watching the boys' reactions.

The boys answered, "Yes, sir," No, sir," becoming very polite.

"Don't give us that polite stuff. That's not the way you are. You're hard-nosed guys! You think you're tough!" The prisoners wouldn't let up for several hours.

The boys were given a tour of the prison, the lifer cells, the isolation cells. As they left the prison, the boys were very quiet. Then, as they neared home, the boys began talking about their experience, how they never wanted to be in a prison, and how they wanted to transform their lives.

When the boys returned to school the next day, I asked them to come to my office for a chat. I asked them how their day went. They said, "Mr. Zook, you'll never catch us doing anything wrong again."

"That's a pretty big commitment," I said. "Are you sure you can manage that?"

"Yes, we can," they replied.

"Please understand that if you do fall, and in all likelihood you will, remember the lesson is: take the punishment, do it willingly, vow to yourself you won't make that same mistake again, square your shoulders, and go on."

Both boys have their own businesses now. One has a wallpaper business and years later was really proud to be able to do some paper hanging in my school. Seven years after he graduated, the other boy, who now owns a construction business, came by. "I saw your car out front," he explained. "I want you to know what kind of a man I made of myself. I have a wife and three children." He gave me a picture of his beautiful wife and three beautiful children.

This same boy had been in an English class with a large male teacher who ruled by sheer size and intimidation. This young fellow wasn't about to be intimidated, so when the teacher asked him to move to a different seat, he refused. The teacher couldn't do anything about it, which greatly upset him. When the student was sent to my office, I said, "Why is this so difficult for you?"

"He doesn't have a right to do that to me."

"Maybe he doesn't have the right, but he's an adult and he has the authority," I responded. "It should be you who yields to that authority. If an officer stops you on the highway, are you going to argue with him, telling him he has no right to stop you, and get yourself into a lot more trouble? It takes a bigger man to yield, to just obey. Maybe he was out of line, maybe he didn't use the right tactics, but someday you're going to be an authority figure. You'll be a parent, a boss, somebody in authority, and you're going to expect another person to obey you. What are you going to do about it? Do you want to be a man or do you want to be a little kid? Why don't you surprise Mr. Clark and do what he wants you to do? Do it willingly without making any bones about it?"

"I'll do that," he said, because I had him feeling like he would be a bigger man than the teacher if he could do that.

The boy returned to the class and sat in his seat. The teacher said, "Are you going to listen to me? I told you to move back to the back of the class."

The boy obediently moved to the back with no problem. Several weeks later, the teacher came to me asking, "What's with this guy? He does everything I tell him to do."

"Isn't that what you expect?" I asked

"Yeah, but I don't understand the guy. He doesn't give me any more hassles!"

"Isn't that what you want?"

"Yea, but I want to know what happened."

"Your problem student decided he wanted to be a man and that's what he's trying to be. Just respect that!"

This student, now a man, when he returned asked, "Mr. Zook, do you remember Mr. Clark, that English teacher?"

"Yes, what about him?"

"Do you remember what you told me about respect? I want you to know I'm a boss now. I have three men working under me doing construction. Two of the men are great guys; the other has all kinds of ability, but he's an ass. I can't make this guy follow orders."

"Why don't you fire him?" I inquired.

"Because he's a good worker. I'm here to tell you that I thought about what you told me back in my English class. I took this worker aside and told him about all his abilities, about how it's difficult for me to be a boss when I have a workman like him. I said, 'I thought about firing you, but I remembered something that happened to me in school,' and I related that experience to him. I want you to know that today that guy is my foreman. What you taught me at Indian Valley does work, even in my dealings with my workers!"

He also thanked me for the Rahway Prison experience, telling me he never messed up after that.

Benny [not his real name], who was in a life skills class and was sheltered in elementary school, was afraid of a new environment. He had never ridden a bus. I talked to his parents, whom I had taught, and remembered them as sweethearts in seventh grade. I asked them why they were driving Benny to school, suggesting it was time for him to venture out by riding the bus. The parents were afraid he wouldn't behave on the bus but agreed to try it because of who I was. Before long I received a call from the bus company, stating they were excluding Benny from the bus because he couldn't stay in his seat. He was on the floor, on his knees, and all over the place. The driver had tried seating Benny directly behind him, but Benny wanted to talk. Everyone loved Benny in spite of his disabilities, he was so active and outgoing. But the bus driver said Benny's activity on the bus was too dangerous.

I felt we must solve this problem. When Benny was removed from the bus, his parents said they didn't think it would work. I slept over it and after a few days an idea came to me. Why didn't we ask students to solve this? I presented the problem to the student council officers, suggesting we work together to solve Benny's situation. I had in mind using two students and a backup student in case one of the two was not on the bus. We would put Benny in the back of the bus where everyone wanted to sit. The assigned two students would sit with him and play games or entertain him in some way.

The student council suggested two students who liked Benny and who had egged him on to do funny things that would annoy the driver. When I called the boys in and explained what we would like them to do, asking them how they would feel about it, they said they would love it. They sat in the backseat and played video games with him, et cetera. A chart was developed so each day Benny got points, red or gold stars, depending on his behavior. He took the chart home each day for his parents to sign. Even when the problem was solved, the driver didn't like Benny and didn't want him on the bus. I told the president of the school bus association that this boy would ride the bus because he was doing well and getting gold stars every day. The driver had to accept him.

When students brought me pictures, I slipped them under the glass on my desk until it was full.

One time in the lunchroom I saw a boy hadn't returned his

tray, so I offered to take it back for him. I told him I hadn't done my good deed for the day and took it back.

There were other very serious cases with which I had the opportunity to deal. One young girl came to me from Philadelphia and was now living with her sister. She was very tough. After coming to our school, she told a girl who had befriended her all about her past. The friend suggested she talk to Mr. Zook about it, which she did in part. She was so hard, so unreachable, that I felt there was something deeper going on. I asked, "Angie [not her real name], has anyone ever sexually abused you?"

Angie sat back in her chair exclaiming, "How do you know that?"

"I don't. I'm just asking the question," I replied.

Then she told me about seeing her mother stab her one-year-old brother to death. She described her mentally ill mother holding the baby, stabbing him repeatedly with a butcher knife. She described the bloody mess. She told me about her father sexually abusing her. She never knew that wasn't a part of normal family life. She began crying, losing her hardness.

I allowed her to regain her composure; then rolling my chair to her side, I took her hand in mine reassuringly. "Angie, take your time. This obviously is very important to you. Tell me as much as you want to tell me."

She balked at telling me anything more, but she again began sobbing, eventually telling me how she came to live with her sister. While her sister was in the hospital with a new baby and Angie was baby-sitting the older children, her brother-in-law raped her. It was a brutal rape, since she tried to resist.

"Please don't tell anyone," she pleaded.

"Angie, we can't do that. We must tell someone about it," I said.

We waited until her sister came home from the hospital; then I asked her to come to school. I told her what was happening and she was devastated that her husband would do this to her sister. I went with Angie to court about the brother-in-law rape. Then, later we went to a court in Philadelphia to deal with her father's past sexual abuse, since Angie was at one time under the Philadelphia Children's Youth Services because of her mother's stabbing the baby. When it came time to take her father to court, it was extremely difficult for her.

I kept reassuring Angie, "Look, Angie. I'll be there. I'll be there with you. This could turn out to be OK, if you just trust me." Again, I feel this was God's doing. I said, "Angie, I spent several hours in prayer just before going to court. This could help your father, who may have been a victim of things about which you have no knowledge."

When we got into court, she was sitting by my side until it was time for her to testify. I could see her trembling. It's amazing to see how much abused kids love their parents. Even though they don't like what has happened, they don't know how to deal with it. Something in their innocent souls tells them that sexual abuse and rape aren't correct behavior, but they don't know what it is.

As the judge called her father to the stand, I could see Angie steeling herself for the worst. When the judge asked her father if these charges were true, he broke down, crying like a baby. He asked the judge for leniency and begged his daughter for forgiveness. Angie ran to her father, hugging him and crying as they held each other. Later she told me the one thing she wanted in life when she learned such behavior wasn't appropriate was to have her father confess that he had abused her. The judge was lenient with the man, putting restrictions on visitation and ordering counseling for the family.

I wonder what happens to these children if no one is there to intervene and to bring a solution to these situations. Another boy, Sam [not his real name], whose father had killed his sister, came to my school from a halfway house. There had been a half hour between the mother's and father's work shifts when the children were at home alone, and during that half hour the father would lock the boy and his sister in a vacant woodshed outside the house. On a very cold day in the dead of winter, the father was suspicious the children were slipping back into the house after he went to work. He laid a trap for them and discovered they had indeed gone into the house, so he went after the little girl in a rage and beat her to death. In trying to defend his sister, the boy went after his father with a butcher knife, slicing him several times. Though only in elementary school at the time, the boy was put away for a while, then later released to a halfway house, after which time he came to my school. The courts asked me if I would be willing to take him, which I said I would.

When Sam arrived at my school, he was simply bad news. All he had been through made him so hard. On one occasion, his art teacher asked him to do something and he told her to "F—— off!" That language just wasn't used in my school, so he was sent to me. He chided me, "You think you're gonna straighten me out. You think you're so hot." I let his tirade go by and sent him to lunch. At lunch, he pulled a pocketknife from his pocket and began toying with a boy's neck, pretending he was going to cut him. That was before pocketknives were banned from schools.

The cafeteria monitor saw what was happening and told me about it. "Ask Sam to come to my office," I said.

"I did," he replied, "but he won't come up."

I went to the cafeteria, saying, "Sam, I have something to discuss with you. Will you come with me to my office?"

To my surprise, he came with me. After I told him I had learned what he had done with his knife, he challenged me with, "You think you're gonna take that knife from me, don't you?"

"No," I said. "I'm not going to ask you for that knife. I would like to ask you what you had in mind. I'd just like to talk to you about it."

He blustered on for a while, periodically saying, "You think you're gonna get this knife!"

"No, Sam," I said. "There are other people who can do that. I

151

can ask an officer to come and remove it from you, which I don't plan to do. I can ask your mother to come to school."

"She'd never get it," he bragged.

"Let's not discuss that," I answered.

After more than half an hour, when the lunch period was over, I said, "Don't worry about your lunch. I'll get that for you." After a while I said, "Sam, you're a nice guy; I can see that. You're a nice guy and I'd like to have you as one of my workers."

"What did you say that for?" he asked.

"Because I think you're a nice guy who has made some mistakes. There's something wrong, something that's eating at you. You wouldn't ordinarily act like this." After probing a bit more, I said, "I know there's something bothering you."

All of a sudden this hard young man began crying uncontrollably, sobbing aloud. I stayed by his side during about five minutes of crying, and I asked, "Sam, would you like to tell me about it?"

Sobbing through the story, he told me about his dog that was like a human being to him—his only friend in the world.

"I don't have a sister," he sobbed. "I don't have any friends. That dog was faithful to me every time I was with him. Last night some guy killed my dog. He ran over him with a car. The guy didn't even stop or come back to talk to me about it. He just let the dog lie in the road. My dog died in my arms." He sobbed through the whole story.

I said, "You know, Sam, I can't bring that dog back to life. Today is Thursday. On Saturday we'll go to the SPCA to look for another dog."

On the way to the SPCA, I asked Sam, "What kind of dog have you always wanted?"

"I always wanted a police dog," he replied. He had said his dog had been a stray he found. When no German shepherd was at the pound, I suggested we look elsewhere. The person at the pound knew of someone who had a litter of German shepherd puppies he wanted to sell. We went to see the puppies, but they were too young to leave their mother that day. One of the puppies came to Sam wanting to play.

"That's the one I really like," said Sam.

These were purebred puppies so they were rather expensive. When I got home, I called the owner of the puppies, telling him Sam's story and the situation that had brought us to his home. I asked when the puppies would be old enough to leave their mother and we agreed on a time to pick up the puppy. I was planning to pay for the puppy myself. When we picked up Sam's puppy, the owner dropped $300 from the price and I only paid $100 for it, although Sam never knew about that.

The art teacher didn't want to ever have Sam back in her class because he had been giving her a lot of trouble, but I begged her to give him another chance, letting her know I would be right behind her lending my support. Because of the act of getting him that puppy, Sam turned around in a matter of weeks.

No one else knew what had happened, except the guidance counselor, whom I told about it because he had asked why Sam was crying. I explained to the counselor, saying, "Never give up on a youngster. You can always bet that somewhere deeper there's a cause for an action." I wanted him to learn that. I was always very private about things I did for kids. I didn't want staff or anyone else to feel I was trying to bribe kids. Sam went back to class, doing his art work and his other work.

It was a thrill for me in my career to see these almost instant transformations in human nature. It rivets in my mind that if you find the cause and treat it, there can be transformation in lives or circumstances. These are just a few examples of some very hard cases I was privileged to deal with. I say "privileged" because it was those difficult cases that made me what I am now, that gave me hope and faith in the fact that you can have faith in people who are seemingly hopeless. That's why I loved my job.

Upon receiving invitations from other districts in the county, I would give talks at in-service programs to teachers about dealing with difficult students and handicapped students. I told teachers not to go overboard in making it easy for them but to hold them responsible for misdeeds just like anyone else. Teachers have some difficulty knowing how to deal with misdeeds because state laws are strict about handling slow learners and students with learning disabilities. Many problems came from students with learning disabilities. I never treated those with learning disabilities any differently when it came to discipline. I assumed they had a mind that was bright enough to know what they were doing, and I acted on that premise.

I used to say there was only one time when I was glad I had a disability and that was when I was dealing with students with drug or alcohol problems or deep into misbehavior. I would say, "Look at me. I can't even get off the floor if I fall. Look at you. You can do so much." Fortunately, I never put bad substances in my body. I don't know why; I just never did. I would say, "You know, I would give everything I have just to have your body right now." Somehow it got into their heads; I don't know how or why. I never preached to kids; I just talked to them. I never mandated; I suggested.

I would tell students, "Until you become a young lady or a young man nothing else really matters. Your grades don't matter. But when you become a young lady or a young man, everything else will fall into place. I do know if you are not a young lady or a young man, a lot of other things don't shape up." Character, honesty, forthrightness, kindness, love, those things all matter. If those things are in place, then everything else kind of slips into place, too.

Harold believed the small things were what counted. He says, "One of the hardest things for parents to understand is that it's the small things that count." He believed in telling the truth, that honesty was always the best policy. He told the school superintendent and board president, "I am a man of my word and I will never lie."

Whenever I was working with a teacher regarding a difficult

student, I would ask, "Just give me some small reason why I should praise this student, even if it's just a good vocabulary score. Even if he just comes into the homeroom without his hat on. I don't care what it is, just anything. If you see him pick up a pencil for someone who dropped it, or if he picks up a piece of paper from the floor, let me know."

One difficult boy got a perfect score on a vocabulary test, which was very unusual for him. When the teacher told me about it, I made sure I was in the hall between classes. I pulled him aside and said, "Phil, I heard you got one hundred percent on your vocabulary test today. Good guy!" and went on my way. Later in the day I told him, "You know, Phil, I can't forget about that test. I've been thinking about it all day."

"That was nothing," he replied.

"To me it's everything," I said. "I think it's really great! How many more of those are you going to get?"

"I'll prove to you I can get more of them," he promised. And he did.

When I would see him, I congratulated him on any achievement—no matter how small.

"How do you know about this?" he asked me. "Did the teacher tell you?"

"How else do you think I'm finding out about it?" I assured him. "You're doing great. You're making your mark in that classroom. Do you know what? The kids are starting to look up to you; they're looking at you as a different kind of guy, you know!"

It's that kind of stuff that makes a difference. When I would call parents about their child caught smoking in the lavatory, the parents would often say, "Wait 'til that kid gets home. I'm gonna—"

"Whoa, whoa, whoa!" I would say. "Just wait a minute. I want you to understand he [or she] will be suspended for three days by school policy, but your son [or daughter] made a confession. I didn't have to force it. That should mean a lot to you. Why don't you use the element of surprise with your child? Your son [or daughter] thinks you're going to cream her, that you're gonna ground him [or her] for two months." That's what many parents are prone to do—go overboard in their punishment. I would continue, "Your son [or daughter] agreed with me to tell you what happened. Wait for him [or her] to approach you." I would always encourage the students to tell their parents when they got into trouble. If for some reason they absolutely felt they couldn't, I would do it for them.

I said, "Let your son [or daughter] tell you about it. Then use the element of surprise. Stop whatever you are doing, sit down, lay your hand on your son's [or daughter's] shoulder or lap, and say, 'I'm so proud of you for telling me what you've done. I'm really concerned about your smoking and I would like to do whatever I can to help you break that habit—if it is a habit. Just sit down and love your child." It makes all the difference in the world in children, helping them want to be better. To top that, I would call the student in the next day and thank him or her for being faithful in following through. I would tell the student to latch onto that feeling by doing a nice deed for his or her parents the next day. "Why not voluntarily clean the house, do the dishes—something that is out of the ordinary for you? Watch your mom's reaction when you do that." Students would often say, "My mom's mad at me all the time." I would tell them parents need to have an opportunity to show how they feel about something their children do that's good.

I really felt I made a difference when I became an administrator. Previously there was a lot of what I called educational politics going on. People did things to appease other people; they lied, if need be, to appease parents. I never believed in that. My principal used to tell me, in his words, "You're too damned honest. It's going to get you into trouble sometime." I said, "Well, that might be true in the short term, but I think in the long run I'll be better off for it." When I first became an administrator, I would keep students after school doing work detail instead of giving them detention. I believed that work makes a man. I would take students to the nurse to have their fingers taped up, then give them a scratch pad to remove black marks from the floor made from students' shoes. I would have them work until about five-fifteen, then I would take them to my office. I would give them a break every forty-five minutes or so, give them a soda and snack, and sit on a windowsill to talk about why we were doing this and how I appreciated the labor they were putting into beautifying the school. Sometimes I got a lot of flak from parents for doing these things, but it made a difference in their children's lives.

It took me most of a year to get people to understand what I was doing and why I was doing it. My principal said, "Sometime you're going to find yourself in a court of law for doing these things." Those were not fashionable things to do, since student rights were coming into play. I always said, "I'll take my chances."

During my first year of administration, I had parents scream at me, but I would listen to them and let them unwind. I knew it was because of the man who was in my position before me, who had let anything go. He was from the Philadelphia area and thought he was in a utopia when he came to Indian Valley, but his mode of discipline wasn't right for our area. Gradually parents began to see results in their children's behavior at home as well as in school. All of a sudden things began to get better and better. My name stopped showing up on the lavatory walls. At Halloween, my name would be sprayed all over the outside of the school. It was very painful and I almost quit several times. I felt I was alone against the world, because my ideas seemed to be so out of sync at the time.

As things began getting better, they just mushroomed! Students began confiding in me. Earlier when bus drivers told me they saw students exchanging drugs on the bus, I couldn't get names from them because they were afraid. I would get calls from parents who had overheard drug deals being made but were afraid to come to school for fear of retribution. There was a church on the other side of our school property. The pastor gave me permission to use an office in the church when necessary. I asked the bus drivers and parents to come to that church to give me information. I would then go back to school and get to work based on this information. The students could never figure out how I got this information, which was obviously accurate.

I wanted to call in the police, but school district officials didn't want that. They said, "Oh, no! We'll sweep that under the carpet. It would make the school look bad." Everyone was afraid, but I told them, "We've got to get this under control." The superintendent reluctantly gave in and allowed me to do my thing. I called the officers in. We did lab tests, we made prosecutions. I found students with drugs under their waistbands, so we would strip-search them. It was a nightmare for a while, but I stayed the course. It started to pay off. The kids decided it wasn't worth it because "This guy's (meaning me) going to catch us. If he does catch us there's a price to pay."

Eventually, the district began looking my way for advice. Kids would call in a bomb scare. Instead of hushing it up, I would get on the intercom and say, "Students, I just received this information. We're going to evacuate. If there's anyone who can help me with any information, I want you to come to me privately and we'll discuss it. I would like you to give me any leads you can." After I had this network in place, I got leads all the time, and in short order we had the problem solved. Eventually, students would voluntarily come to me without my asking, saying, "I just heard so-and-so," or "I know so-and-so," or "you should know such-and-such." That's how it was when I left for retirement.

Recently, when the school shooting happened in Colorado, someone in my school wrote on the wall "BAM" in big black letters. A teacher was in a meeting with some administrators when they were discussing how to find out who wrote those letters. Someone said, "If Harold Zook were here, he'd have the name of

158

that person within minutes!" And the superintendent, who was new to the district, said, "How would he have done it?" He was told about the network I had set up and how students freely came to me. Someone always knew something and would give that to me anonymously, because I never blew a kid's cover. I never divulged my sources of information.

A girl was writing graffiti on the lavatory wall one day, thinking she was alone. Another girl heard the squeaking of the Magic Marker and, quietly looking under the stall, noted the shoes the writer was wearing. She described very explicitly the kind of shoes the girl was wearing. I roamed the halls looking for that pair of shoes and found them. Before calling the girl in, I looked at the handwriting and matched it with hers, so I could give her the exact time and period when she was writing on the wall. She told her parents I must have hidden cameras in the girls' lavatory and her parents chided me for having hidden cameras in the girls' lav. I assured them there were no such cameras in the lav, telling them, "If you wish, you may have an expert come in and check. You may also come in and look at the handwriting for yourself." The girl did confess she had done it, but she could never figure out how I got the information.

The Reading Eagle *reported:*

"That Harold Zook has endured a puzzling degenerative muscular disease for all of his 53 years is both utterly irrelevant and undeniably important. Irrelevant because . . . he has by most accounts earned a deserved reputation as one of the best educators in the area. His particular talent has nothing to do with the lack of strength in his legs or his back. It is his mind that has given him his ability to devise ingenious, sometimes unorthodox, and usually highly effective methods of bringing straying kids back into the fold.

But his physical impairment cannot be ignored as part of the equation. That and a strict Mennonite upbringing on a farm near Oley have knit the kind of heart that can embrace all the misfit behavior of early adolescence because its owner well understands what it means to be different.

Zook spent many hours helping the students work through the difficult situations by listening to them, disciplining them, and running interference with parents and police if need be. . . .

His critics on the faculty don't doubt Zook's dedication, but they do accuse him of being stubborn, opinionated, perfectionistic, and out of touch with the realities of the classroom.

He readily concedes to the first three charges, but disagrees that he doesn't know what is going on in the trenches.

Harold knows that he can't please everyone. He says, "Some say I'm more student oriented than faculty oriented. I do what my heart tells me needs to be done. Kids have an instinct. They can tell whether someone really cares about them or not. I care."

Harold did not have one rule for students and a different rule for teachers and administrators, as the following account illustrates:

I was very strict about gum in the school because kids would stick it everywhere. So we had a very strict no-gum rule and if a student was caught with it he or she did work detail. That student sat under the cafeteria tables scraping the gum off the tables. Or he or she would scrape the gum from under the serving bar, where there were always hundreds of wads of gum snuck there by students when we first started this rule.

One morning I had bad breath, so while in the office I put a piece of gum in my mouth. A student came into the office commenting, "Mr. Zook, is that gum you're chewing?"

"You're right," I replied. "I am chewing gum. I'm sorry. I apologize."

I had never had detention for twelve years, but this gum was such a hard thing to get under control that Brooke Moyer, the principal, said, "Let's have detention just for this." I eventually agreed, but only if students were made to do something productive. The rules stated that a student had to bring something to study; they couldn't sleep or talk. I would always set up the routine for the teacher on duty, reading the rules and making certain there was no misunderstanding.

I told this particular student who caught me with gum, "You know I believe in doing what I preach. Would you like to place me in detention?"

"Yes," he said. "I'll put you in detention."

I took my detention and this student monitored the detention, along with others in detention that day. Brooke came into the room to talk to me about something after seeing me sitting there. He said something to me, but I ignored him. He said something again, but because there was a no-talking rule, I refused to answer him. I noticed the student watching me very carefully, certain I would talk because he knew Brooke was my authority.

That incident soon spread throughout the school. It was what made kids understand that I walked the talk. When I was given detention as an assistant principal, I became the model and wouldn't talk to Brooke, the senior administrator, when he came in. Kids couldn't believe I would be that strict in my modeling. It goes a long way over a period of time in setting up standards of behavior.

Robin MacMullen, a guidance counselor, testifies: "I worked with Harold for about sixteen years. We worked closely together with students. Character is that which distinguishes a person, and no word accurately describes Harold's character, but it is good. He wants to do things right and I think he believes if you do things right, good things will happen. I really believe he allowed his heart as well as his mind to determine what was right. One of his best qualities is his ability to listen. He has a gift of allowing a person to feel he was genuinely being heard. Many students, as well as adults, benefited from that quality. He has helped me many times by listening to me; he was a tremendous listener. I really liked working at Indian Valley because it had a special quality.

"There was a spiritual quality to his belief that if you do the right things, good things will happen. It went beyond mere right and wrong. There was a special quality to Harold.

"I liked working at Indian Valley because Harold was at that school. I felt I worked at a school where the disciplinarian was the best counselor I've ever seen. I felt he was a mentor to me. He viewed discipline as an education. He never held a grudge, but anyone making a mistake had an opportunity to rise above it. Kids all knew he was firm, an enforcer, but he did it with a lot of love and care.

"Harold's strength seems to come from his father's teaching him perseverance as a child. I also think his Mennonite upbringing and faith gave him strength. I understood some of Harold's difficulties because I had an older brother who was both mentally and physically challenged. I knew the abuse he took from other kids, and I knew Harold endured some pretty tough stuff. I knew from the experience with my brother that when Harold referred to what he took from kids growing up it was very credible. He withstood a lot of pain and humiliation. That and the support he gains from his family have helped make him who he is.

"Indian Valley was Harold Zook. He and Brooke Moyer provided outstanding leadership. They complemented each other. I look at that time as the Golden Era of Indian Valley. Harold was at the school all the time—like the fabric of the school. He really had the 'Spirit of the Eagle.' He provided so much motivation. During the magazine drives, he would use farm humor, such as, 'The fox isn't getting into the henhouse with this homeroom!' He always showed a lot of humor and was very entertaining. Many things in the school had his signature on them in a contributing way, not a controlling way.

"The assistant principal is usually viewed as a disciplinarian, but Harold was more. He helped more wayward kids by planting seeds where sometimes the results weren't immediate, but many times they came back later to tell him what a difference he had made in their lives. Many parents who are very thankful say they

162

don't know where they or their children would be without Harold's intervention.

"Much of his success can be attributed to his genuineness, which is a major defining word for Harold. He's definitely one of the most genuine persons I know. He's not fake at all nor trying to fool anyone, but he tells it like it is.

"Harold was a strict disciplinarian, which he viewed as a form of education. He recognized that kids will make mistakes, but he would take a big mistake, take it through to closure, and never hold a grudge and would provide an opportunity for the student to do the right thing. Kids knew he was a disciplinarian and would say, 'Watch out for Zook, because he's tough.' He was; he was the enforcer, he was firm, and he stuck to the letter of the law. He used his disability as an advantage, as a blessing, and as a wisdom builder.

"Harold has a tremendous amount of courage. Sometimes he took on an unpopular stance, but he stood his ground. There was one boy who missed school one day, telling his parents he had been kidnapped. Harold was the only one in the school who stood by this boy, saying if the boy said it, we'll take him at his word. He helped the boy work through the experience whether or not it was a real kidnapping.

"Harold makes me glow! He was a joy to work with and was always a role model. He is just a wonderfully good and caring person, ranking up there with others in my family. He has made more of an impression on me than anyone else in my life. He is totally surrounded by good. I'm a lucky person to have known him. Harold always finds what is good in the world."

8

Disability: An Asset for Personality and Character Building

A person is not defined by a disability. One's disability is only one aspect of a full life. We need to learn to view persons with a disability as whole persons, only different in the sense of having a disability. The views of society make it difficult for persons with a disability to accept it and fit into society as complete persons.

Harold became a model and an example for the thousands of students, teachers, and parents whom he touched. His success and humility helped others realize that a disability does not define a person. Personality and character determine the individual.

Harold states: Everyone, even a person with disabilities, learns about life in the struggles. I was fortunate in that I had my disability from early childhood, because I grew accustomed to it, so it wasn't like a sudden shock. I had time to adjust and put things into perspective.

The kind of caring exhibited by my geology class in college gave me an immense self-confidence, just to say, "It's OK to be who you are." (Refer to chapter 4, pages 74–75.) I remember the little girl with cerebral palsy who didn't want anyone to carry her tray. I knew there would be a time when she would drop it and almost fall. That time came, but I let her go as long as possible. When eventually she dropped her tray in the cafeteria, she cried with embarrassment and humiliation. I took her to the nurse's office for a long talk, telling her, "I know exactly what you're feel-

164

ing. You're embarrassed, you're angry that you didn't take my advice, all those things mixed up in your mind. I have three girls out there just waiting to help you."

I had been secretly preparing these girls for this time. After talking to her for a while along with the nurse, I said, "Would you let me bring these three girls in?" She had no idea who they were, but I had chosen girls who were her friends. We had talked about procedure, about taking her out of class a few minutes early so she could get her tray without anyone else seeing her. The girls thought it was an extra privilege to be able to help their friend as well as being first in the cafeteria line! This student is now doing a marvelous job as a cashier in a restaurant.

Disabilities are strange! I don't know how many people in the real world realize what it's like to have a disability. I feel good because I think I've had a large part in influencing hundreds and hundreds of young people in that aspect alone, because by the time they were through our school at Indian Valley they were very comfortable dealing with disabled people, including myself.

I fell twice in my school, and students saw this. One time I fell right at the top of a ramp. It was rather funny, because I was lying on the floor when this girl came by. She walked around me, looking rather strange. I looked up and said, "Hi! How are you today?"

She responded, "I'm fine. How are you? May I get you some help or something?"

I told her I was fine, but that I had just slipped as I was trying to get onto the seat of my Amigo—my chair on wheels. I told her I had seen a certain teacher go into the faculty room nearby, and I suggested she knock on the door of the faculty room to see if there might be several male teachers who could get me up, which she did.

Instead of going on her way, this student came to me, knelt down beside me, and said, "Mr. Zook, are you sure you're OK? Are you lying comfortably there? Are you sure I can't get you something?" She said, "They'll be here to help you real soon," staying by my side until help came. Then she went on to her class.

The other time I fell was during a school assembly program. I happened to be in the lavatory during this school assembly showing a boy whom I was disciplining how to remove graffiti from the walls of the lavatory. I can't recall his infraction, but he had done something to merit my work detail. I would always show a student how to do anything I would ask of him or her. I got off my Amigo and was standing to show this student how to use a scratch pad to remove this graffiti. I slipped on the floor, falling right under the urinal, scaring the boy half to death. He exclaimed, "Man! Are you OK?" I told him I was fine, that he should go to the auditorium where the assembly was being held to get Mr. Moyer, the principal, and tell him to bring another man with him. This boy took off and I could hear him running down the hall. In a matter of seconds I could hear men running down the hall, yelling, "Which lav is he in? Where is he? I'll go this way; you go that way!" The boy was yelling, "No! He's over in this lav!"

When Brooke saw me lying under the urinal, he asked, "What in the world are you doing?" I explained that I had just slipped as I was showing this boy how to clean the lav walls. Brooke and the other teacher wanted to take me to the nurse, but I said, "No! You guys just go on and I'll finish my work here." So that's how the students sometimes saw me in action.

I very kindly showed the boy how to do the job. That student was never a problem again for me or for the school. Several years after he graduated from high school, he stopped in to tell me, "Mr. Zook, I just want you to know that you had a tremendous effect on my life that day when you fell in the lav. It scared the heck out of me, but I couldn't believe you were so helpless. I never knew you couldn't get up. I started thinking about all the things you told me I had going for me." I had seen this boy several times because he was having difficulty with drugs. He said, "I began thinking about all that I had with a sound physical body, so I decided I wouldn't give you any more hassles." He knew that if he gave anybody else any hassles, he would have to deal with me, too.

My disability has taught me how to be flexible. Maybe I would have been flexible anyway, I don't know, but I can say without a doubt that my disability taught me how to be flexible, how to be patient, how to be accepting of myself and others. It's taught me how to see through somebody else who has a difficulty. There's just no substitute for feeling it. It's like having a mediocre spiritual life and then some catastrophe comes along that puts you on your knees. All of a sudden you become a man of faith, a man of God. There's no way one can say you are happy you've had that catastrophe or have to live with a disability, but it's hardship that brings out the steel in us, that brings out the quality in us. If we accept the disability and have the courage to go forth being the best we can be, I think it brings the mettle out in us.

Believe it or not, it's made me love life, because I appreciate the little I have—or how much I have. I love ballet, even though I don't know that much about it; I've never studied it. There's only one reason I love ballet. I sit there mesmerized by the way people float in air, the way they twirl on their toes. To me, it's refreshing. I say, "Wow! How do they do that?"

I love to watch football. I never watch it without being amazed. I ask myself, *How do these football guys all get up again after being tackled and ending up in a pile on top of one another?* I watch their movements as they get up. I bet most people don't even think about it. But to me, it's miraculous.

It makes me appreciate that I can do what I can. I can see. I have a mind that's fresh, which is something I appreciate immensely after my latest hospital experience. The doctors thought I would be brain-damaged. They weren't even sure they should keep the tubes in. It's a miracle to have been gone, "dead," as long as I was without having any brain damage. I appreciate that more than if I'd have been a normal person. I would never have known twenty-eight wonderful caregivers had I not chosen to live. It's immensely gratifying to have met these people who have been so dedicated and so great a part of my life when I couldn't even raise my arm. To be brought back to the degree of health that I have now, in spite of all my medical difficulties, is awesome. I enjoy life almost more than I did prior to all this because I'm enjoying it with people I love and who have become important to me. I can't quite say I would want a disability. I would never want that brought on anybody. And yet, at the same time, I can honestly say I don't think I'd be what I am today without my disability; I don't think I'd have experienced the joys of life that I did by affecting so many people. Had I not had a disability, I believe I would have chosen marriage and devoted my time to my wife and family.

During Harold's younger years, his father had advised him that when being teased by a student he should stop and say, "Look! I want to talk to you about this. I wish you wouldn't do this. There's nothing I can do to change it. My parents are doing everything they can to make life easy for me. How would you like to be in my shoes? How would it feel to you if you were me and I were you and I did to you what you just did to me? I'd like to know how it would feel to you?"

That was the exact strategy I used with my students. I could speak from the heart and somehow kids seemed to grab that message. Each year we got a new group of seventh-graders, I would introduce myself and talk about my disability. I would let them know that I had deep concerns about other people who were being made fun of. I would say, "I know teasing goes on and some of you have had that experience in elementary school. It may have happened to you and nobody did anything to correct that experience or to go to bat for you. I want you to know that I don't care how minor it may seem to you; if anyone hassles you or makes fun of you because of your glasses, because of your freckles, because of your weight, because of your size—because of anything—I want you to personally come to me. I want to know that and I want you to know it's something about which I will be very, very concerned." I would tell them if we didn't correct that, we were only enabling that other person to become a bad individual. "It won't only be you who is hassled, but it will be Johnny and Sam and Sue and other people out there. They will develop these bad traits going into adulthood."

It took me years to develop that message, but in the last ten years of my career it became an automatic reaction in the school. When a student came to me about being teased or hassled by another student, I would ask how long he or she had been putting up with this individual. Many students said, "Oh, since second or third grade."

I asked, "And nobody helped you?"

The response frequently went like this: "Well, the principal called me a baby, telling me to grow up and take it." I responded that was not the way we do things in this school.

I felt this was one of my real successes at Indian Valley—helping students recognize the damaging effects associated with teasing and making fun of people who might be different. I welcomed handicapped students—Easter Seals students—even though our school didn't have elevators. There were twelve steps going to the gymnasium and shop area. I had volunteer teachers who would carry disabled students in their wheelchairs down the stairs. These students never lacked for anything. They did everything any other students would do. Sometimes parents would suggest that some arrangement might be made for their handicapped students to have a special class in the library in order to avoid negotiating the stairs. My reaction was, "No! They get the same experience as all the other students."

When our ninth-grade students went to Washington, D.C., the handicapped students went, too. One girl confined to a wheelchair needed therapy twice a day. She even needed help going to the bathroom. When it came time for the class trip, her parents felt there was no way she could go with the class. I said, "There is a way. I've already discussed this with her class and her classmates

169

have already chipped in extra dollars so a special wheel-chair-accessible bus can be hired to accommodate her." It was a small bus, with room for twelve students, equipped with a ramp so her wheelchair could be rolled into it. That year there were three handicapped students—one with cerebral palsy, another student on crutches because of a malfunctioning leg, and this girl in a wheelchair. They all went with us that year. It was wonderful—a miracle—to see how the other students all wanted to help in any way they could. Even the boy on crutches wanted to take his turn pushing the girl in the wheelchair! Her chair was an easy one to push, so he got his turn along with many others pushing her around the sidewalks of Washington.

A wheelchair was obtained for the student with cerebral palsy so she could ride when she became too tired to walk. The greatest miracle of all was receiving a call about a week later from the parents of the boy on crutches. He got so much exercise that day, walking and pushing his friend in the wheelchair, that his leg got stronger. He discovered he could strengthen his legs with exercise, so he eventually threw away his crutches, never to use them again.

My junior high school years were very difficult years. Sometimes I would come home crying to my dad, telling him how students were making fun of me. He taught me how to confront students who did that so I would no longer have trouble with them. There was always someone who was making fun of me. However, I felt it was just ignorance about disabilities. It's not that way anymore, and it doesn't need to be. My goal in school was to help students with difficulties to face those difficulties, deal with them, and overcome them. The second half of that equation was to teach regular students how to respect those with disabilities and how to feel comfortable around them. When I had a student who was distressed about his or her disability, I would tell them this story.

"There were three high school boys that I confronted on my way home from work one night. It was about ten-thirty at night when I was driving through Boyertown; there was hardly any traffic. I noticed a ruckus about a block ahead. I saw a lot of flailing. Many times previously I had seen a blind man tapping his white cane as he walked along, and frequently I saw him sitting on a bench at the square. Now I saw this man on the ground being burned on his arms with cigarette butts. I brought my car to the curb, got out of the car, and asked, 'What's going on here?' I could see this blind man with his stick flailing all around. These three high school guys were laughing, saying, 'This guy's an idiot.'

"I asked, 'What do you mean, he's an idiot? He's a blind man.'

" 'He's stupid,' they said.

"I really got upset, telling the guys to be on their way. I helped the blind man get up and reoriented, showing him where the traffic light was, where the square was, where the bench was. I asked if he wanted me to take him to a doctor, but he said he was all right. I told him to go on his way and I would go to the police station about a block away. Fortunately, there was a police officer at the station. After I told him my story about the blind man and the three boys, he got into my car and we drove down the street until we found the boys. I said I wanted these boys arrested. The officer told the boys to get into the car and we went back to the station.

"Even after hearing me tell the officer everything that had happened, the boys thought it was funny. I said, 'Officer, I want these boys charged to the hilt. You probably have noticed I have a disability myself, and I won't tolerate this kind of behavior. I will go to court if that's what needs to be done to see that these boys are prosecuted properly.' The boys were shocked. The officer 'threw the book at them.' We did go to court."

My disability has definitely made me a better man. No question. I don't think I could have had the same impact on students without my disability, especially dealing with youngsters who had drinking and drug problems. I also worked with girls who had pregnancies. I always tried to work ahead of problems; I didn't wait for disaster, but I tried to prevent disappointments and disaster. Whenever I counseled girls who were difficult, who were wild and reckless with their bodies, whether it was sex, drugs, alcohol, smoking, whatever, I tried to instill self-worth within them. Several times, girls came to me with issues about wanting to be popular; that's one of the things that is so important in junior high school, and they make the mistake of giving their bodies to become popular with some older guy. I remember one girl in particular who was in my office. I usually took care of the problem at hand, then talked in generalities: "How are you? How are you getting better? How are you becoming a young lady?" This girl said she didn't want to do drugs, but she had a boyfriend who was pretty heavy into drugs and she was going to try to reform him. After many consultations with her and her parents, she finally broke up with her boyfriend, which I had encouraged her to do. To her, it was a matter of being popular with a handsome guy. She was a beautiful girl. She said the guys want this and they want that and she felt that to be accepted she needed to give in to what they wanted.

I said, "Denise, [not her real name], you're in junior high school. Do you have as a goal that someday you may want to be married and have your own children?" She nodded her head. "Now, think about it. I can't tell you what to do. I can only challenge you to do what I believe is right for you. Let's say that I'm your boyfriend; you're my girlfriend. I want to get married after high school. I'm looking for that wife whom I want to cherish and love, to be the mother of my children. Am I going to look for a girl who's been trashed by every guy on the street? Am I going to risk having a life mate who's diseased because of a careless sex life? Is that who I'm going to look for when I'm out of high school in my early twenties?"

She said, "Probably not."

I said, "If that's the case, why would you want to be that girl now just to be popular? Trust me. Those guys will not want you as a mate. They will want you for what they can get from you now.

They will forget about even thinking about you when you're in your early twenties. Then what will you do? It's done. It's finished. You can't reverse it. It's over. You lost your virginity. You lost everything that is beautiful within you. *You* have to make that decision. Your parents can't make it; I can't make it. Only you can make that choice. Trust me, Denise, if you hold true now, in your high school years and after high school, you'll be the one the decent guys will want. Trust me." That was the end of it.

In Denise's junior year, I was sitting in my office about six in the evening, when I heard a voice in the outer office.

I asked, "Who is it?"

A young female voice said, "Mr. Zook, please close your eyes."

I said, "Why? That's a strange request!"

"Please just trust me. Just do it!"

Even though I didn't recognize the voice, I agreed, calling, "Come in!"

I heard some rustling as she entered my office. "Now turn your chair this way," the voice pleaded. "Now open your eyes!"

There stood Denise in a prom gown with her boyfriend, a great guy, a guy who believed in the goodness of women. She said, "Mr. Zook, meet my boyfriend. What you said was right. I have the most handsome guy, the greatest guy I could hope to have in high school." There she stood in her white gown in all her glory! I hadn't seen her in all those years! Today she has a great family, a great husband, and great kids.

I could give you hundreds of examples like this. How do you put a value on something like that? I will tell you that in my first years of administration I was criticized a great deal by administrators for spending too much time with "jerks and bad kids," until several years later when administrators saw these kids come back from high school thanking me for staying with them and helping them.

A disability is not an embarrassment but an opportunity.

Harold learned to use his and students' disabilities as a means of learning to accept all persons. Diversity was something to be honored and encouraged. These accounts indicate the value of including disability as part of the curriculum of our schools. Curriculum is the experiences of the school through which students learn.

Harold's cousin's wife, Lorraine, remarks, "There's an endless list of things I hear that he has contributed to kids—troubled kids, kids who would have fallen through the cracks. He had so much love for kids; he had the patience to persevere in showing them love. Many times there were kids who had learning disabilities, or problems with alcohol. He worked with parents, with police.

"God is essential to Harold's very core. It's easy to tell God has given him the strength to fight the disabilities he has. He wouldn't have talked about his disabilities in years past. God and his family have given him his strength. The kids also have given him a lot. He loves those kids.

"All through Harold's uphill battles, I've never seen someone so determined to overcome difficulties. I think working with kids helped keep him going because he saw positive results in kids who he saw were headed for trouble. Many still return to him years later, giving him credit for caring so much. That gave him the motivation to keep going. When working with children, he used his disability to motivate them and him. He would tell students that if he had their abilities there would be so many things he could contribute. That motivated him to rise above his disability, which was a shining example to the students. When Grant and I were married, I was only nineteen years old and lived thirty miles away from home. Harold would pick me up once a week, even after I had a baby, and bring me home to my mother for the day, then take me back home in the evening. I was so young and still needed my mom. During those long car rides, we had a lot of time to talk.

"After Harold retired, we would be invited to weddings of people we didn't even know because word got around that Grant was good at transporting Harold and they wanted Harold to have a way to get to the wedding. These folks always treated us so special just because we were related to Harold. They made us feel as though they knew us forever. In fact, there is a couple moving next door to us and the lady was a flower girl at one of those weddings. We feel so honored to be a part of Harold's life. There were many parents who called to tell us they were inviting us to the wedding so we could bring Harold, since it was so very important to their son or daughter that he be at that wedding. Next to my husband, Harold has meant more to me than anyone. He has helped give me peace in my physical situation, dealing with severe headaches most of my life. The attitude we bring to life is more important than anything else.

"There are so many unique things about Harold. I knew Harold's lifework at school was meaningful to him, so when Harold had his retirement dinner I decided to develop a scrapbook with contributions from friends, family, and colleagues. I asked Harold to give me a list of students who had meant a lot to him. I sent out a letter to each person on this list. I never expected so many positive responses from everyone on the list. Some people sent one page; some sent three pages. It was so uplifting to read the stories that came in.

"Back in about 1986, I came across a quote by Louis Stunningham that I did for Harold in calligraphy, and it described him so well: 'What life means to us is determined, not so much by what life brings to us as by the attitude we bring to life; not so much by what happens to us as by how we react to what happens.' That's Harold. He can turn a bad situation into a learning situation, just by his attitude. He could have had just the opposite reaction and be a bitter person. But he has not and has touched so many lives because of his attitude."

Harold and his cousin Grant converse on where Harold got his courage, strength, and motivation:

Grant: I feel I must attribute a lot of your courage and motivation to your mother. With her handicap, she struggled so hard to work her gardens and flower beds, and to help with the barn work. You have learned from her to keep on going.

Harold: She was a tremendous inspiration to me because as her multiple sclerosis got worse, she refused to yield to it. The Amigo I used was initially purchased for her, but she refused to use it. She would fall frequently—falling from the top of the stairs to the bottom more than once. She strove so hard to do her work. She was such a kind, loving mother, allowing Dad to be the disciplinarian. I didn't even know until Mother passed away why she put so much effort into preparing certain foods. After returning from a family viewing at the funeral home, the sisters-in-law were telling about how Mother knew each child's favorite food. When Don would come home, she would make whoopee pies. I asked her why she struggled so hard, since she would have to lean against the kitchen counter, but she would never reply; that's just the way it was. If one of the other children was coming who loved shoefly pies, she would stand all afternoon to make shoefly pies. The same was true if someone was coming home who loved fruit salad. That was the answer she never gave me. That was why she did those things.

Grant: I remember seeing your mother making beautiful quilts. We wondered how she could sew when she hardly had control over her arms and hands. Even then she could thread a needle.

Harold: She would work hard at threading a needle even though it was difficult for her.

Grant: I think you learned a lot of perseverance from your mother.

9

Humanistic Administrator

In an article titled "Proud to Be an Assistant Principal," published in the Souderton Independent, *June 7, 1989, Harold wrote:*

Recently, a staff member asked, "Don't you ever get tired of being an assistant principal and disciplining all those kids?"

Reflecting on the question for just a moment, I realized that nearly 15 years have sped by since I became an assistant principal.

"No, I really don't tire of being an assistant principal or a disciplinarian, for that matter," was my reply. Actually, I'm proud of the fact that for the past 15 years of my total 29 years in education, I have been an assistant principal; and I have no desire to use the position as a "stepping-stone" to become a principal.

As an assistant principal, I feel I am able to reach and assist more young people than I ever could as a principal. The positive impact, the building of self-discipline, and the encouragement to be positive, productive citizens is paramount in my daily duties.

Yes, I am the disciplinarian; yes, I build various schedules for students and staff; yes, I supervise in the cafeteria; yes, I help build the budget and make sure it's not being over-spent; and, yes, I spend many hours meeting with parents and even occasionally have an opportunity to observe teachers.

However, the highlight of my duty is to assist students in becoming more responsible, responsive young men or women in our current and future world. Sometimes this means directing help for the pregnant girl, or the youngster who has fallen victim to chemical abuse, or the student faced with severe depression.

The numerous hours I have spent just listening to students and parents have been a noteworthy investment of time. There's an old formula I still use with students: Listening + Sharing = Caring. After listening to a student and exploring possible solutions to overcoming a problem, I still observe that special "light" in his or her eyes that is comparable to the light that I had seen so often as a teacher years ago when a youngster resolved a problem or reached an understanding of a concept in a teaching situation. The "I got it," also occurs as they progress in their problem-solving skills and make better, more responsible choices.

I'm reminded of a young fellow earlier this year whom I had seen many times for discipline in the previous months and year. After football practice one evening, I called him into my office to briefly relate what had transpired in a parent conference just hours before. He was first told about the positive things discussed in the conference and then I carefully laid out some self-discipline that still needed to be worked on.

Suddenly, near the end of my encouragement, this young fellow stood straight up and stepped toward me with his hand extended. Upon shaking my hand, he said, "Consider it done, Mr. Zook!" and walked out with his shoulders squared. It's seven months later, and I have yet to see this "young man" for any type of serious discipline.

I know we are supposed to be tough, thick-skinned, and seldom smile or show emotions, but that really does not work for me. I do care! I share my feelings and emotions with students. I let them know I expect better choices next time, and usually there is a "next time." I express my appreciation to that student who has the courage to face a mistake honestly no matter what consequences may lie ahead.

And, yes, I do "preach" that it's not the mistake or "sin" that concerns me as much as what that individual learns by having made the mistake and how he or she is able to effectively close that "chapter" of his or her life and walk ahead with a renewed determination not to commit the same error.

To me, there is nothing more rewarding than to see a youngster progress from that immature, troubled sixth-grader to a responsible, self-disciplined ninth-grader ready to "take on" high school and know he or she will succeed.

Yes, I am proud to be an assistant principal in a middle/junior high school setting. And I am especially proud when those so-called at-risk students come back to see me during their years in high school or after they graduate and tell me, "Thanks."

I know it was worth all the time I spent dealing with the trouble they caused, while they were simply struggling to find their place in the world. I am glad that I had the opportunity to make a small contribution to their lives.

I received my master's degree at Lehigh University in 1966. My principal, who was an older man ready to retire, asked me to get into a program to receive a principalship. He had already convinced me to become head of the English department four years into my teaching career. I didn't think I was qualified for that, but it turned out that I was very capable and was very successful because I had some experiences that helped me.

Prior to becoming vice principal, I had been very involved in teacher affairs, having been president of the teachers' association and negotiated seven contracts. I was a hard negotiator, getting what I felt teachers deserved and needed to be honored in the profession. I was a bit of a maverick in a way. The principal in the junior high school had just gotten rid of his assistant, who was having difficulties with students. I had become certified as an administrator, so the principal said he wanted me to be his vice principal. During my years of negotiating, I had developed credibility with the school board because in my negotiations with them I always gave them the facts as they were. I had taken two courses in budgeting at Lehigh University, so I broke down the budget and consequently knew everything about the budget for the entire school district. I knew more than the school board did about the budget. The financial manager let the superintendent know that I knew a lot about the budget.

Since I knew what moneys were coming in and what was going out, I gave a detailed report to the school board showing them why my requests in negotiations were financially feasible. Therefore, the board generally relied on me for the facts. One time during negotiations, when I was giving my input, the superintendent interrupted me saying, "Well, this is—"

The board president turned to him and said, "Look! I don't want to hear you. We want to hear Mr. Zook!"

My figures were most often less than the central administration's figures. I never started with a far-out figure to get to my desired figure. I began with the desired figure and stayed with it. That became my pattern, so the school board usually relied on me to give the correct figures. At this point in my career, the superintendent, the assistant superintendent, and the director of pupil personnel didn't want me as an administrator in the district, yet the junior high school principal wanted only me as his assistant. They asked him for a second choice, but he refused. Even though it was standard procedure for a principal to name his assistant, this particular time they wanted him to give them a second choice so they could present that second choice to the school board for their approval. The principal and his superiors were deadlocked concerning the naming of a candidate.

When it was time for the interviews, the superintendent said to the board, "I don't think we need to interview Mr. Zook. He's been in the system for fourteen years and you know him well enough without an interview." This ploy was being used in hopes that I would somehow be overlooked as a serious candidate for the job.

The board president disagreed. "No," he said. "Mr. Zook gets an interview like everybody else." The superintendent had told the board that because of my disability I wouldn't be able to get around fast enough if there were problems in the building. In his view, my disability would disqualify me from being a vice principal.

Just a year earlier, I had been directly responsible for getting two new board members elected by conducting a "write-in" campaign. Months before the elections, I had organized "coffee klatches" with parents to introduce these two members who were opposing the existing structure. One of these board members was now chairman of the committee for personnel, in charge of hiring teachers. Consequently, I was interviewed by the full nine-member board along with the superintendent and his assistant. During the interview, the committee chairman said, "Mr. Zook, would you mind if I ask some very personal questions?"

"No," I replied. "You may ask anything you wish."

"We all know you have a disability. Do you think your disability would hinder your work as a vice principal?" Other questions followed as to how I would handle my disability in the job.

As the interview drew to a close, I could see the superintendent just bristling, because he recognized that the board was clued into my honesty and forthrightness. At the end of the interview, I said, "Gentlemen. I would like to take this opportunity to thank you for hiring me as a teacher in this district fourteen years ago." Had it not been for Mr. Warner, my former principal, I would not have gotten a teaching job. I had heard the superintendent (who has since retired) arguing with Mr. Warner about the insanity of hiring me as a teacher because the students would just "walk all over me." At the time I was hired, teaching positions were very scarce and I was still recovering from my foot surgeries.

"I just want to thank you," I continued, "for putting the faith in me and giving me this opportunity to have a very successful teaching career. It is your decision whether to place your confidence in me once again for this administrative position or allow me to continue teaching, which I also truly love."

Four candidates were interviewed for the position, including a lady who was the superintendent's preference because women were beginning to take administrative positions at that time. Eventually, the board voted unanimously for my candidacy to get me into administration.

That summer prior to my candidacy for the administrative position, I was in the process of working with the administration and school board to hire a full-time nurse for our building. We were having too many injuries in the school—we had a gymnasium as well as a wood and metal shop where students could become injured. It wasn't good not having a full-time nurse in the building with so many students. I was doing battle, as the teachers' association leader, trying to get a nurse full-time for Indian Valley. I had created some ripples because I was pushing for things I felt were necessary.

I had been attending all the school board meetings, and by October the battle for a full-time nurse at Indian Valley was building up. Months before, I had laid the groundwork with parent groups concerning the need for a full-time nurse, but the board was refusing to accommodate them. About a hundred parents attended this particular meeting—even reporters from three different newspapers were in attendance, because they heard rumors that this was possibly going to be a "pretty hot" board meeting.

When I was hired as vice principal the previous month, I was told I needed to resign my membership in the teachers' association as all previous administrators had done. I said, "You can fire me, but I'm not going to consent to that kind of irresponsible request. If you don't trust that I will be a part of management and break my ties to a certain extent with the teachers, then I don't belong here." I was told that I was now management and needed to follow management protocol.

The superintendent evidently thought he had "trained me" to his management styles, so when the issue of hiring a full-time nurse arose at the board meeting he turned to me and said, "Mr. Zook, you're here as a vice principal at Indian Valley. We've been meeting on this issue and Mr. Zook knows what we're planning to do about this." He was making it sound as though we had planned to hire the nurse when we really hadn't. He was only trying to appease the parents and get out of a hot situation, especially with the press sitting there. "Mr. Zook, you can speak to this," he said.

I said, "Well, I wish that were the case, but I regret to indicate that in my best understanding the nurse situation isn't going to be addressed, at least during this school term."

The superintendent got red as a beet. He could see the reaction of the parents. He had committed himself far enough so that with my response, the parents recognized there was no intention of hiring a full-time nurse. By this point, after fourteen years, the parents had never known me to lie, never to be less than honest. During negotiations, I had been looked upon to lay it out like it was. We could all feel the tension in the room. Immediately the superintendent brought the meeting to a close. I was inundated by reporters and parents. I said, "I've made my statement. I've nothing more to say."

The next morning, the superintendent called me into his office. The school board president was already there. I had worked closely with him on many occasions during contract negotiations and I thought we had a lot of respect for each other. When I asked if I should close the door, the superintendent said, "No, leave it open." I understood then that the secretary might be planning to tape the discussion. The two men asked various questions for quite a while and I had a feeling I knew why I was there, but it didn't come up. I finally said, "Gentlemen, it seems as though we're beating around the bush. Why am I here? Is it because of my statement last night at the board meeting?" They answered that it was.

"What do you want me to do?" I asked

"You must understand that you are now management and you do what management desires."

"Even if I have to lie?" I asked.

The superintendent said, "That's correct."

I stood up from my chair and walked toward them, looking straight in their eyes, saying, "Mr. Board President, I'm disappointed that you haven't spoken up on my behalf. You two gentlemen know what the truth is and you know the truth is that you have no intention of hiring a nurse at Indian Valley. I want to make one thing extremely clear right now. I will not become a part of educational politics. I'm a man of my word and I will never lie. As an administrator, I will give you my best. I will work my heart out for the students—that's why we are all here and that's why we need a full-time nurse; it's because it's in the best interest of students."

Just prior to that board meeting a girl went off the high bar in the gymnasium, causing what we thought was a serious hip injury. A boy cut off the tip of his finger with a band saw in shop. Another student broke an ankle in a physical education class. I told these gentlemen about these injuries, asking them, "Is that enough reason for you to hire a nurse?"

I continued, "I will never lie, and if that's not good enough you will need to replace me." The superintendent never spoke to me from that October until the following June. The board president called me several times, but I never returned his calls. I felt that if he wanted to see me, he could come to me in person. I wasn't about to do any "around the bush" discussion.

In June, the administrators had a retreat in the Poconos. One evening several of the guys went out for beers while I went back to my room to get some work done. As I walked back to my dorm room, the board president and director of pupil personnel asked if they could talk to me. The board president apologized for his actions regarding the nurse issue, saying, "I admire your Christianity and your stand for honesty." The other man was also a very straight shooter.

I tell this story because it was the end of any further harassment in my administrative years. From that moment on, I had established myself as an honest straight shooter and as a no-nonsense kind of guy. It was the best thing I could have done, because it gave me leeway to work for the betterment of schools, children, and parents. It was the stepping-stone to my successful career in administration. I was looked up to and respected when there were difficulties. My voice was heard, because they felt my gut feelings were pretty accurate most times. I marvel at those things sometimes and I can't tell you why I have such strong convictions about almost everything I do, but I can only tell you that honesty does pay—not always in the short term, but in the long term it does pay.

One of the greatest feelings of euphoria I ever experienced was when I became an administrator. The school at that time was less than desirable. I had been hired to be Indian Valley's new assistant principal in August, and the first day of that school year in a welcoming assembly, Mr. Warner, the principal said, "I have another introduction to make." I was standing in the back of the auditorium along with some teachers when Mr. Warner continued, "I want to introduce you to your new assistant principal for Indian Valley." The student body didn't know who that would be. Mr. Warner said, "Mr. Zook, I would like you to come forward. Mr. Zook will be your new assistant principal." Immediately the whole student body stood and, facing me as I walked to the podium, broke into a thunderous applause. "Well, I see," commented Mr. Warner, "that Mr. Zook meets with your approval." The students remained standing, continuing their lengthy applause. He asked me to speak, but I was speechless—the words wouldn't come.

I stood at the podium for a while. After I could gather my emotions, the students sat down. I said, "I'd like to welcome you into my family." That's all I could say.

I know teachers were shocked to see an entire student body receive their new assistant principal in such a positive manner—a genuine vote of approval. I was immensely shocked. It made me feel as though I had accomplished something in my fourteen-year teaching career. It also made me want to be the very best I could be as an administrator with that kind of vote of confidence.

My first year as assistant principal was tremendously hectic. I almost threw in the towel that first year because the school had in previous years deteriorated so much: there were a lot of fights; it was overcrowded—it was a school built for 650 and now we had over 800 students in it. I had been a teacher in my own island with my own students doing things the way I felt they should be done. The word was around that I was fair, that I understood, and that I cared. Those three things the students respected.

Harold's first secretary, Diane, remembers:

"When Harold first came on the job, he tackled it with zest, working hard at whatever needed attention. He was very particular and serious about his work, and put in unbelievably long hours. One of his greatest strengths was he never thought much about his disability. I can't think of any weaknesses he might have had.

"Harold had a great concern for his students. When they were in trouble, he didn't just discipline them, but he tried to make them better people. He seemed to have an especially close relationship with the teachers, developing a great family feeling.

"Working for him was rather unique because we knew many of the same people, which put me at ease with him. We had a great working relationship having a lot of fun. One Christmastime, he put mistletoe over my office chair. After several teachers came by giving me kisses, and seeing Harold's impish grin, I finally looked up and saw what he had done. He always had little tricks up his sleeve.

"Harold always wanted to be fair to everybody. He was dedicated, not letting anything get in the way of his work. He had a special concern for his students, always wanting them to succeed, and did what he could to help them succeed. He also worked very closely with teachers. He had an inner toughness that may have come from his living with his disabilities. The way his parents raised him, his faith, and his persistence kept him going."

Another secretary, Elaine, remarks, "Harold was always very caring, always wanting to give students second chances. He followed up with students to make certain they were on the right track. He was very forthright and supportive of teachers and staff. His support gave me confidence in my work as a secretary. He also put a lot of trust in us. Working for Harold was a lot of fun because he loved jokes and having fun. He would get an impish grin on his face that would warn us something funny was about to happen. Harold had so many friends who supported him; he knew he was never alone.

"Harold lived his Christian beliefs. He had a lot of perseverance, was strong-willed in a good sense and very determined to live up to his potential. He was always complimentary to people, and his confidence in them helped them live up to their potential, too. Students and faculty knew that when they brought problems to Harold they would be dealt with—not shoved under the rug."

Harold continues: Just prior to my years as an administrator, drugs had begun making their appearance in schools and a prevailing atmosphere had developed in which marginal students seemed to have gained the upper hand. Noteworthy students were reluctant to receive public praise for their good deeds or accomplishments for fear of being looked upon as nerds. An achievement I think most appreciated by others was that Brooke and I were able to move Indian Valley from a school where students didn't want to be recognized for doing good things to a school that wanted to be recognized for its worthy achievements. I know the staff really appreciated that because they were able to teach in peace. They now had a school where we were a family, a school of which they could be proud, a school that the nation recognized as being a school worthy of praise. I think parents appreciated what we had done for their children. Again, I don't take full credit for that. It takes more than one person to do these things. You have to have a stage—an atmosphere—in which to do these things. Brooke, the principal, and I were able to develop that atmosphere with time.

Our school district had had about four different superintendents. One superintendent, Dr. Alexander Grande, admired my abilities and my character, my personality, and what I had done for kids. He was getting a lot of letters from parents praising my efforts, asking to promote me to principalship. However, although I had other opportunities for that, I never wanted to be a principal. I felt there were too many meetings. I never liked being the front man. Brooke Moyer, for whom I had developed a great deal of respect as a fellow teacher, was an assistant principal at the high school when the position for principal opened up at Indian Valley. It was a dream of mine to work with him in administration. I felt Brooke was a better front man, so I told the school board if they hired him, I would like to stay in my position as assistant, making that my career. That was rather unusual, since most people used the assistant principal position as a stepping-stone to a principalship. I explained my situation, why I wanted to stay an assistant, and that I felt I was best suited as a disciplinarian working with children, which was my reason for going into the profession.

The faculty also wanted me to move up, which created another kind of problem. I told the staff they would have the best of both worlds if they would accept Mr. Moyer as their principal. They all knew him as a fellow teacher who had a tremendously strong reputation as a teacher.

During this time, I was secretly discussing my situation with board members, also telling them of my desire to have Mr. Moyer as my principal. I told them if that were not possible or if Brooke didn't want the position, I would take the principalship so I could choose my assistant. I didn't want to be in a position as an assistant without having some input as to who would be my principal.

Brooke Moyer did accept the position, immediately telling me, "I want you to know you are not my assistant. We're coworkers." Nicholas Chubb, who was then an assistant principal at the high school, had the same concept about child-centeredness as we did. Brooke and I knew that sooner or later we would be retiring, and eventually Brooke did retire four years before I did. We started grooming Nick years before to take over our school. We invited him to visit our school on various occasions, involving him as much as possible. When Brooke retired, Nick came in as principal. We served together for four years.

Harold and Brooke describe their team approach:

Harold: Brooke and I worked together as administrators at Indian Valley. Brooke came in at a time when the school was having a lot of difficulties, so we spent one entire summer planning how we could turn the tide. Brooke was always one of my mentors when I was still a teacher; even when he was a fellow teacher, we somehow clicked. Prior to his move to the high school, he served as assistant principal at Indian Valley, during which time we frequently conferred with each other about educational matters; I admired him in his role, and he obviously admired my role as a teacher. Brooke is one of those administrators who was a tremendous "front man." He would roam the halls in the school and was always visible. My job was more behind the scenes as a support person, giving him time to be the visible person. It was a team that worked very well. We developed goals right at the outset. I well remember one of the first things he said: "Honesty is important. If you have something on your mind, don't withhold it. Speak up and say what's on your mind." We didn't always see eye-to-eye, but we could always walk away in accord with each other. I appreciated that so much during those early years together.

Brooke: There are so many things I could say about Harold, it would take me three days. He's a unique, remarkable human being. He wears sincerity. He focused on his career; in fact, it was his life. I saw him as a catalyst in so many ways. Before becoming an administrator he was very active with the teachers' organization, and while serving as negotiator for teachers' contracts he maintained credibility with central office personnel and board members. As we worked together, we could see Harold becoming very involved with students, noting how kids bought into Harold's sincerity. His handicap was an asset with students because they admired his courage and the fact that he never complained. I don't think Harold ever complained to me, which has given me strength.

Even as a teacher we could see there was a future for him. When he first began teaching, this poor guy's classroom was on the second floor. I can't imagine going up those stairwells with his handicap. However, he never complained about it.

When we worked together as administrators, I told him our purpose was to serve the teachers and students. We had to make this place one of the best places for people to get to their maximum in terms of potential, both teachers and students. I looked to Harold as a coprincipal more than an assistant. When Harold was behind closed doors working with a teacher, I had no concerns about what their discussions were. I trusted him and he trusted me. We had such a trust that when we had differences of opinion we never walked out at the end of the day without having that cleared. Teachers sensed our mutual trust and they felt secure in it.

We believed in establishing positive attitudes that developed into tradition and expectations. We told our students this was a great school with great teachers and this is the way it is going to be. Teachers bought it, students bought it, and we eventually developed a great school that became a National Blue Ribbon School.

Harold confided in me and I confided in him. We never asked teachers to do anything we didn't do ourselves. We set goals and objectives for ourselves and were evaluated in terms of meeting those goals. Teachers also set goals and objectives for themselves and for their students, and it was my job to meet with the teachers several times during the year to ask how things were going for them. We eventually had students develop goals as well. Each year in January, I gave a "State of the School" speech in an assembly, reviewing where we were in light of the goals we had set for the school. We used that at final exams, too. Many teachers wanted to teach in our building.

Harold developed such a great handbook, called *The Agenda,* which I think is one of the best in the state of Pennsylvania. *The Agenda* is a large attractive spiral notebook containing a wealth of information, including, among other items, the school philosophy, academic practices and policies, the alma mater, the schedule of events, and the student support team, as well as inspirational sections. One example is a section titled "We Dare You!" with challenges such as "To use your full human potentials in achieving your goals" and "To be strong, to persevere, to be determined to have the stamina it takes to lead instead of being led." One means of bringing attention to *The Agenda* was a weekly drawing of a few student *Agenda* numbers. Renee, the first recipient of the "Spirit of the Eagle" Award (see the middle of Chapter 10, pages 220–221) explains: "Each Monday Mr. Zook drew numbers from a box that corresponded to a student Agenda number and announced the numbers over the intercom. Those lucky students went to the office at lunchtime to receive some kind of prize. It was a great morale booster and motivational tool. I was so pleased to be able to sometimes draw the numbers for Mr. Zook."

Brooke: Harold didn't leave school until seven o'clock at night. I'd be entertaining guests in my home on a Saturday when Harold would call me about a problem. He lived at school almost twenty-four hours a day. Late one afternoon, not realizing the microphone was on, Harold said, "I think I'm going to leave early today like the teachers do." It was piped into every classroom. All the teachers laughed because they all knew he stayed so late every evening. It wasn't offensive to them, but they never let him forget it!

I don't think I can give a total picture of what this guy's about—he's so unique. He's courageous, a taskmaster when dealing with students. If he couldn't get very far with students, he would call me in and I took over. We always maintained dignity with a child. When parents sent their students to our school, they knew what our tradition was. Older children passed it down to their younger siblings.

I don't think anyone in the school looked on Harold as disabled; I know I never did. And yet in his later years, I helped him get to the lavatory. I could tell you some very human stories about him. Other handicapped students were much more at ease with their handicaps because of his own situation. He was always steady, fair, consistent, but very firm. Their respect for him was unbelievable. He could go everywhere in that building on his electric cart and I never heard a student make a caustic remark about him. Some parents insisted they wanted students in Mr. Zook's school. We weren't miraculous, but we were different.

About three days before the end of the school year, we issued invitations to high school seniors who had gone through Indian Valley to come back for a visit. The yearbooks were spread out on tables while teachers and administrators sat with the visitors and reminisced about their school years at Indian Valley. Initially not many students came, but gradually more and more came back to share in this terrific event even though it was held after school hours. There was something there that brought them back. Two teachers brought up that idea. The students were so proud to tell what college they would be attending or other future plans.

In many schools, teaching shuts down about four days prior to the end of the school year. At Indian Valley, we taught up to the end of the year and mailed the report cards to students. Our last day was a dress-up day with an awards assembly to which the parents were invited. We presented awards in every subject, memorial awards, and other awards, including plaques. It was such a dignified occasion. When students went to the auditorium, teachers were seated on the stage. As each teacher presented a student with an award, the student took that teacher's seat, so that by the end of the assembly all teachers had left the stage and only students were on the stage. I gave a speech, we sang the alma mater, and the chorus sang "We've Only Just Begun." Many students cried, as this was their farewell event.

Harold was a master at developing motivational ideas and events. There were motivational banners all over the school. Letters went home to parents when students were on the honor roll. Excellence in academics and behavior was always recognized.

Harold was an anchor to me, contributing support, reassurance, and confidence. He gave me everything. He was the best assistant anyone could ever have. He gave the same support to teachers, going into their classrooms to show them how to teach, or spending time talking about their problems.

To students, Harold gave expectations and accountability. Nobody likes cafeteria duty in a junior high or middle school. Harold developed table captains who remained behind after other students left to straighten up everything, wipe the tables with a wet cloth, and put chairs back in an orderly fashion.

Harold: I frequently chose marginal students for those cafeteria jobs and at the end of the month I wrote a letter to their parents with high ratings stating how responsible their child had been at this job. At the end of the month these students were allowed to choose whether or not to clean the cafeteria for another month. Also, at the end of the month they were allowed to choose a special dinner from Burger King or McDonald's or Chinese food, which we ate together in my office. This was a special treat from me to them. Likewise, at the end of each week I gave them some small thing such as a coupon for a free ice cream. They always looked forward to receiving a small reward for being responsible.

Brooke: We had school pride pins with an eagle on them, which were given to students when they earned it. Those pins were much desired by both students and teachers.

The student council in our school was a very functional organization. Harold would sit down with the officers of student council and give each one of them a paper on which to list how they felt they would like to spend the activity funds raised by the students. On a yearly basis, Harold thoroughly explained the budget to student council representatives and followed up on their suggestions. Harold taught the students how to take minutes of their meetings, keep accurate records, et cetera. Everything was always well researched, carried out fairly, and well documented. Harold's penchant for meticulous records paid off. When the auditor came to the school district, he was always sent to our school because the records were well documented! Later it became law that all student activity funds must be audited. All dealings with students and teachers were out in the open; there were no hidden agendas.

I believe Harold's faith helped make him a unique person, as well as his dedication, sensitivity, and consistency. Any time a problem came up, I knew that together we could handle it. He was that way with my successor, Dr. Chubb, as well as with me. I think Harold's greatest achievement was his total advocacy for every student. In a good way, he was more of an advocate for students than he was for teachers or parents. He would often say, "You're reading this student wrong. I want you to respect what I'm saying to you because I think this is the way to handle it." I think the community knew he was committed to developing students through that very traumatic period of adolescence. He dealt with students experiencing all kinds of problems, such as those involving drugs and alcohol, and students who were suicidal.

Early in his career, Harold was criticized for his concern for marginal students. The comment was made that "we can't afford to have a highly paid English teacher spend so much time with one student."

Harold has meant so much to me and now, ten years later, we are still very good friends. He is one unique guy! It has been said that it's amazing how much you can get done if you don't care who gets the credit. Harold built on that.

Harold: We believed in decency and were both decent. We modeled what we preached. It is unusual for two leaders in a school to have a genuine Christian faith, and teachers sensed that. A fair number of teachers also had a strong Christian faith. When one prospective teacher was being interviewed, the principal, near the end of the interview, asked, "Who is your hero?" Without hesitation, this young teacher, applying for a public school teaching position, said, "Jesus Christ." Immediately, Nick closed the interview telling her she would be hired. This dynamic teacher never flaunted her religion, nor wore it on her sleeve, but she lived it.

As an assistant principal, my goal became more focused because my primary role was discipline. My goal was to prove that I could take a so-called bad kid—I even hate to use that term—and help that student become a human being and a lady or a gentleman. I wanted students to learn that their school was their life during those three years at Indian Valley. If they made Indian Valley a better place they would become a better person. I wanted them to know it was *their* school, not *my* school. It was their home for three years. I proposed the idea of having students in the same homerooms for three years in a row so we (students and teachers) could develop a family relationship.

My goal as an administrator was to help every girl and every boy in our school become a responsible teenager—a young person. I never called them kids in school. I called them ladies and gentlemen. I would show them the virtue and the gains to be had in becoming that—how life could be so much better for them by becoming ladies and gentlemen.

The following stories illustrate Harold's relationships with others and his adherence to what he taught.

A fellow English teacher and personal friend, Ginger, comments, "In 1969 Harold hired me as an English teacher. We shared many teaching ideas with each other. As a young teacher, Indian Valley was my first long-term teaching job. Harold had an uncanny sense of knowing what were the best qualities of a young teacher and how to cultivate and bring out those best qualities. Some teachers have horrible experiences their first year. When teachers asked Harold questions, he would help them understand they had the answers inside themselves and would encourage them to discover those answers.

"He encouraged me to apply for department head, but I felt I couldn't handle the job. He kept telling me I was ready, so I applied and became department head and was successful. He helped me believe in myself. He gave me a real sense of who I was as a teacher and why I was a teacher. He gave me the freedom and opportunity to use my creativity in the best way I could for kids. He helped me develop a program called Creative Arts for Kids as an elective, knowing it was the very best course I could ever teach. He supported the ideas that were "pushing the envelope" for curriculum when it was in the best interest of the kids. I still apply that when I work with younger teachers. I try to recognize what is best in a young teacher and to create an environment for that teacher to flourish. That's what Harold did, not only for me, but for all the teachers on his staff.

"I would describe Harold's character as well grounded, someone with a deep faith—a nondenominational faith. I'm not sure I know what his church affiliation is, and it doesn't matter. His character never changed. There was integrity about him; one could always count on him. There was never any doubt about where he stood and why he stood there. Whether he was working with adults or children, the well-groundedness and faith were always there. They couldn't snow him. He always knew where he was and where he wanted the students to be.

"Harold not only had an inner faith from his religious background, but his family gave him a lot of strength. I never saw Harold as disabled because he never made an issue of it. That seemed to have come from his supportive family.

"Harold had a number of opportunities for other administrative positions, which would have taken him out of direct contact with kids. When I watched him work with kids who had problems, kids of whom another teacher would be afraid, he would say, 'I'm making progress. He's coming around.' Sometimes it would take years, but many of them came back and said, 'You were the person who believed in me.' No one else could have done that like Harold did. That's why he is so beloved in the entire community and why he turned down other administrative positions.

"All the relationships Harold had with people were genuine. What you saw was what you got. He was not a role player. Everyone knew what he stood for and why he stood for it. Such integrity is so unique in the world. So often people compromise to get ahead, but I never saw him do that. It was not what was important for Harold Zook, but it was what was important for the kids that mattered. Harold was always respectful of a parent's role in working with kids.

"I believe his faith and strong belief in himself kept him going when things got tough. People were amazed at how he kept going. He had an inner strength that was more important than what was outside—that was his faith in God and his faith in other people. Harold didn't view his physical condition as a disability.

"Harold's love for children was very strong. He was very close to his nephews and nieces. The children at Indian Valley were also part of his family. It was amazing to me when he shared that he had been in love with a young woman, but he didn't marry because he didn't want to be a burden to anyone. I wonder if I could have shut off that love were I in his situation. He was thinking more of the other person than of himself.

"Although Harold was my administrator, I felt he was more of a mentor. I always knew I would get a very positive response when I shared a lot of professional or personal things. He is a wonderful friend. I have been able to share things with him that I wouldn't have shared with most people. He was very understanding, always willing to listen, and always honest with his answers. I may not always have wanted to hear what he had to say, but he said it constructively. I miss him greatly and I continue my friendship with him. I don't think anyone will ever be able to take his place at Indian Valley.

"I think the most unique thing he did was when he took a group of students on a trip to New England at a time when such trips weren't done. He made these things happen at a sacrifice to himself, but it was because he wanted to broaden the experiences of the students.

"When I was in charge of talent shows and I needed students to stay late for practices, Harold would say, 'I'll stay late.' Harold asked me to start a Future Teachers of America club in the school that resulted in a wonderful organization. Because of that I went on to become a Pennsylvania regional and state representative in the Pennsylvania State Educational Association. This was because of his initiative and prodding."

Brenda, Harold's secretary of over seven years, comments, "Harold always liked to listen to the kids' stories or anyone else. He really cared about people. He was very understanding when I had problems with my teenage children. He also helped me realize my dream of going back to school to become a guidance counselor. He was always there anytime I needed to talk. He was a great listener. He helped me stay on track with my life.

"Harold was a very easygoing, patient, caring, and understanding person—a go-getter. With his disability, he knows he can't sit around feeling sorry for himself, but he has a good time and keeps on going. He relies on family and friends. He was very generous with time or money, staying many hours at school to work on projects or to call parents. He kept the school on track. He worked hard to complete the many forms when applying for the National Blue Ribbon School Award, which was quite an honor. I am glad I was here during the process.

"He was a financial wizard, keeping the books straight. He helped me learn what I needed to know. After he retired, he told me he would be at home and if I needed anything I should feel free to call. He also contributed a lot to the community, keeping his eyes and ears open to the community needs and organizing Walk-a-Thons for people who needed help. I'm amazed that even after he's retired, he picks up right where he left off. When he meets someone, he never forgets him, and people don't forget Mr. Zook.

"Students knew they could go to him if they needed someone. They all knew he was a tough disciplinarian, but years later they would come back appreciating what he had taught them. He did whatever it took to accomplish his goals and it made them a better person. He was able to keep parents calm when their children were in trouble. He helped them understand their children were not angels, that they needed discipline and were normal teenage kids.

"Harold had a good relationship with his fellow workers. Most felt they could talk to him when they couldn't talk to anybody else. Sometimes they made fun of all the forms he had created and his ultraorganization, but it kept everybody in line. We still continue to use many of those forms.

"Harold knew there were always going to be hurdles in his life, but he kept a positive outlook, saying there were people out there who were in worse shape than he. I think that's what kept him going. I know his parents had Amish background and I think some of that may have rubbed off on him. He felt he could make a difference in the world and make it a better place to live. Keeping in touch with other teachers and friends made a difference in his life. When he was in the hospital, his brother said, 'You're going to see Harold, aren't you?' We hadn't planned to go that evening, but we did and our visit and the visits of others seemed to make a difference in his getting well.

"Harold used his disability with the students, showing them they can do anything if they put their mind to it. They shouldn't let anything hold them back no matter what, whether it is a disability, a handicap, or a learning problem. Life is tough at times, but you just get through it. I remain friends with him and still turn to him when I need someone to listen to me. His whole life is unique. He touches all the hearts with whom he comes in contact."

Harold describes his relationships with staff: When I first became an administrator, administrators were considered people to be set aside. They weren't to fraternize with staff, custodians, or those who were a lower echelon. Michael, our head custodian or engineer, as he was called, had abilities and smarts that few people had. He knew everything about boilers and any kind of machinery. I had been a friend of his during my teaching years because I spent so many hours in the building. Shortly after I became an administrator, I invited Mike to lunch with me. The principal asked me later that morning to go to lunch. I said, "I invited Mike to lunch. Why don't you join us?"

My principal remarked, "Harold, you're an administrator now," insinuating it was inappropriate to be having lunch with the custodian.

We happened to go to the same restaurant. Mike and I were sitting at one table while the principal was sitting alone five tables away. Those things never made sense to me.

One day, Mike played a trick on me. He knew the chief of police, Mr. Clemmer, in town very well. Mike knew I always came to school about an hour earlier than the teachers. He told Chief Clemmer to wait for me some morning, follow me to the parking lot, and pretend he was giving me a ticket for speeding. I was really speeding a little. It was a thirty-five-mile-per-hour zone and I was going about forty-five. As I got almost to the school driveway, I heard a siren, so I pulled into the parking lot and stopped.

Chief Clemmer came to my car with his pad, asking, "Do you know why I stopped you?"

"I suspect I was speeding up Maple Avenue," I admitted.

"I'm afraid I'm going to have to talk to you about this," he said.

I thought he was acting a bit strange for a police officer, because he wasn't getting to the point of giving me a ticket. While we sat there, other staff members began driving in while this officer was writing me up. I wanted to get it over with and get him out of there.

Mike had told the officer to detain me a bit so I'd be there when the staff came in, but I was getting frustrated.

"Officer," I said, "just give me the ticket."

"Suppose I just give you a warning," he replied.

"Officer Clemmer," I urged, "just give me a ticket. I was wrong."

I believed in being a model for students and I felt that if I was wrong I should pay the price.

I said, "I was wrong. I could have killed a child. Please give me a ticket," but he wouldn't give me one.

Eventually, he gave me a warning and left, but by that time half the parking lot was filled with teachers. When I went into the office with my "tail between my legs," there was a sign on the counter: "Zook Fine Fund!" Everyone was to make contributions. There were screws, washers, lots of pennies, nickels, and dimes.

"For gosh sakes!" I exclaimed. "Get this out of here. Students will be coming in here before long!"

My school nurse, Eleanor, and her husband were responsible for helping me break my workaholic habit, even encouraging me to take a trip to Hawaii. On my return I wanted to give them a special dinner as a thank-you, so I made a "dry run" to a Hawaiian-style restaurant in the area. During this visit, I observed the hula dancers performing, so I explained to the manager that I was bringing my dear friends Eleanor and Harold and their daughter to his restaurant. I made arrangements that my guest Mr. Hillegas would be asked to participate in the dance.

During the entertainment, the master of ceremonies said, "We have a special guest, Harold Zook, with us tonight, and he has his friends with him. We would like Mr. Harold Hillegas to come to the stage." Being quite a "crackerjack," Harold went onstage, where they tried to teach him the hula dance, and he made a rather awkward attempt.

At one point, the dancer said, "Come on, Mr. Hillegas. Shake it!"

"Honey," replied Mr. Hillegas. "It's dead! It doesn't move anymore!"

We were laughing as hard as we could, when I heard my name: "Mr. Zook, we would like you to come onstage also."

"Oh, my!" I told Eleanor. "I can't even go up those steps to the stage."

One of the dancers came to my table, urging me to come with

her. I explained that I couldn't go up the steps, but she said there was a back way to the stage, so I went with her.

They got me up onstage with one person on each side of me and a hula dancer telling us how to do the dance. We all had on grass skirts over our rolled-up pant legs. One of my pant legs dropped while the other one stayed rolled up! I was up there stepping around, with everyone saying, "You're doing fine!" It was so crazy! That was one time my joke backfired on me.

During my teaching years we moved into a new building, which required choosing a new mascot. I'm not sure who chose the Eagle as our mascot, but I felt as a teacher we should know why we chose it. I asked, but nobody seemed to know. I spent three days in the Reading, Pennsylvania, library reading everything I could about the eagle, such as its habitat, et cetera. Their nests alone are phenomenal—their size, weight, and height. The heights at which eagles can fly and see a fish in the water, how they use their talons, and their power are extraordinary. I got so enthused about it that I took this information back to my classes, always making sure my students understood the tremendous abilities of this bird and how it fits into our school and why we should emulate these characteristics and how we become better because we strive to do so.

I was not responsible for choosing the Eagle as our mascot, but I felt responsible for giving it meaning. That is why, when I retired, I spent over $3,000 to put a bronze plaque in the front hall with my message to the school, which I wanted to remain there permanently. I wanted students to be inspired after I left the school. I included on the plaque some of the things I had discovered about the eagle. I spent over six years developing that plaque knowing that when I would retire I would donate it to the school. (*See the foreword for the wording.*) An additional gift I gave to the school when I retired was a large porcelain eagle that is now in a display case in the new library named in my honor.

It took four men to put the bronze plaque in place in the front lobby. Every day since that plaque was put in place, a little vase of flowers has appeared on a little pedestal underneath. For years no one knew how those flowers got there, but every day the flowers were there. Finally, one night, someone was in the building at eleven o'clock and saw the night custodian putting a vase of flowers on the pedestal. This night custodian—whose daughters I had always respected as students—was responsible for the flowers and he has done that every day since.

I saw him one day and said, "John, I understand you are responsible for the flowers. What makes you do that?"

"They're just flowers from my garden, Mr. Zook. I can never repay you for what you did for my daughters. The least I can do is make that plaque just a little more attractive."

John, the head night custodian at Indian Valley, comments, "I knew Harold as assistant principal when my two daughters were going through school. He helped my daughters a lot in getting them through school. It is amazing how he would take the time to write letters to them, encourage them, and help them have a positive outlook. Our daughters always felt they could go to him for help at any time and for any reason. At first I wondered who this guy was to do so much for my daughters. To this day they continue to talk about him and come back to see him. My oldest daughter invited him to her wedding, which she talked about for many years.

"I helped hang the large bronze plaque, the *Spirit of the Eagle,* which was Harold's gift to the school upon his retirement. It represents what one person can do and the positive effect that person can have on a school.

"Years ago when my girls were little, I put flowers in their rooms for them. I thought of the beauty of flowers and the beauty of my girls and I think that's what life's all about. I began raising the kinds of flowers that grow in the shade of the woods where I live. One day when I saw a teacher carrying flowers to school, I offered to bring flowers from my flower beds. I began putting poinsettias by Harold's plaque at Christmastime and thought it looked so nice; therefore, I decided to put a small arrangement there each day. I felt it gave people something nice to look at when they read the words on the plaque.

"I could take several days to talk about Harold. He was so dedicated to his work, always managing to help anybody in any way he could. When I felt I needed to help him, it would soon turn out that he would be helping me somehow. He was very precise in everything he did. There wasn't a thing in the school that he didn't know about and know where it was placed. He didn't mess around. He knew how he wanted to do things and they turned out right.

"Because Harold loved his work so much it kept him going. I don't know what else it could be. He spent many hours at the school, always working, always working. He worked very hard for what he achieved. His problems never held him back. He gave a lot of encouragement to others, helping them strive to do their best and be their best. Just talking to him made one want to be the best possible person. When I went to him with a problem, if he didn't have an answer, he helped me find an answer.

"Harold did so much for the school, often spending his own money to have things nice for the students. He built a nice showcase for trophies, et cetera, but he did it quietly, not taking any credit for himself. He was always looking for ways to improve the school.

"Harold never used his disability negatively. He went about his work as if the disability wasn't there. It seems to be a gift that's built inside him to be able to keep going when times are tough. After working with him over the years, I can't believe what he's accomplished for himself and what he's done for others. I think it's so great they named the library for him. I asked for the responsibility of cleaning that library so I could be certain to keep it like he would want it to be kept. He's done so much for the school."

Harold was interested in people whether or not they were students or teachers in his school. While eating at a restaurant he was impressed with the waitress serving his table. After praising her service, he said, "You are the kind of person who should be a teacher, the type of person I would like to have in my school."

"I am a teacher," she replied. "I just graduated, but there are no jobs."

I asked for her name, address, and telephone number. About a week later an opening arose at Indian Valley for a teacher's aide in special education. I told her this could be an opening for a future teaching position. She took the aide job and the students loved her. Four years later she got a teaching job at our sister junior high school, and today she is again teaching at Indian Valley.

On another occasion, a very shy high school student with no self-esteem attempted suicide three times. She was a former student at Indian Valley with whom I stayed in touch. After talking to her, I got her to agree that if she was ever tempted to make another attempt, she would call me first. I received a call one night at three o'clock. She said, "Mr. Zook, I can't make it through the night." I talked her through the night until six o'clock, when I told her, "I am taking the day off from school. I want you to take off, too. I will meet you at a restaurant where I'll buy you breakfast and we'll talk person-to-person."

After we talked through the morning, I got her into counseling. This had been her junior year in high school. We prayed together and gradually she got through it. Later she became the prom queen in high school. Today she is happily married, with three young daughters.

There was another girl who wanted to apply to teach at an elementary school in the Souderton Area School District, which already had over 200 applications and was not taking any more. She talked to me about it, and when I asked her if she had applied, she told me they refused to give her an application because they weren't accepting any more.

I spoke to the director of personnel, whom I knew very well, telling him, "I know you are not taking any more applications, but I would like you to do me one favor. Interview Jennifer even if she

can't apply. You are possibly turning down one of the most potentially successful teachers." I explained how she had received the
Dean's Award in Education from Kutztown University, as well as
my dealings with her. He agreed to interview her and hired her on
the spot without an application; today she is teaching at Indian
Valley.

A student who as a sixth-grader was very shy but very bright
desired more advanced English work. She wanted to become a for-
eign exchange student but had no backing. No one in high school
appeared to recognize her ability. After she told me her dreams
and disappointments, I talked to the Rotary Club about her, asking
them if they would sponsor her, which they did. Halfway through
her term abroad, she had a nervous breakdown. Her parents came
to me, and when she came back to the States I spent a lot of time
with her. Today she is a very talented writer and has her own inter-
national editorial business.

Another girl had bouts with severe headaches. I believed her
and permitted her to stay at home or to come to the nurse's office
to get rid of her headaches. I trusted her not to misuse my trust. In
high school, no allowance was made, so her parents came to me. I
explained to the personnel at the high school what I had done for
her in my school, so they made allowances for her and she made it
through high school. I believe today she is nearly cured of her
migraines.

In about 1983 I started using my Amigo—only for long runs
from one end of the building to the other. In 1986 I began using it
for shorter distances as well. I had tremendous difficulty accepting
the use of a wheelchair. Walking was having an adverse effect on
my back. My doctor told me it was either take an early retirement
or concede to using some kind of mechanical wheelchair. He
thought I could stretch my career eight or ten years if I used a mechanical device. I really struggled with that. I would hide my
wheelchair in the school. Maybe it was pride, but it took a long
time before I accepted using the Amigo. Then, I noticed when I

used it in the high school students looked at me very strangely; but in my school nobody paid any attention.

When we had school dances, I would always guard the front entrance to make certain nobody could go in or out without my seeing them. It was also an opportunity to chat with parents. Students would want to pay me a dime for a jog on my Amigo. I refused the dime but would sit on a bench while they took turns going to the end of the hall and back on my Amigo. They got the feel of it.

The art teacher wanted to do a caricature of me in my chair to use in an art lesson. She drew me with a big head and smoke coming from my wheels. The students loved it. They were very accepting of me in my Amigo.

I had back problems that gave me a lot of pain. Sitting on my chair at length for twelve hours or so became very painful, although I tried not to show it. One young girl who always had a smile on her face would walk up to me in the hall, put her arm on my shoulder, and say, "It's OK, Mr. Zook. I'm praying for you." How do you put a value on that? I thought I was hiding my pain, but she had an instinctive sense that I was in pain.

Another girl I would call my hugger often came flying into my office between classes. Entering the inner office without permission was normally forbidden, but she would run in no matter who was with me, give me a big hug, and say, "You needed that!" Off she would go to her next class. I told her one time, "You know, young lady, if you're ever late to class I'm going to have to discipline you like anyone else."

"It's worth it, Mr. Zook," she would say.

One day the superintendent came to see me in my office when all of a sudden this young girl came flying in, wrapped her arms around my neck with, "You needed that," and off she went.

"What was that all about?" the superintendent asked.

"She's just my hugger, Dr. Grande," I said. "She does this almost every day."

"You're kidding me," he said. "What a testimony to you that some kid would want to do that."

She has four children now, but she still sends me letters. She is such an inspiration to me.

When I was first teaching, I could carry a typewriter from my car to the school. Later, I had such difficulty walking that I had to lean against the auditorium seats to get enough strength to walk the rest of the way. Before long a parking place was made for me at the front of the building, and eventually a ramp was put in place because I could hardly negotiate the two steps anymore. As my condition worsened, I would have to stop about halfway from my car to the building, set my briefcase down, and put my hands on my knees because my back was giving out. Then, after regaining some strength, I'd make it to the railing and lean against that. After a while I couldn't carry anything, and eventually I was in my Amigo all the time.

My family and friends wanted me to get a car phone, which I didn't think was necessary. I always got to the school early, and the custodian was there to help me get from my car to my Amigo, because I could no longer get out of my car to a standing position. Yet I was still hard-nosed about giving in to more help.

One January morning there was an ice storm. It was school policy that when schools were closed all administrators still went to school. On the way to school, there was a very icy hill on which a lot of cars were stuck, and for three hours I was hung up there, not able to get to school. Nobody could move; even salt trucks and snowplows couldn't get through until they began carrying salt in buckets to get people moving. Everybody was frightened. My sister called the school and learned I hadn't gotten there. The state police were out looking for me. That was too much consternation for me, so I installed a car phone, which put everyone at ease. From then on, when I got to school I called Brooke or Dr. Chubb in the office, who would call the custodian on the intercom, saying, "The eagle has landed." Mr. Kulp would then bring my Amigo out to my car. At home in my garage, I had a lift to help me get out of my car into a standing position, at which point I used crutches for about five or six years before going to my Amigo.

Craig, chief of buildings and grounds at Indian Valley Middle School, met Harold at his car every morning with his Amigo. Harold would call and say he would be there in one minute and fifty seconds—and he was. Harold was very prompt. Craig worked with Harold for about thirteen years. He says, "I pulled him out of his car every morning and put him on his Amigo. I also kept his Amigo in good shape, fixing anything that might go wrong. I kept him mobile. I saw what he went through every morning to get out of his car and to get to the building. Every morning we would be laughing about something. He was such an inspiration to me.

"Harold and I were buddies. We did a lot of unique things together. When he needed something done, he wanted it done right. For example, when we hung pictures, they had to be exactly the right distance from the ceiling to be at eye level—to the tenth of an inch. When we planted flowers together outdoors, he would have me measure exactly where the flowers would be planted. He was very intense, working many hours. When he left, I felt so sorry for him, because it was like giving up his family. We were all sad to see him go. It was a hard decision for him to retire. His determination gave him the perseverance to keep going. He's stubborn, just like me. When there was a job to be done, we kept at it until it was done. We're a lot alike.

"He contributed so much to students. He helped kids in many ways; I'm sure he helped them with money, but he never told anyone. There are very few administrators who put in as many hours as he did. This was his life. Things at home were put on the back burner if he was needed at school. He put his heart and soul into the kids. If he knew they needed help and were genuine, he went full throttle to help them. He is a genuine person, straight forward, and never lies. Everybody loved him. He treated everyone the same. He knew all the custodians by name, even part-time workers.

"After Harold retired, someone was putting a small bouquet of flowers at the base of the plaque Harold donated to the school. We would ask everyone who put them there, but no one said anything. After almost a year, I caught John, a night custodian, placing the flowers there. When I told Harold that John was placing the flowers under the plaque, he got all choked up. When John is asked why he puts the flowers there, he just brushes it off. John was often at school with Harold in the evenings and just loved Harold.

"Harold's stubbornness, pride, and church life keep him going. He won't let anything get him down. He has accomplished a whole lot more than I have ever accomplished. He was always upbeat and would never give up.

"Harold loved jokes. I would tell him a joke, and he would tell me things the kids had done but would never reveal their names. We would laugh so hard. He was very precise about the maintenance of the building. I learned to notice things on my own because I knew he would tell me about a crooked picture or a squeaky door.

"One snowy morning Harold didn't show up at school. A half hour later we received a call from a snow truck driver telling us Harold was all right but was caught behind some vehicles on the snowy road. When he got to school, I yelled at him for not having a cell phone. Within the week, he had a cell phone installed. I think that's the only time I ever yelled at him.

"When it was snowy and icy, we worked very hard to shovel a path, salt it to melt the snow, and then sweep off the snow so he could make it into the school. It was especially hard for him in the snow and ice. He was always very patient with us. He never missed a day of work."

Harold fondly remembers: It was a great surprise to me when the decision was made to name the new library at Indian Valley the

J. Harold Zook Library. Earlier the school district wanted to name an elementary school in my honor, but I didn't want that because I never felt I was worthy of that honor. I guess it's my Mennonite upbringing, but I couldn't face my name being on a building for posterity.

My school district was very reluctant to accept my resignation, but I felt it was physically necessary because I couldn't put in the hours I really wanted to. I felt if I couldn't do my best, I wasn't getting the job done. I was still putting in more than twelve hours a day, and it took me all weekend to rest up. I was so exhausted at the end of each week. I was offered various opportunities, but I felt it was time for someone else to make his or her mark. Parents were very unhappy to see me leave because they had other children they wanted to send through the school. We had just become a National Blue Ribbon School, which was a great thing. I didn't even go along to Washington to receive the award, because I felt it was important for teachers to have that experience, even though in their eyes I was responsible for making ours the Blue Ribbon School. I wanted the honor to go to other equally deserving people.

I attended the final board meeting when they reluctantly accepted my resignation. A board member composed a motion that the new library be named the J. Harold Zook Library. I felt honored—I don't know how else to say it. They had just built a new addition to Indian Valley. The enrollment went from 650 to 1,000 the year after I left. We became a middle school instead of a junior high school. The motion was immediately accepted. It was an emotional thing for me, and it still is. My night custodian friend asked for the opportunity to clean that library every day to be sure it was shipshape. The beautiful library is located in the center of the school, complete with a computer lab and all the most modern equipment. I'm surprised that it's still an emotional thing for me. I suppose it speaks for the parents.

Two bronze plaques hang in Harold's bedroom today. One plaque reads:

J. HAROLD ZOOK
1960–1996
36 YEARS OF DEDICATION TO
SOUDERTON AREA SCHOOL DISTRICT
AND INDIAN VALLEY MIDDLE SCHOOL
1960–1974 ENGLISH TEACHER
1974–1996
INDIAN VALLEY MIDDLE SCHOOL
ASSISTANT PRINCIPAL
*   *   *
Your Guidance Has Helped Us To Soar.
You Truly Are The Spirit Of The Eagle.
Your Wisdom, Dedication And
Strength Have Carried Us To Reach
Our Highest Potential. Thank You
For Teaching Us To Fly.
With Deepest Appreciation,
THE INDIAN VALLEY
STUDENT BODY
1995–1996

The second plaque reads:

Presented to
J. HAROLD ZOOK
*   *   *
In Recognition Of Your Thirty-Six Years Of
Dedicated Service To The Souderton Area School District.
In Your Twenty-Two Years As Assistant Principal Of
Indian Valley Middle School
You Were An Educator Who Taught School Pride

And Individual Responsibility;
An Outstanding Leader Who Was Generous And Supportive;
A Disciplinarian Who Remained Open-Minded And Empathetic;
And A Confidant Who Was Fair And Forgiving.
Your Unwavering Dedication And Personal Integrity Have
Made You A Role Model To Students And Teachers Alike.

WITH GRATITUDE AND RESPECT
WE SEND YOU OUR BEST WISHES
ON YOUR RETIREMENT.

Teachers and Staff of
INDIAN VALLEY MIDDLE SCHOOL
May 10, 1996

213

10

Blue Ribbon School

For years, Dr. Grande, the superintendent, had asked Brooke and me to apply for recognition for our school as a Blue Ribbon School, but we both knew what we had and didn't feel like tooting our horns. We also knew it was a tremendous amount of work and we felt we had other work to do.

Dr. Grande kept encouraging us, telling us, "I know you can win hands down." He was on the national review panel that chose winning schools. He knew what was required, what had to be done to become a Blue Ribbon School. Knowing I was going to retire at the end of the year, Nick Chubb, the principal, felt it was the best thing he could do as an outgoing honor to me to win that award. Nick got together a committee of teachers to investigate the requirements and necessary steps to apply for the award. He gave released time to teachers to accomplish this, preparing the documents that must be completed because it took a tremendous amount of work.

An educator from New York, who was a member of the National Blue Ribbon School Review Panel, spent a week in our school district to make sure that what was on paper was indeed happening. He spent hours interviewing students, teachers, parents, community members, stopping people on the streets asking, "Tell me about Indian Valley." He verified that our documents represented our school activities. We became one of six schools of all levels in Pennsylvania, and eventually we were one of sixty-four in the nation to receive the honor. Representatives from the school were called to Washington to meet President Clinton, who gave the award at a ceremony in the White House. I sent the teacher who had worked on the application in my place. I was just as happy because it meant a lot to the teachers to be recognized.

The National Blue Ribbon Schools Program was established in 1982 by the U.S. secretary of education. Its purposes are to identify and recognize outstanding public and private schools across the nation, to provide research-based effectiveness criteria so schools can assess themselves and plan improvements, and to encourage schools to share information about best practices of educational success.

National Blue Ribbon Schools are models of excellence and equity. To be recognized, a school must demonstrate a strong commitment to educational excellence for all students. Schools applying must demonstrate sustained success in achieving these values for at least five years.

The chief state school officer of each state nominates the schools to be recognized for the U.S. Department of Education. The national review panel, consisting of approximately one hundred outstanding public and private school educators from all levels, evaluates the nominations. Based upon the quality of the applications, the most promising schools are recommended for site visits. The purpose of the visit is to verify the accuracy of the information the school has provided in its nomination form and to gather any additional information needed.

The categories considered are student focus and support, school organization and culture, challenging standards and curriculum, active teaching and learning, professional community leadership and educational vitality, school, family, key community partnerships, and indicators of success.

Indian Valley Middle School submitted a forty-three-page application to a Pennsylvania Department of Education panel of judges. After evaluating the application, they passed it on to the national level. The national committee, after evaluating the application, decided the school qualified for a site visit by a Department of Education representative who would check out the claims made in the application to make certain they were factual. The site visit produced a thirty-page report. Based upon its strong leadership, clear vision and sense of mission, high-quality teaching, challenging, up-to-date curriculum, policies and practices that ensure a safe environment conducive to learning, a solid commitment to parental involvement, and evidence that the school helps all students achieve high standards, the school was awarded the status of a National Blue Ribbon School.

Indian Valley was one of six middle schools in Pennsylvania receiving such a high honor in 1996. The person conducting the site visit was amazed that there was not a single negative comment concerning the school. The principal commented, "This award was built on the hard work of Mr. Moyer [the previous principal] and Mr. Harold Zook." He also offered special thanks to the teacher, Lois Smoot, for the many hours she had put into preparing the application and to "Assistant Principal Harold Zook, who epitomizes what Indian Valley represents—a child-centered school which cares about both its own school community and the community at large."

Harold is quoted as saying, "We really were a family. I think that what they saw was a family environment. They saw a school that was very child-centered and had a curriculum that engaged children in learning. Parents believe in this school. Administrators believe in this school. Teachers believe in this school. Kids believe in this school. If a parent and school work together there's no way you can't affect it in a positive way." Indian Valley Middle School had strong leadership, high-quality teaching, and a clear sense of mission shared by all.

Harold noted: On the last day of the school year, we didn't show movies as is customary in a lot of schools. We loved faculty–student interactions. One field day we had a big tug-of-war, which led to developing school spirit by dividing the school into red and blue teams that represented our school colors. Students were given points for everything they did. If they were on the honor roll, they got points. Points were given if they went out for a sport, for being student of the month, student of the week, or whatever.

Each month these points were placed on a big board. With every candy drive, or any other drive, points were given for high homeroom sales. Everything we did was geared toward points. Student government had a committee that dealt only with these points. This competition developed school spirit among the students.

The reviewer for the National Blue Ribbon School was present during our final tug-of-war featuring the Blue Team against the Red Team—homeroom against homeroom and grade against grade. This was then narrowed down to the best homeroom from each grade in a tug-of-war with the teachers. I was captain of the Blue Team and Nick was captain of the Red Team. The kids really got into it. The final teams were nip and tuck in their tug for supremacy. I was running up and down in my Amigo scooter cheering on my team. Nick was on the other side cheering on his team. The reviewer was watching all this. He later said he had never seen anything like the camaraderie, respect, and enthusiasm shown by the students toward one another and their teachers.

To develop enthusiasm during the magazine drive in my final year, I got on the intercom and sang a song or two. I also challenged Nick and his team to beat my team, which became a real competitive thing. One of my favorite foods is apple pie in bean soup, something our family ate many times, even though lots of people think it's gross. I had often tried to get Nick to try it, but he always said, "No way!" We decided if Nick's team lost he would have to eat a piece of apple pie in bean soup. As time went on, kids started hearing how Nick would have to eat apple pie in bean soup because his team was losing.

During that final week, there were virtually no discipline problems because everyone was focused on other things. Well, Nick's team lost, so I decided to make this a whole school event during an assembly. I asked interested students to write an essay indicating why they should be chosen as a contestant to eat apple pie in bean soup; and from about two hundred essays I chose the four most outstanding. I asked for an equal number of teacher volunteers. The four students and four teachers were seated at a table set up in the gymnasium. The table was covered with a fine linen tablecloth on which was placed my best china and crystal. A large scoreboard was erected behind the taste testers to record their vote after the taste test. The governor of the student council, dressed in a chef's apron and hat, dished out the bean soup I had made. The lieutenant governor cut the apple pie and inserted a piece in the bowl of bean soup. Other officers of student council and a few cheerleaders wearing waitress outfits were the servers. The table, decked out with flowers, fancy china, goblets, and silverware, was a sight to behold. In the background I played Tim McGraw's famous country song, "I Like It, I Love It, I Want Some More of It." Nick sat at one end of the table and I sat at the other end with the other eight taste testers seated along the middle. The remainder of the student body and teachers were in the bleachers on either side of the gymnasium as observers. The rating system for the taste test was Excellent, Good, Fair, or Poor, with each taster giving a rating. The final score was Good—almost Excellent. It was such fun.

The students became so enthused and excited about "the Great Assembly" that they couldn't stop talking about it at dinner tables at home that evening. I got so many calls from parents telling me about the enthusiasm of their children. Things like this help tie the administrators, teachers, and students together as a family—we were all family.

Renee, one of the students chosen as a taster, remembers, "That was one of my most vivid memories of my school life, and I was surprised to find the meal really delicious!

"Mr. Zook was the disciplinarian helping students overcome negative things. He was very sensitive, but when necessary he could be all business. It was amazing how he could switch back and forth as required; I really respected him for that. He was always around to answer questions or to help people. He was just a pillar. I think it was probably tough for Mr. Zook sometimes to get up and go to work every day, but I like to think we students provided the motivation he needed to do his job. He wanted to show the students by example not to give up.

"Even though I don't live close to him and we correspond only several times a year, he continues to be a positive influence in my life. His interest in what I'm doing is good for my morale."

Harold continues: After we received the National Blue Ribbon School Award, the observer told me that he could not find one individual in the community, on the staff, or among the students who had any negative thing to say about Indian Valley School. We got a very glowing report as to why we had received it. It was a highlight of my career and I praise Nick for doing it. He did it not only for me but for the teachers and students as well. That would be the last year we were together as a school family, because the next year Indian Valley moved from a six hundred to a nearly one thousand student body. Needless to say, I went out on a high note!

When I recently visited the school, I was so pleased to see the administration and teachers working very hard to keep up school spirit and the traditions Brooke and I had started. As we went through the hallways during class passing time, a little girl ran up to me saying, "Oh, you're Mr. Zook, aren't you?"

"Yes, I am, but how would you know?" I asked.

"I know," she responded, "because you had my older brother and my sister. I wish I could have had you." How that warmed my heart!

Dr. Chubb, principal at the time Indian Valley gained recognition as a National Blue Ribbon School, said he believed the school qualified as a Blue Ribbon School because "we have a very professional staff that's child-centered, because the kids are engaged in their learning and they take an active part in all areas, and that what they're learning has application in their everyday life. I think the site visitor saw a family . . . that embraces the community, the staff, and the kids."

Dr. Nicholas Chubb, principal who succeeded R. Brooke Moyer and was Harold's coadministrator for five and a half years, described Harold thus: "Even though Harold had his way of doing things in a detailed way, he was open to other ideas, and had a world of patience with a lot of staying power to see a situation through. He never gave up on a student or family situation. Harold did all he could to make the situation better. There's a sense of tradition and of family at the school and Harold was the glue that kept that together. When new administrators or teachers came in, Harold provided a smooth transition. I am firmly convinced that Harold saved hundreds of students by developing that sense of family. Even when an alternative situation had to be found for a student, he left with a positive feeling about the school.

"I was an idea person, and Harold could put those ideas into a plan and make them happen. This was true in applying for the Blue Ribbon Award. Working that through was a labor of love, since it validated what we had been doing. Harold spent hours, sometimes until three or four o'clock in the morning. I respected him for doing that, even though I couldn't do the same.

"We developed the 'Spirit of the Eagle' Award to honor Brooke Moyer and Harold. This award was chosen by faculty and was given to a graduating student from Indian Valley Middle School who best exhibits the qualities espoused by Brooke and Harold, namely, sensitivity, public service, integrity, respect, initiative, and thoughtfulness. If I were a student at the school, I would have wanted to earn this award because it represents what makes the school special. The engraved plaque received by the recipient reads:

" 'R. Brooke Moyer
J. Harold Zook
SPIRIT OF THE EAGLE AWARD
Presented to : **Renee J. Lombardo** Who Exhibits:

Sensitivity
Public Service
Integrity
Respect
Initiative
Thoughtfulness

Indian Valley Middle School
June 17, 1996' "

Renee expresses her feelings about winning the first award:
"I couldn't believe I was chosen to receive the award. I cried my eyes out onstage in front of everybody. Mr. Zook was a great role model for me during my years at Indian Valley and I'm still in awe of having received it. I enjoyed doing volunteer work during study halls or before and after school. This helped me develop self-confidence so that when I went on to senior high school I could excel."

Dr. Chubb says of Harold, "I believe God and family values of a strong work ethic gave him strength to keep going even when things were tough. Harold had to pull his share and he learned to enjoy a challenge. I appreciated Harold for the little things he did. I feel I'm a better principal, father, and Christian because of having worked with Harold. When working with other people, Harold is empathetic, caring, patient, and loving. His relationships are never short-term. He followed students for the long term with letters, phone calls, visits, and gifts. He could tell corny stories to students or pretend to be naive and get away with it. He often got through to students in that way. There have been a lot of plaques, books, et cetera, given in his honor, but I feel his greatest contribution was his heart.

"There were times when his disability made getting around very tough for him, but I feel it was his mental attitude that kept him going. He thrived—and still does—on his relationships with his students and friends. I believe the way Harold lived his life was unique. He has a bit of devilishness in him that shows in his eyes. He loved to play tricks on people, then scamper away. He'll always be a very dear friend."

Anne McCue, a fellow teacher and friend for thirty-seven years who worked on the Blue Ribbon Committee, fondly recalls, "When our school was applying for our National Blue Ribbon School, I helped with the editing of the materials. There were only a few of us who could go to Washington to receive the award and Harold asked that I go in his place. I was so honored, and I felt like I was there for him. Only sixty-four secondary schools in the United States received recognition as a National Blue Ribbon School during the 1995–96 school year, Indian Valley Middle School being one of them.

"I've known Harold as a colleague and later as a loyal friend. We have the same philosophy of teaching: if we're going to do a job, we will do it well. Harold is an advocate of children—children come first. I think of Harold as the Dad of Indian Valley, and the teachers were his children and the students were his grandchildren. Grandpas love grandchildren the best. Harold felt that by modeling he showed children what a good person is like. We were drawn together because we love children.

"During my first year of teaching, when I was so scared, Harold gave me so much encouragement. As I was a very shy person, he stood by me and gave me the courage to keep going. He gave me confidence when I needed it. I was rather insecure, which Harold sensed. He picked out my good qualities and emphasized them. When I left teaching to have my family, Harold kept it touch with me for twelve years, getting my job back when I was ready to return to teaching, which was wonderful.

"Harold is so loyal to his family, to his friends, a child advocate, and especially a champion of the underdog—a person others might give up on. He was a true professional, doing everything with great thought.

"Harold has a physical handicap and we know there were times when he was in great pain, but he never said anything about it. He did his job so well we totally forgot he was disabled. He worked very well with others who were disabled in any way. He also worked well with students having a social problem or dealing with emotional growth. He seemed to be able to appreciate each child's own problem and help them deal with it.

"Harold worked so well with students, remembering them after they left school by writing them notes and letters. There are many things at the school that were not paid for by taxpayer money but came from an elf who decided to dig deep into his pockets because he felt it was important for the school. He never talked about it, but we knew Harold gave emotionally and financially. We knew the school was his extended family. When he retired, he gave me a gorgeous decorative plate as a remembrance of him.

"Harold's relationships were always professional. We never felt alone when he was here. He helped us get out to various workshops to help us improve professionally. He liked for us to have great experiences. He was also respectful of parents, trying to help them in any way he could.

"Harold's philosophy seemed to be to concentrate on the positive side rather than on the negative side. He advocated being proud of what you do when you've done your best. His family and his faith gave him the strength and courage to keep going.

"I was so honored to have Harold come to my retirement party in spite of his most recent illness. When I saw him get out of his van with his sport coat on to surprise me, I was so touched and appreciative. I understand it was Harold's first social outing after getting his tracheotomy."

Lois Smoot, another fellow teacher and adviser to student council, who did a lot of work in preparation for the National Blue Ribbon Award, comments, "I knew Harold for quite a few years. Applying for the Blue Ribbon Award is a lengthy and involved process, detailing all aspects of the school, including the subjects taught, methods used, type of activities and committees, involvement with parents and community, and the type of administrators and their philosophy. The final application consisted of about twenty-seven single-spaced typed pages. We spent months on the application. We knew that with Harold's thoroughness we would have a perfect document. I had known for years we were Blue Ribbon material, but Harold and Brooke were too humble to go through the process until they received enough encouragement from others.

"My first experience with Harold was his work as president of the teachers' negotiating team. I was so very impressed with the volume of work he accomplished for that organization, and I've seen that detail and perfection reflected in everything he has done since then. All of his colleagues see Harold's character as being above reproach. He's totally humble and totally honest. He was brought up in the Mennonite tradition of serving one's fellowman, thinking of others before oneself. That's the philosophy by which he lived.

"Harold told me on numerous occasions how tough his dad was on him, how even though he was disabled, he had to help with the chores around the farm just like his siblings. I believe he grew up thinking, *This is the way I am, and I will overcome it.* He is incredibly positive, throwing himself into his work. There's no time to think about aches and pains. His caring for other people gave him motivation to keep going.

"Harold made me totally love this school, giving all of us teachers the feeling we were a family—a team. He never put himself on an administrative level but was always on the same level as teachers. He trusted our ideas and the work we did. Harold and his coprincipal, Brooke Moyer, made this school what it is today. Harold truly is the 'Spirit of the Eagle.' Even though I'm not teaching anymore, I believe the 'Spirit of the Eagle' continues to be strong. An award is given to a student each year who exemplifies that spirit. The student may not be the highest academic student or the best athlete but is one who shows total enthusiasm in spirit and who is concerned for others.

"Harold's relationships with others were absolutely incredible. Being an assistant principal dealing with problem students isn't the greatest, but that's where Harold shone. His discipline could be very harsh at times. I overheard him insisting that a student get on the phone and tell his or her parent the curse word used. That was tough for a student to do. For another student who had been throwing spitballs, Harold insisted on a whole hour of making and throwing spitballs by this student after school. The student then had to pick up all those spitballs so he would know how the teacher felt cleaning up spitballs.

"Harold's great humor helped bind us all together. On my fiftieth birthday, before making the morning announcements to the school over the intercom, he began telling about a lady in the school who was getting older and older, then sang, 'The Old Gray Mare, She Ain't What She Used to Be!' Every student knew I had reached the big 5-0, and they all loved it and paid tribute throughout the day to my birthday.

"Harold's life philosophy is to be the best you can be at all times, in all situations, no matter how you feel. There's no limit to what one can accomplish."

Another fellow professional, William Maza, describes actions that evolved into a National Blue Ribbon School:

"I have known Harold for about forty-two years, first as an industrial arts teacher, then as a guidance counselor. Harold came to Indian Valley as an English teacher. He was very gifted, well organized, and revamped the English Department. Harold was well noted for his grammar and spelling, that he thought were very important. He was an outstanding teacher, to be sure.

"Mr. William Warner, who was the principal, believed in Harold, saying he would not remain a teacher but would become an administrator, since Harold was a real educator. We developed an excellent school. Harold became the vice principal, but he should have been called an associate principal. Every principal who had Harold as his assistant had it quite easy, because Harold could assume responsibility and do well with it. He had a good relationship with parents, police, and the children about whom he was concerned. He was a disciplinarian but a very kind and outgoing associate principal. Harold was an educator. He had a good relationship with teachers, too. I've seen him in conference with a teacher bringing a complaint about a student. Many times he straightened out the teacher as well as the student, because he did a lot of counseling. The teachers were very loyal to him, since he was a very fair man. Many times people said Harold was the most fair man they ever met.

"Harold's character was above reproach. He was a man of God. He had a good family upbringing, sharing his family experiences with all of us, which was commendable. Harold's personality reflected all of this. He lived the way he taught. He helped many, many people. As a counselor, I sometimes did all I could with a child, but then I would send the child to him. There were some students who were in real trouble, but Harold never gave up on anyone. One time Harold mentioned that he felt bad for having neglected many students when he spent one, two, or three days with one student who was having a very hard time. I told him he was like the Good Shepherd who left his flock to seek out the one that was lost.

"I'm sure Harold was hurt by students, teachers, and parents, but he never held it against anyone. That was a real tribute to him. He didn't try to get even with anyone. When he had to discipline a person, whether it was student or teacher, he did it with love and caring. When it was over, it was over. I don't believe anyone will ever forget him, and I never knew him to hold a grudge. He never pitied himself. Children can sometimes be cruel and take advantage of someone, but I never knew anyone who did that with Mr. Zook, because they respected him. It was part of his character that he persevered. To sum it all up, Harold was a father in every sense of the word to so many children.

"Our school was a Blue Ribbon School years before we got the award, and it was because we had good leadership. We had top-notch teachers who worked well with the administration. Harold's strength came from his belief in God. He didn't brag or show off his knowledge, neither did he wear it on his wrist, but we could see that his strength came from the good Lord."

Dr. Alexander Grande, fellow administrator and a former superintendent of the Souderton Area School District, gave another description of Harold's work that helped create a National Blue Ribbon School:

"Harold has been a real source of inspiration in many, many different ways, not just to me personally but to faculty and thousands of students. Over the years I have worked with Harold as a fellow teacher, as a member of the teachers' negotiating team, and as an administrator. We worked together very closely. Harold was almost a super human being. He was so dedicated that at times he literally slept at school rather than going home. He had an arrangement in the nurse's room where he slept. Sometimes we tried to throw him out. His work was very, very detailed and extremely thorough. Even today, twenty-five years later, the procedures Harold set in place at Souderton are still followed. Some precise people may not like having associations with people, but Harold was the exact opposite. Harold loved people. I doubt that Harold would ever know the number of people he helped get on the right path, either financially, religiously, morally, or ethically. He was very giving, a superpositive role model.

"Harold had a great sense of humor along with his strong work ethic; we were constantly playing tricks on each other. He showed total love and dedication for children and family, and the true meaning of giving in every sense. He helped people work through many problems. He was always thinking of others, not of himself. Sometimes this was to the detriment of his own health. He would get very weak and tired.

"Harold would have been an effective principal, but he was extremely happy as an assistant; in fact, that was the position he preferred. His character is one of integrity, honesty, and a work ethic that is second to none. When Harold was given a job, I knew it would be done well. Even though Harold had difficulties, he gave encouragement to others. He never wanted to be treated any differently because of his handicap.

"Harold's faith gave him the strength to persevere. He's a very religious person. Harold made a sizable contribution to his church, helping to finance restoration of the chapel. I also think his desire to help others who were less fortunate than he was, as well as giving them the desire and faith that they could be what they wanted to be, kept him upbeat. He understood that life is a journey and a challenge, not an obstacle. He was able to overcome the roadblocks and hurdles that life brought. I always enjoyed being around Harold because he was so upbeat. His strong work ethic helped shape me. I've always considered him a good friend.

"When working with students, Harold's work ethic elevated him to a status that students knew he wasn't just mouthing words but was living what he said. For faculty and staff, his modeling what he believed went a long way in their development. We'll never know all the ways he contributed to the community—financially as well as giving advice and participating in various community organizations such as the Jaycees and the United Way. I'm sure there would be a waiting list of people who would like to give testimony to how he has shaped and changed their lives. Many of his students who could have been juvenile delinquents went on to be contributors to society in a variety of professions.

"Harold's philosophy of life revolves around one word—*God*. That's the core of his life, his childlike belief that God is there to help us, whatever comes. His actions and words were very powerful. It was his faith, as well as people with whom he worked, that helped to keep him going. He thrived on close working relationships with people. When hiring new staff, Harold had a good understanding of who people were. I believe that contributed to our receiving the National Blue Ribbon School Award.

"I wish Harold well and I hope this book serves as the same source of inspiration to its readers as he has been to those who knew him personally."

Jonathan Graff, former student and governor of student council, describes some of the factors that helped make a National Blue Ribbon School:

"I first met Mr. Zook as a sixth-grade student at Indian Valley. He remembers me as a shy little kid who became the governor of the school. It's true that I was very shy, and when people such as Mr. Zook sat with me and asked for my opinion, it helped me develop my abilities. I felt he believed in me. I am now in my second year of teaching.

"When my friends and I arrived at Indian Valley the first thing that struck us was that we were going to be working with someone on a daily basis who had a disability. But it wasn't long until that feeling went away and we learned to know him for who he was. When he called us in, he treated us very warmly and kindly. There was one student who could have been known as a 'nerd' or someone who had some social problems, and Mr. Zook called in another student and me, asking what we could do to help this boy feel more welcome here at Indian Valley. I'll never forget that meeting with Mr. Zook. The fact that he was willing to do that has always impressed me.

"When my friends and I saw Mr. Zook's car at the school at

229

all hours, we used to joke that Mr. Zook slept in the building. It wasn't until later that we learned he really did sleep in the building some nights. I don't think he did it because he had nothing else; it was because he loved the students and what he did here. He was so good at what he did. The school has the reputation it has because of Mr. Zook. I have not met anyone who had bad things to say about this school, and I think it's because of Mr. Zook and his desire for this school to have such a great reputation.

"Mr. Zook had a model character for people to follow. He was a leader. People admired him because of how he carried himself. He never bragged about what he did, but his dedication came naturally. His objective was not to gain credit for what he did. They say character is what you are when people aren't looking, and that's how Mr. Zook lived. He wanted to instill in his students that character is important. He wanted them to treat each other with kindness and let others be who they are. It bothered him when people were harassed because they were somehow different.

"I don't think Mr. Zook's character is stronger because of his disability. I think he would have been the same without his disability. He was just being who he is. He realized that just because he had a disability didn't mean he couldn't be who he is. I believe he kept going because of his love for the school. The teachers were the constant, stabilizing factor of the school that helped him focus on his job. He wanted this school to be a premier school and he persevered until it was a perfect school. When he set his mind to something, he got it done.

"A sixth-grade mind wonders how a disabled man can be strong. Then I saw what he accomplished in the school and I was amazed. I felt he genuinely cared about me, and that stays with me forever. That's one of the reasons I wanted to become a teacher. I saw in him someone who reached out and cared for students, liked them, and asked students for their input. He even invited six of us students to help develop the school budget. That stays with me. I know that I relate better to my students because of Mr. Zook. I try to follow in the tradition of Mr. Zook and other teachers. I want students to say that I cared about them. I love teaching so much; I don't want to be anyone except a teacher. I don't feel I could do as well as Mr. Zook has done as an assistant principal. Those shoes are too big to fill.

"After I left Indian Valley, I received the nicest note I had ever received. I was only thirteen or fourteen when I received a two-page handwritten note thanking me for what I had done for Indian Valley Middle School. My role as governor of the school was only because of what he had done for me. I felt so special that I continue to cherish it. That made such an impression on me that after my first year of teaching I wrote a note to the parents of one of my students who I felt was very outstanding, knowing it would be important to them and knowing the student would also see that letter."

11

The View from the Summit: Retirement

As his health continued to decline and it became difficult to function as assistant principal, Harold composed the following letter which set in motion a series of events leading to his retirement:

Dr. Mark G. Garis, Superintendent

Dear Dr. Garis:

Please accept this letter as an official declaration of my retirement from employment with the Souderton Area School District to become effective as of July 1, 1996. Should Dr. Chubb need me during the summer months beyond this date to assist with the present transition or in the training of a new assistant principal, I will freely give of my time at no cost to the district.

At this time, I also wish to express my sincerest thanks to the Souderton Area School Board and district administration for giving me the opportunity to serve the Souderton constituency and school system these past thirty-six years—fourteen as a teacher and twenty-two as an administrator. It has been a wonderful career which I have found to be very rewarding and memorable. Literally, hundreds of students with whom I have come into contact have left a most positive effect on my life and helped mold me into the man that I am today. During this span of thirty-six years, I have never lost sight of my mission and tried to give back to the system, parents, and students my very best efforts in both time and talents.

Therefore, as I approach this time of employment separation

and retirement, I do it with no regrets—realizing that I was given a unique opportunity to serve a district whose Board of Directors employed me at a time when disabled persons were not as readily employed in education. In appreciation, I trust I have been able to repay the Souderton Area School District with my loyalty and dedication. Together, hopefully, we have all become the benefactors.

Sincerely,
J. Harold Zook

Harold said of his thirty-six years at Indian Valley, "It has been a great career." The principal and staff believed that Harold embodied the "Spirit of the Eagle," the school mascot.

The chairman of the school board's Educational Personnel Committee, upon making the motion at the board meeting to accept Harold's resignation, said, "I really hesitate to make this motion. I know he is looking forward to his retirement, but we will surely miss him." Crediting Harold with a large part of the excellence the school has achieved, another board member stated, "Mr. Zook always put the welfare of the students first."

The board president said, "He's a good disciplinarian. He is respected by the students. He will be sorely missed."

Harold had worked hard to put an end to all the drugs, fighting, and smoking that went on in the school when he became assistant principal. He was instrumental in turning the school from a negative to a positive one. His fifteen-hour school days paid off. "His total commitment and the extra hours he put into his job and the many little things he did for the school will be missed by teachers and students," commented a teacher with thirty-one years of teaching at Indian Valley. He cited Harold's strict handling of discipline, efforts at fund-raisers, the pride and spirit he displayed, and the fact that he worked really hard at everything he did as some of his greatest accomplishments. He concluded by stating, "He has made his mark."

Another teacher with twenty-eight years at Indian Valley said, "We will never forget his ways. He is a perfectionist, works far too hard; the sixteen hours he works is too long. But, I can't imagine the school without him. He is an institution here."

Students believe he is the one true "Spirit of the Eagle." They know that "there will never be another Mr. Zook. He really gets through to kids. He will be in our memories forever."

Harold said, "It's the story of my life. People always saw things in me I didn't see in myself." Beginning his career at a time when disabled persons weren't easily hired, he said, "I know the question came up: 'This man is going to have difficulty with discipline.' " Recognizing his human quality and hoping it would rub off on kids, the principal at Indian Valley insisted that Harold be hired. He wanted Harold's honesty, integrity, the ability to listen to kids and to understand kids.

Harold's farewell message to students and staff revealed his love for Indian Valley:

Farewell to a Legacy of Love

It has been said, "If a man has any greatness in him, it comes to light, not in one flamboyant hour, but in the ledger of his daily work." For thirty-six years I have been in the business of learning and sharing that knowledge with thousands of students and adults—each a unique individual responsible for leaving his/her indelible mark on my personal and professional life.

During these many years at Valley, I have served in the presence of the very best teachers and staff members—not to mention the hundreds of students who have inspired me to rise above adversity and value the simpler things associated with honesty, integrity and humility. I have learned that the highest reward for a man's toil is not what he gets for it, but rather what he becomes by it. Mine has been a magnificent career blessed with many varied opportunities to serve; and now, the time has come for me to pay tribute to all those who have helped me to never lose my love for life nor my belief and willingness to face each day with anticipation, love and happiness.

I leave Indian Valley knowing that the "Spirit of the Eagle" is alive and well. This "King of Birds"—strong, swift and majestic—has for centuries been recognized as the undisputed ruler of the sky and made the emblem of freedom. May its attributes continue to find a prominent place in each of your hearts so that you can aspire to even greater heights of personal satisfaction and academic freedom. And to each new student and staff member privileged to become a part of this great school, I challenge you to likewise proudly acclaim the great American eagle as your mascot symbolic of power, courage, dignity and independence.

As a teacher and administrator, I came to Indian Valley eager to learn and serve; and now, I leave the joy of my labor for others to carry on.

Respectfully yours,
J. Harold Zook

The staff of Indian Valley created a testimonial album, titled A Legacy of Love *for Harold. Following are comments they inscribed in that album.*

A previous superintendent of schools composed these words:

To HAROLD, Administrator, Teacher, Co-worker, Confidant and Friend: You have earned so much more than your degree. You have earned a place in the hearts of many persons—persons whose lives have changed direction by your being the wind beneath their wings. Countless hours were so devotedly spent challenging and motivating so many students in reaching seemingly unattainable goals.

Perhaps the most valuable contribution you have given to those of us who are fortunate enough to touch your world is reflected by the life you live. The obstacles that have to be overcome just to perform a simple task have not swayed your determination or disposition.

You will never be forgotten—nor will you forget these "special" students, teachers and friends who so willingly and eagerly contributed a page in this album. This small tribute seems inadequate to convey the thanks and appreciation from those of us whose lives are so positively affected.

Don't think your career is over. You are a friend for life.

WE LOVE YOU, MR. ZOOK

The current superintendent of schools, Dr. Mark Garis, wrote:

What a privilege it has been for me to know you these past thirty years. You are truly an inspiration to everyone and have modeled for me what it means to be committed and dedicated to your work.

I admire the thorough way in which you deal with every situation, the way you review and analyze to assure that everything is accurate and well thought through. You have always displayed a positive, even disposition when many times I knew you weren't feeling well or facing discouraging obstacles. You are always reluctant to accept praise, but quick to give it to others.

We will never know all of the lives that you have impacted, but I feel safe to say that you have never made any enemies. Every one of us should try to be as dependable as you are, as encouraging as you are, and as determined to go on in the face of adversity as you have represented through your life. And now you have the opportunity to look forward to retirement full of many wonderful memories which are the fruit of a life well lived in service to others. You will continue to brighten the world around you, to encourage those who are discouraged, and to support those who are in need.

I'm sure you must be familiar with it, and perhaps it has been the guiding principle of your life, but you represent to me the embodiment of the Prayer of St. Francis of Assisi which goes like this:

"Lord make me an instrument of your peace,
Where there is hatred . . . let me sow love.
Where there is injury . . . pardon.
Where there is doubt . . . faith.
Where there is despair . . . hope.
Where there is darkness . . . light.
Where there is sadness . . . joy.
O Divine Master, grant that I may not so much seek
To be consoled . . . as to console,
To be understood . . . as to understand,
To be loved . . . as to love, for it is in giving that we receive; it is
    in pardoning . . . that we are pardoned; it is in dying . . . that
    we are born to eternal life."

Thank you for challenging us to a life of service to others, and best wishes for a long and happy retirement.

In Harold's evaluation, Dr Garis wrote: "Thanks for the top quality performance you have given this school year. Your students have benefited and their parents very much appreciate it. I am proud of you and realize that you have impacted the future because you have invested in our children. Thanks so much!"

These words came from Dr. Grande, another former superintendent of schools:

We want to congratulate you and thank you for the thousands of lives that you've touched over your career. Your sense of caring, respect for the goodness in people, finding time to help all, leaving skid marks in the hall with your buggy, and even using your whoopee cushion when Dr. Chubb was on the phone at the most inappropriate times, will be deeply missed; well, at least some of them will be. You're truly one in a million!

Harold, you have laughed, been respected, loved, been loved and most certainly have made the children educated at Indian Valley better as a result of being with you. You have truly succeeded.

237

Harold's former principal Brooke Moyer wrote: "You have accomplished more in your profession than anyone that I could ever recall. So many lives have been touched by your gifts. I will always be indebted to you for all that you have done for me. Thanks for being such a source of strength for me personally. I can think of no educator who has impacted the profession as you have. Countless students, parents, colleagues and community members will be forever in your debt because you gave so unselfishly of your time and talents."

Dr. Chubb, current principal, contributed these words:

Someone once wrote: "Fifty years from now it will not matter what kind of car you drove, what kind of house you lived in, how much you had in your bank account, or what your clothes looked like. But the world may be a little better because you were important in the life of a child."

Harold, the world is certainly a lot better because of the important role you have played in the lives of thousands of young people at Indian Valley Middle School. You have also had an impact on our staff, parents, and myself.

It is with great respect that I take this opportunity to thank you for all you have given Indian Valley for your entire career. I have been very fortunate to have learned from the "best." It is through your daily commitment to students and staff that I have learned many lessons about middle school, my daily job, and myself. It is your daily approach and attitude to life that serves as an example to everyone.

You leave us with a National Blue Ribbon School—a tribute to your work and devotion to your "home and family" for 36 years. We thank you for helping to show us the way. We thank you for your love and friendship. We have been blessed and we are grateful.

You truly are the "Spirit of the Eagle."

Glenn Wimmer Sr., managing director of Virtual Communi-
cations, with whom Harold dealt, has these kind words:

To me, you exemplify a man with a special gift. This light inspires all those around you and is evident in all that you do. You are unselfish in trying to lead others to be their own person, and to do their best and help others.

It has been about 30 years since I have been working with Harold. I first knew him when he wanted nice labels for his famous chow-chow that he made and gave to friends. Since then, he brought me into his business life working with the school yearbook, letterheads, thank-you cards, and school forms. It was quite an honor for me to work on the bronze plaque given to the school in his honor.

In describing Harold's character I would use a few key words such as harmony, in control, with presence, patience, persistence and reverence. He really excelled in getting others to perform their task, whether it was a teacher or a student. He always strove for that person to reach his or her potential. Harold's relationship with other people is remarkable. He's frank, sincere, inspiring, and enlightening. He always had the ability and thirst to say, "Why? Explain that to me." I think that the spirit in which he worked with his people is the character that has reached beyond himself.

Harold has the ability to inspire people to work well with others. When you work with someone like Harold, it inspires you to want to be someone who contributes in the spirit of likeness with Harold. When one starts contributing on the level that Harold has, it becomes a fulfilling mission, and I think it's only at that time that you can finally fully grasp the concepts Harold faces on a daily basis.

There are no parts of Harold's life that are hard or difficult. He didn't greet life that way. He dealt with life on an everyday basis. Harold has a philosophy that I only know two other people on the face of the earth to have. Harold doesn't run from life; he runs to life. I think the freedom Harold has shown is truly to be like an "eagle"; we're free, we see, we hear, we fly; there are no boundaries. What we do within our lives is within our control, not the control of others. Harold has practiced this and I have nothing but admiration for him; maybe even a reverence of his Christian sense. If this is what Christian is, then what a wonderful man Harold has become. Harold is so consistent that it draws attention. His Christian spirit is consistent with everything he does. When looking at Harold's character, he lights up and people are attracted to him. Miracles come from the light. One has to wait long enough for miracles to happen. There is no such thing as running out of time.

The school secretaries expressed their appreciation:

Diane: "I consider it such an honor to have known you. From your dedication to the kids who went through Indian Valley and making everything run so smoothly—I have the utmost respect for you. . . . Working against a deadline, or tackling a project, we had such a great rapport. I feel almost like you're part of my family! . . . We laughed a lot."

Gail commented:

Being your secretary for only one year has been one of the most enjoyable years of my secretarial career. It has been a wonderful experience for me. I knew before working with you what a caring person you were and how you care about your students and how dedicated you are to your job because of my being a parent of two boys who went through Indian Valley. I know the deep impression you made on them and I believe that helped them, in part, become the fine young men they've grown up to become. . . . Thanks for all of your help, knowledge, and making me feel important as a secretary.

A former shop teacher, now guidance counselor, Bill had much to say about Harold:

A popular song, "Tie a Yellow Ribbon Around the Old Oak Tree," was a hit tune made famous by Tony Orlando in 1967. In contrast, you can have for your theme song "Tie a Blue Ribbon Around Indian Valley Junior High School (Indian Valley Middle School)."

The latest achievement at Valley can be attributed to your strong leadership, enthusiasm and ability to organize and orchestrate an excellent, caring faculty and you should blow your horn in this recognition, but you declined my suggestion and said, "I don't like to take credit, as I only do my very best." Further, the rapport that you have with the faculty, students, parents, and community can easily qualify you as being called "Mr. Indian Valley Junior High School."

Harold, I remember very well when you came to Souderton as a young, knowledgeable and well-prepared English teacher. Mr. Warner, our principal, believed in you as an outstanding teacher and encouraged you to be a good administrator.

Your caring and compassionate qualities along with your expertise of the subject matter earned the respect of your pupils and their parents.

As vice principal you and Mr. Moyer formed a good team and complemented each other. You involved principals, teachers, nurses, custodians, cafeteria workers, police, bus drivers, students and parents in the day-by-day responsibilities of making Indian Valley a prize-winning school.

Your primary focus was the students. You always were available, and gave much time and effort to them. Your greatest trait that I recall is your fairness in dealing with a student. You listened, gave ample time for discussion, dealt with the pros and cons, weighed the evidence, and always displayed fairness; however, you were no pussycat in your dealings. Stern—yet fair is your forté.

You were very effective as you counseled the more serious guidance needs. You involved the guidance counselors, nurses, teachers, police and parents in making a decision. I remember when you spent one whole day with a student who had a serious problem, and when the smoke cleared you said, "I am sorry that I neglected the other students that day." As I recall this, the Bible story of the Good Shepherd comes to my mind—leaving the 99 sheep to find the one lost sheep. There had been other cases when you left the flock, and saved many lambs lost in the bushes. What a joy you must feel!

I have spoken with many parents in the school area, and you

241

are held in the highest esteem. They are thankful that at one time Mr. Zook had been a surrogate parent to their children.

Speaking of parenting, I feel that although you have never fathered (physically or biologically) a child, you have been a real father in every sense to many boys and girls. You have, by example, measured up to what a father should be as you related to them. For some children, there is a need for this kind of love. I wish that you consider this a compliment because I was blessed with a loving and understanding father, and now I try to emulate this role for my two sons and four grandsons.

After all of this, Harold Zook, I am happy and thankful that you are my friend who Marilyn and I admire and love very much. You are truly an excellent mentor and a great, loving person.

God is surely smiling and happy that His servant, Harold, is truly an example of a happy, caring and compassionate person who loves Him and his fellowman.

I'm sure you have heard the cliché— Relax, relax, and smell the roses—now that you will be retired. Yes, the many "rosebushes" you planted have produced many, many fragrant, beautiful, splendid, and colorful roses for you and all of us to enjoy.

Nurse Freed had this to say: "Please know you have shared a very special place in my heart and memory. I will never forget how caring and thoughtful you have been both to the students, especially the students, and your fellow workers. I will sorely miss you. I know they will never find another person like you."

Kevin, the librarian, commented:

I can think of no other educator who has impacted his profession as you have. Countless students, parents, colleagues, and community members will be forever in your debt because you gave so unselfishly of your time and talents. . . . Thank you for being such a source of strength for me personally.

I have never worked in a place where I could confidently say that one person was the soul or sinew of that place, but you are truly the soul of Indian Valley. Thank you for hiring me and inspiring me, for your support of the library, and for touching the lives of thousands of students in a positive way.

There were many testimonials from teachers:
Gina: "Harold, your love of children has been what has made you the great educator you truly are. You not only wanted students to learn their ABCs, but especially the ABCs of life."
Ruth, the art teacher:

I felt you were my advocate as art teacher and department head even before I came to Indian Valley. There were many days when thoughts of your energy and persistence helped me stick to my battles. At Valley you were behind me from day one. I hope you know I was behind you, too. You supported everything I did, even though there were some activities and some requests that may have made you shake your head, such as the life-size plaster sculptures in the lobby during my first spring arts festival or your fight to the finish purchasing the drying rack, the kiln, and tables for the art room. Everything you did helped me and, in turn, made a much better Fine Arts Program for the kids. You knew, and some days I felt you were the only one who knew, that I was only in it for the kids, too.

Jill: "You have shown great courage and leadership to all who have had the privilege to know and work with you. In my career I have not found another administrator who has had more compassion for both his faculty as well as his students consistently over time. I can only hope that through your influence on me, my students can feel the benefits of a caring and supportive educator after they leave the classroom."
Kristin: "Thank you for your dedication to watching me grow into a Godly Christian woman. I only pray I will approach my teaching and my life and marriage with the same dedication."
Doug and Julie:

Testimonials, notes, tributes, letters, and remembrances—all well deserved—will attest to an enviable assortment of character traits which define Harold Zook. Themes of loyalty, dependability, compassion, understanding, gentleness, courage, diligence (and more) could rightly fill several pages. We will focus on a quality that you have shown us to a degree that few others have—INTEGRITY. Integrity is defined as, "soundness of moral principle and character, uprightness-honesty."

A man of integrity knows what is going on around him, but is not greatly influenced by it. The measuring stick for such a man is not public opinion or circumstances, but the truth.

A man of integrity sleeps well at night, not because he is without burdens, but because he is at peace.

A man of integrity has a walk that matches his talk.

A man of integrity is comfortable enough with himself that he is willing to go the extra mile (or two) with others.

A man of integrity will say what he means today and it will mean the same tomorrow.

A man of integrity makes mistakes, but not excuses.

A man of integrity gives counsel that can be trusted.

A man of integrity realizes that it is more important to be respected than popular.

A man of integrity models what he expects from others; he doesn't need to preach it.

A man of integrity will often see his own glass as half-empty, but others' are always half-full.

A man of integrity exhibits a nature that is beyond reproach, that will endure well beyond his years.

Mr. Zook, you are a man of integrity. During our years at Indian Valley, we have seen it from 7:30 till 3:30 each day, which is about sixty percent of *your* normal workday! Then again, a man of integrity would rather finish a job instead of watch a clock! ~ Thank you for your example to us and others.

Dave: "You always made me feel great after you observed me. I appreciated your comments very much."

Stephen, a former student and current teacher, said:

I need to go back to September of 1959 [when] . . . I was a very naïve 7th-grader in your homeroom. . . . At that time I would have never imagined working with you as a teacher for 27 years. . . . As a first-year teacher . . . I began to understand the personal qualities that made you such an outstanding educator.

You have been an inspiration to me and a role model for me as a person who has worked hard to become an effective teacher. Your leadership here at Indian Valley has helped to direct this school toward greatness. I have been so impressed by your leadership because you always are willing to do what you ask others to do.

Your heartfelt concern about the lives of kids is something that no one can replace. I can remember many students over the years whose lives are better because of what you did for them. You never gave in to the short-term solution to a problem. I can still hear conversations you had with me about troubled students and trying to get to the "real" solution. This took you way beyond your expected job description.

The quality that I absorbed so much from watching your career is your relentless *thoroughness.* I learned from you how to do a task well. No matter what job was at hand, you attacked it with the idea of doing it *right* and doing it *completely.* This is a personal strength and quality that I see slowly disappearing from our world. I have never seen anyone maintain your level of commitment and dedication for such a long period of time. Harold, you are a credit to this school, community, and world—your life as an educator has made a real difference in people's lives. I include myself as one who has benefited from your life.

Kim:

When I think of you at Indian Valley, some words and phrases come to mind: spirit, caring, leadership, dedication, hard working, loving, inspiring, example to others, never giving up on anything or anyone, details, enthusiastic.

I have only known you a few years but you have influenced my teaching and life greatly. Thank you, Mr. Zook, for giving so much to every person who entered through the doors of Indian Valley! You will be greatly missed!

John: "Working with you has helped me develop my own style in meeting the many character needs our kids bring to school. Your example of firmness tempered with kindness has been a daily inspiration. Your ability to see through a smoke screen of excuses has shown me the value of being an active listener. Finally, your patience with young people over a long period of time made me realize there is always hope."

Ruth: "You always had the time for positive feedback both in writing and in conversation. . . . Long hours of discussions before and after school come to mind as our real 'bonding times.' I was always so psyched to have you come into my classroom—you got as excited as the kids did when we were running through lectures, demonstrations, studio work. Your spirit got into them and me and will continue on in my heart as long as I am an educator."

Brenda: "You have given me the strength I need to become who I want to be in life. Your words of encouragement will never be forgotten. You have been a great counselor when I had 'teen' troubles with my own children and they didn't even attend Valley, but I know they also look up to you."

John: "You have given me a lifetime of memories from the words, cards, and letters you took time to write to me and my family—especially to my daughters which helped direct my girls in a positive way through their teenage years. If everyone would only take half the time and heartfelt friendship and kindness you have given, the world would be a better place."

Dick:

What a wonderful twenty-eight years of association and friendship with you. Over the years our time together has grown to a brother relationship. When I think of you as my "older brother," I have seen a man after whom I have modeled my life—a man I am proud to have as a mentor, an encourager, a helper, a man of excellence! Nothing you did was ever second rate. You are the reason this school is filled with great teachers because we saw in you a leader who demanded excellence for himself and we had to strive to be like you! The greatest form of flattery is to be imitated!

There are only two things that live for eternity—God's Word and people. You poured your life into the lives of all—the great and the small. I never saw you deal unfairly or in favoritism to a student or teacher because of who they were. Your honesty and fairness were a second set of my brother's qualities. When Indian Valley goes places, your excellence goes with them. For over twenty years we have been able to have our students produce great science work because you supported us. You were there for the 6:00 P.M. phone calls, the money for the buses and equipment and the interest that spurred me on. When I was down, I always had a listening ear in your office. When I needed a good laugh you always had the right "Dutchman" humor that got me back on track.

Most of all, your life was our kids! The most important thing a teacher can do is to pour his life into another. You have done that ever since I have known you. I will remember you as my brother, a man of excellence, a man of honesty and integrity, a mentor and encourager.

Drew:

You have been a steadying force for me. When I didn't know exactly how to handle a situation, you were always there with great advice and many strategies to solve the problem.

I appreciate how you supported me throughout my teaching career. I appreciate your honesty, integrity and lack of personal hidden agenda which too many people bring to their job.

As Bette Midler sings, "You are the wind beneath my wings" —all of our wings—enabling the great Eagle to soar.

Gretchen:

I feel I can say that you are a teacher of all—children and adults alike. I've witnessed your patience with both, your unique strategies and techniques to show each of us how to better ourselves. Your target is a person's heart and soul. Your aim is often a perfect bull's-eye!

I will miss your smile, your laugh, our chats, our brainstorming, the sound of your "Zook mobile," your announcements, and most of all . . . your stories. Indian Valley has been blessed. We benefited from your child-centered attitude, your professional dedication, and your unequaled perseverance.

Susan: "When I think of you, I think of the word DEDICATION. Your name and that quality are synonymous. Personally, I would like to thank you for your patience, your encouragement, and your enthusiasm for the art of teaching. I absolutely loved having you visit my class and getting together with you to discuss how things went. You were almost like a professional father to me. I respect you greatly. Your opinion has always mattered a great deal to me. You have touched my life in a profound and unforgettable way."

Katie:

Mr. Zook, I sat in your office and you spoke to me about the proper behavior of a young lady. You provided guidance, direction, and an openness that showed you truly cared about me and my junior high experience. For that, I am eternally grateful.

I sat in your office and you spoke to me about your teaching experiences, relating them to mine. You provided guidance, direction and an openness that showed you truly cared about me, what goes on in my classroom, and my state of mind. For that, I am eternally grateful. Thank you for helping to keep me on course for the past 16 years. You truly are one in a million. With much respect, admiration and love, Katie.

Nan:

I have not forgotten the many hours you found to chat with me, and I will hear your voice and see your face always. Many an afternoon—as the hour grew late—you offered me ideas about how to put events into reasonable perspectives. You reassured me of my worth when disappointments crept into my life. You always seemed interested in my ideas and enabled me to carry them forth because I knew that if you valued them, they must be effective. I know I wasn't the only life you enhanced. I have watched parades of people enter your world and leave in better shape, but I want to offer a personal "Thank you." I am grateful that I have been one of the lucky ones to have known you.

Mervin, Harold's brother: "It was you who got me into teaching in the first place. You purchased a plane ticket for me to fly into Philly from Cleveland for my interview. Without your encouragement and help I doubt that I would have gotten the job. I marvel at your determination to keep going even when you could hardly walk and needed to switch to the wheelchair. I felt good about your calling me into the office to tie your shoes or give you a pull to help you up when you needed help."

Lyndell:

I can't believe I've only known you for 9 years. I've learned so much from you in that time. I think observing you guide and care for children has been the most inspiring thing for me. Whenever I become frustrated with my students, I think about your words of kindness and encouragement to them, and it helps me keep things in perspective.

The staff and students at Indian Valley have grown to be better people through your caring and leadership. You have also shown that a person with a handicap is just as good and even better at his/her job than one without physical handicaps. Our students will take that knowledge and make the world a better place.

Diane: "Although I have only had the privilege of working with you a year, I have seen the level of dedication you bring to this profession. It makes me very proud to see someone leave still fired with enthusiasm and a genuine caring for each student as an individual. I know how fortunate every student whose life you touched has been, but I feel the faculty has been even more enriched by our time spent under your leadership. You are truly a role model we should all aspire to emulate."

Thea:

I remember many days of agonizing about how to deal with many troubled students through these years, often to end by seeking your advice. I guess many of us sought your advice on many issues throughout the years!

You have a special talent for looking at each human being as an individual and then dealing with that person as such. Not many people take the time nor care that much. It's been valuable to me to observe you in dealing with these individuals.

Jane:

As I have traveled through life, I could probably count on one hand the rare individuals who truly live by the high code of morals set forth by the Lord. You are such a person. You live your faith. What I enjoy most about working with you is your love and respect for the worth of all individuals. Although at times we may disagree as to the technique to be used with a student, our long-range goals are always on line. With you I can speak my mind openly on any subject. When advice is needed, your patience is endless. Together we have thrilled to the success stories and grieved for the failures.

I have no doubt that you leave us only to pursue yet another avenue with which to help others. May your legacy here continue to set the tone in the "Spirit of the Eagle."

Andy: "Thank you for letting me see that I should be working on enjoying the little triumphs in teaching and worrying less about what my students haven't learned. Although I have only been at Indian Valley for two years, you have spent hours talking with me about the students and their special needs. You have a very special gift that few people have. You touch the hearts of those around you in many ways because you take the time to care. Your perceptive attention to others can never be matched. Add to that the fact that you never give up on people and we have the definition of an unbeatable man."

Debi:

I have only had the privilege of working with you for one short year. I was able to experience firsthand how dedicated you are to the Indian Valley students and staff. I remember when last summer you told me how very lucky I was to be coming to a top-notch school with a top-notch faculty in the beginning of my teaching career. You also said that the Indian Valley Staff is like a big family. You were absolutely correct on both accounts.

I thank you for your wise words, for recognizing and valuing the good in each person, for the respect you instill and show to children, for making a difference by challenging us to make a difference, and giving yourself selflessly to your chosen career of educator.

Thank you especially for your support with my students, and being a fantastic role model, who shows us not to let the little things get in the way of our dreams.

Nancy:

Finally gaining a sense of myself as a teacher, I feel that I can truly begin to follow in your footsteps. Always setting a good example, modeling fairness, showing a genuine interest in each and every student, guiding our young people to become good, responsible, respected citizens—these are standards that you have set, that you have taught to me. Trust that they will be carried on to the best of my ability. I will do my part in keeping the "Spirit of the Eagle" alive and soaring. I will miss the sound of your cart, not to mention your reckless driving! You don't know how that sound perks up the ears of students and teachers alike! It makes people sit up straight, pay attention, and generally "fly right."

Charlotte:

You were always so kind, caring, and sensitive to the needs of our students. You also spent hours with us teachers helping us to find ways to work with our "troubled" students. You were/are always fair and honest.

I remember the kindness you extended to me especially these last few years. Without your help, I couldn't have survived.

Carole and Nadeen contributed this poem:

How to Conduct the Eagle Spirit

As a prelude, teach young eagles,
    listening to the music of their tender souls:
    how they soar on the high notes,
    how they tremble on the low.
Practice your scales,
    the do-re-mi of grammar and usage,
    the la-ti-do of literature.
As you mature,
Accept the baton to lead the whole orchestra—
    the melody of children growing,
    the harmony of helpful teachers.
Blend the ballads of troubled teens
    with the drumbeat of budget and bid list.
Syncopate the march of cool-kickers and weeples
    with the rock and roll of cafeteria.
Harmonize the notes of discord,
    with your patience and advice.

Cue the cymbals of school spirit
    to the swelling notes of praise from parents.
Lift your baton to conduct
    sing-alongs
    walk-a-thons
Amplify the bass-line—dedication, self-sacrifice—
    your steady beat,
    your faithful resonance.
Then, after thirty-six years,
When your orchestra wins a blue ribbon,
Acknowledge them with a sweep of your arm,
And turn again to face the crescendo of applause.
Take a well-deserved bow.

Terre:

Back in the eighties when I was a substitute teacher, yours was one voice I didn't mind hearing at 6:00 A.M. It meant I'd be spending a day at Valley, where I would be welcomed and treated as a professional. I came to respect you so much then because you were one of the few administrators who really supported substitute teachers. That respect and support extended to the entire faculty. How I envied the staff members here!

When I began teaching here, Valley was all I remembered and more. I was so delighted that you were still here. Little did I know how great a help you would be to me. Your kind words of encouragement and your obvious willingness to help me eased this new teacher into place. Your own first year experiences must have greatly influenced you, because your empathy was more helpful to me than you'll ever realize.

You've served as a tremendous role model to us all. Your tireless devotion to the children here reminds us how important each child is and what a great influence we are on them.

We wouldn't be who we are without you and we won't be the same when you're not here, but your great influence will be a part of all we do.

Nancy: "I can't tell you how meaningful it was for me that you took special care in welcoming me as a new and first year teacher. Your special attention, encouragement and kindness will never be forgotten."

Helyn:

From the first day I came to Indian Valley, for my job interview seven years ago, to the present, you have been a constant in my professional life. Your relentless dedication, integrity and moral strength have in large part shaped our wonderful school. Although it is difficult to imagine Indian Valley without Harold Zook, the foundation, legacy and traditions that you leave in your wake will make it that much easier for us and your successor.

Thank you for many things. Thank you for your support with the difficult students. I always knew you would respond to any problem with respect and sincerity. You set high standards for both yourself and the students. You dared to be "old-fashioned" about values and responsibilities, and it worked! Thank you for your facility with the little day-to-day details that can matter so much. Thank you for the wonderful way you showed us all that a person with a disability is not disabled. Thanks for your even temperament, sense of humor, dedication, and more. But especially, thank you for helping to make Valley a place where I could enjoy coming to work.

Barb: "The 'Spirit of the Eagle' soars with you."

Karen:

Harold, I will be forever grateful to you for "opening the door" and your heart to me. Perhaps the following thoughts can best express my ongoing philosophy of truly educating our youth:

The Teacher's Prayer

I want to teach my students how to live this life on earth
To face its struggles and its strife and improve their worth
Not just the lesson in a book or how the rivers flow,
But how to choose the proper path, wherever they may go.
To understand eternal truth and know the right from wrong
And gather all the beauty of a flower and a song
For if I help the world to grow in wisdom and in grace,
Then I shall feel that I have won and I have filled my place.
And so I ask your guidance, O God, that I do my part,
For character and confidence and happiness of heart.

—James J. Metcalf

255

There were many newspaper articles announcing Harold's retirement. The following are only a few of those:

From the February 19, 1997, *Souderton Independent* in the Opinion Column by a Principal:

Mr. Harold Zook is a former Souderton Area School District administrator and teacher. He recently retired as an employee but left a positive impression on everyone with whom he came in contact. Mr. Zook would not tolerate rudeness or cruelty from his students. He always treated students, teachers, or fellow administrators with respect.

    We all knew Mr. Zook cared deeply about his students at Indian Valley. He showed us not by what he said, but by what he did. He spent countless hours after school helping students, teachers, and parents. Mr. Zook listened—really listened—when students had something on their minds. Students knew that Mr. Zook valued them. Yet, he didn't let students get away with misbehavior. They respected him.

The school newspaper, the Eagle Reporter, *reported: "Harold says of his 36 years, 'It's been a great career!' With Indian Valley earning a National Blue Ribbon School of Excellence status this year, it is a perfect send-off for an impressive career. Principal Dr. Nick Chubb and the remainder of Indian Valley staff believe that Harold embodies what is termed the 'Spirit of the Eagle,' the school mascot."*

The Student Assembly at Indian Valley Middle School honored Harold's years of service with various testimonials. The moderator of the assembly, Richard Hawkins, spoke the following:

There is a story about a father who, after a hard day's work, was too tired to play games with his son. He found in his magazine a picture of the world that he cut into pieces. [See chapter 5: "Philosophy By Which to Live" for the story, page 110.] This story of the father and the boy always reminds me of Mr. Zook and all the times and years he took with students. They were the boy in this story that he tried to straighten out. He tried to straighten them out for their own good, for the school's good, and the fact that the world would turn out okay.

Students! Now this is where Mr. Zook's talent really shines through. With his natural leadership ability he helped thousands of students learn and mature during his time here at Indian Valley. He taught everyone vital life skills of determination, generosity, courage, honesty, and sensitivity. He did this through fundraisers, walk-a-thons, gifts for the needy and everyday influence in our very lives. There is one major thing that we need in order to achieve and that is encouragement. Mr. Zook provided so much motivation that every goal that was established was reached. For 22 years Mr. Zook has used the energy of the "Spirit of the Eagle" to strive for the very best at Indian Valley. We will miss him.

The former governor of the student council Jonathan Graff testified of Harold:

I was governor last year. During my three years here, I met a lot of caring people, people who went out of the way to help you out. There was one man, Mr. Zook, who would always be in the cafeteria, calling people over, buying your lunch with his own money. Mr. Zook helped everyone in one way or another. He was here all summer and worked late at night; many people don't realize it. The school would not be the National Blue Ribbon School it is today without Mr. Zook.

Some of you may not realize how lucky you are to attend Indian Valley. This school is very special to many people. The teachers and staff are some of the most dedicated I have ever known. The programs and activities are some of the best we've ever had in the district. This school keeps getting better and better and we should thank Mr. Zook for that. (*applause*)

Every one of you has the right to take a lot of pride in this school, and I think you all should. The gentleman who is the most proud of the school and all its students is retiring after 36 years of the most dedicated service any individual can offer in a lifetime. Former President George Bush said that any definition of a successful life includes service to others. If that is true, then we should all believe that Mr. Zook is the most successful man we have ever met. I can remember when I was here, Mr. Zook was more enthusiastic about school functions than the kids. One of the first projects our student body worked on was a candy sale. I can remember Mr. Zook called all the officers and myself into his office, giving us a pep talk about how activities like these establish school spirit and school pride. He asked us to put on an assembly to promote a candy sale.

Mr. Zook was a real inspiration in setting the tone for that school year. And the Indian Valley graduating class of 1992 thanks him for his dedication and his enthusiasm. It is clear that Indian Valley means a lot to Mr. Zook, but what is more clear is that Mr. Zook means a lot to Indian Valley. Thirty-six years is a long time and we are very lucky that Mr. Zook spent those 36 years at Indian Valley and nowhere else. Indian Valley's success story is a credit to Mr. Zook. Mr. Zook, on behalf of the Souderton graduating class of 1996, I thank you for your years of time, your inspiring energy and tremendous dedication to the causes that were important to you and every student at Indian Valley Middle School.

A former student, currently a teacher in another district, remembered:

It's been almost eleven years since I met Mr. Zook, but I'll never forget the comfortable, safe and secure feelings I had. Junior high is a real tough time in a lot of people's lives and I think it seems to be a turning point. It's almost like society seems to decide which direction you're going to take in your life, where you'll begin your journey. I was feeling as if I had no direction and Mr. Zook helped me define my own spirit and gave me the encouragement to renew my dedication to myself and others. I felt I had an advocate, yet never a superficial one. He always made me feel special and appreciated. He's an inspiration to me. He could have been a bitter person. Any one of us could be bitter or angry about what life has dealt to us. It's all in the choice—what you do with what you have.

Mr. Zook, you've inspired others. Look around and see the positive and integral impact you have on life and others. I could not ask for a better role model, teacher, father figure, mentor, or friend. You wrote to me on my graduation from high school that your wish for me is to always have the strength and courage to seek my dream each day I live, so people will be able to see the special beauty that life is capable of giving. I think I certainly chose the right career in being a teacher, but my greatest wish for myself is to give that legacy to others. If I can reach but a portion of the people you have, my dream in life will be complete. I will miss you. But your faith in me and your spirit will live through me as long as I live.

A former student remarked:

"I would not be who I am without his incredible motivation and devotion. I remember one time when I was in eighth grade and during lunch we talked to Mr. Zook about getting cheerleader uniforms. By the end of lunch, we were promised the cheerleader uniforms. It shows how he tried to help with whatever we needed."

Another former student, Ferne Hillegas, currently a teacher in another district, described Mr. Zook thus at his retirement assembly:

I was asked to complete a page in Mr. Zook's memory book. It is very difficult to put memories on a page that would capture the essence of a man, essence of my teacher, and the essence of my mentor. I decided to use music from "To Sir With Love"—which is a movie that portrays a teacher that I've never once been able to view without thinking of my teacher, Mr. Zook. When an artist surrounded the poem "Others" with meaningful items Mr. Zook loved, Mr. Zook chose to add a video representing "To Sir with Love." When I learned this, that was the first time I knew I had been able to capture a portion of the man who was my teacher and my mentor.

In describing some of his qualities, we must use the words "accurate beyond belief" because he believed in people; he had the courage to care and give commitment to compassion. He was dedicated to detail, yet dared to dream. I know this because he was my seventh grade English teacher and his encouragement has been endless. He gives a whole new meaning to the word "form" especially when he uses his Handbook of Style. And yet he allows perfect freedom of expression. I think the thing I will miss the most is when I dial the number at Indian Valley, especially in the evening, and hear the phone get picked up with his voice saying, "Good evening. This is Mr. Zook. May I help you?" He gives hope and encouragement and did so as my homeroom teacher in seventh, eighth, and ninth grades. I was part of the first group of students when Indian Valley decided to keep the same homeroom teacher for three years.

He had an impact and an influence because he inspired independence and with joy he has shared his knowledge of vocabulary, his knowledge of the English language, his knowledge of grammar, and given to all of us the knowledge to turn us on to books with USSR (Uninterrupted Sustained Silent Reading). He is a leader with his motivation and I know this because he is one of my mentors. He has had many opportunities to observe, he has held the position of power in the Souderton Area School District (SASD) as teacher, vice principal, and educator. He has been able to teach the privileges of education because he understands it is a privilege to be an educator and yet he does so quietly. I am speaking today using a rough draft because no matter what time I had to prepare—if it was one more hour, one more day, or a month from now, it would be very difficult to compose a final draft of memories of what this gentleman has been to me. He has taught me the art of editing by teaching me that with revision you must be responsible, but I don't know if Mr. Zook realizes how much math he also taught me over the years with his sensitivity for statistics and his "Spirit of the Eagle." He has presented trust and truth and given truth to trust. He understands that with vision you can see victory in violation and at the outset, if you don't know what to do, just wing it. When he wants to have a serious discussion with you, he doesn't need an x-ray machine to examine your heart; and if he asks you to yield in the hall, I suggest you do it, but with zest. As I stand before you as a former student of SASD, class of 1971, I am also standing before you as a former teacher at an elementary school with eleven and a half years at SASD in which I relied on the alphabet as the bridge for the vocabulary and lessons in which I taught. And if you were listening very carefully, you may have thought I had skipped the letter "n" in describing the qualities that have influenced my life from Mr. Zook's teaching; but I didn't skip the letter "n" because Mr. Zook has never said "no" without reason or explanation. There has been no limit to what he has taught me.

In 1971, he gave me a book called "The Art of Living." Many times he had the opportunity as a teacher to recognize my achievements. Now, today, I can share the art of his achievements. You hold in your hand the camel's hair brush of the painter of life. You stand before the vast white canvas of time. The paints are your thoughts, emotions, and acts; you select the colors of your thoughts, drab or bright, weak or strong, good or bad, you select the colors of your emotions. The coordinates are harmonious, harsh or quiet, weak or strong. You select the colors of your acts, cold or warm, fearful or daring, small or big, and through the power of your creative imagination, you have the vision and you dream your dreams. You select and make the positive colors of heart, mind and spirit into the qualities of effective living—patience, determination, endurance, self-discipline, work, love and faith. And each moment of your life is a brush stroke in the painting of your growing career and there are the bold sweeping strokes of one increasing dynamic purpose and there are the lights and shadows that make your life even stronger and there are the little touches that add the stamp of character and worth. The art of achievement is the art of making life—your life—a masterpiece.

In the beginning of the book, at the very end of your writing, you said, "Always remember that the truest gift you can give to another is a portion of thyself, and the finest gift you can give to your

261

world and to your time is the gift of a constructive and creative life." I am here today to thank you, Mr. Zook, for sharing your constructive and creative life with me.

Harold sent a retirement Christmas card to staff members prior to his retirement with a Christmas rose, a favorite flower of his, on the face. In the card he said, "As I anticipate retirement from a career that has given me thirty-six years of deep personal satisfaction, please know that you have shared a very special partnership in both my life and work as an educator. Thanks for the memories; they are many and sweet. Happy Holidays!"

At his retirement banquet on May 10, 1996, Harold's message was:

Dear Friends and Colleagues,

Tonight's retirement celebration marks a very special time in my life, a time I approach with confidence and an occasion which brings about many positive reflections and lasting memories.

Early in my teaching career, I came across a poetic prayer entitled "Others" which I eventually accepted as a personal motto. During my thirty-six year career as a teacher and administrator, I pondered on its meaning often and found it to be my guiding light. Then, several years ago, I shared it with my good friend, Allen Hermansader, who as a professional artist was inspired to do the painting which you see reproduced on the other side. In it he included many of my favorite things—roses, forget-me-nots, video, books, etc.

Today, I share it with you in hopes that it too will inspire you as it has me these many years. May it serve as a reminder to each of us, regardless of our careers, that we primarily share a place on this earth to be of service to others. J. Harold Zook

On the following page find the poem, "Others," referred to in Harold's message:

Harold's friend Allen Hermansader, painted the beautiful

Others

Lord, help me live from day to day
  In such a self-forgetful way,
That even when I kneel to pray,
    My prayer shall be for "Others."

Help me in all the work I do
  To ever be sincere and true,
And know, that all I do for You
    Must needs be done for "Others."

And when my work on earth is
      done,
    And my new work in Heaven's
      begun,
May I forget the crown I've won,
    While thinking still of "Others."

"Others." Lord, yes, "Others!"
  Let this my motto be.
Help me to live for others
  That I may live for Thee.

rendition of Harold's motto which included his portrait, as well as his favorite flowers—roses and forget-me-nots, his favorite video—To Sir with Love, *and his favorite books*—On Becoming a Person *and a novel he taught*—The Yearling. *It was then presented to Harold as a gift.*

"The Bridge Builder" (page 264)appeared on the back of the banquet program:

The Bridge Builder

An old man going a lone highway
Came at the evening cold and gray
To a chasm vast and deep and wide
Through which was flowing a sullen tide.
The old man crossed in the twilight dim:
The sullen stream had no fears for him;
But he turned when safe on the other side
And built a bridge to span the tide.

"Old man," said a pilgrim near,
"You are wasting your strength building here;
Your journey will end at the ending day,
You never again will pass this way;
You've crossed the chasm deep and wide,
Why build this bridge at evening tide?"

The builder lifted his old gray head—
"Good friend, in the path I have come," he said,
"There followeth after me today
A youth whose feet must pass this way.
This chasm that has been as naught to me
To that fair-headed youth may a pitfall be,
He, too, must cross in the twilight dim.
Good friend, I am building this bridge for him."
(Will Allen Dromgoole)

A teacher composed the following song, music and lyrics, in remembrance of Harold, which was sung at his retirement banquet:

Teaching: A Legacy of Love

On the occasion of the retirement of J. Harold Zook
Indian Valley Country Club, May 10, 1996
Music/Lyrics by Hilary James
Sung by Becky Damiani Alderfer

What does it mean to teach?
I wonder why anyone would bother,
On a chance—just a chance—that you might be the one to make
    a difference in the life of another.

What does it mean to teach?
To give everything there is inside you,
On a chance—it's just a chance—that you might be the one to
    give the very gift that someone needs to grow.

First day faces can hide children well,
Waiting and watching, they learn what they can tell;
And sometimes you're not really sure how to start,
To open a mind and a heart.

But you take it moment by moment, and day by day,
Patiently showing once again,
Just how we ought to treat a friend,
Moment by moment, and day by day,
Teaching them who you are,
Hoping to reach a star,
And creating a legacy of love.

Tucked between the pages of the stories that they read,
You find the time and place to teach the lessons that they need;
And someone will remember when you listened with your eyes,
And truly tried to understand the child behind the lies.

Trusting faces won't let children hide;
Their eyes reveal what they feel deep inside,
And even if you really didn't know how to start,
You opened a mind and a heart.

You took it moment by moment, and day by day,
Touching them with your laughter,
Moving them with your tears,
Moment by moment, and day by day,
Teaching them who you are,
Hoping to reach a star,
And creating a legacy of love.

For what it means to teach, to touch a life forever,
Is to know that your life's touched forever, too.

Thank you, Harold, for touching all of our lives.

Harold talks about retirement: **After the retirement ceremonies were over and I had given my thanks and farewell, three men brought out this four-by-six-foot bronze plaque (See page 267.) that I gave as a gift to show my thanks and appreciation for all Indian Valley had done for me. It was a surprise. I hadn't told anyone about it. The plaque was on a rolling cart covered with a sheet. When they removed the sheet, I read the inscription.**

I was afraid I would be a bit too emotional to read the plaque, so my secretary was prepared to read it if necessary. All the toasting and the tributes given were such a source of strength that I was amazed to have no problem reading it. It was a gift that brought a sense of awe to the audience because it summarized my

 THE "SPIRIT OF THE EAGLE"
AT INDIAN VALLEY HAS BEEN ALIVE AND
WELL EVER SINCE THE SCHOOL'S BEGINNING.
AS STUDENTS AND STAFF, WE COME HERE
EAGER TO LEARN AND SERVE; AND THEN, ONE
BY ONE, WE LEAVE THE JOY OF OUR LABOR
FOR OTHERS TO CARRY ON. THEREFORE, TO
EACH NEW STUDENT AND STAFF MEMBER PRIVILEGED TO BECOME A
PART OF THIS GREAT SCHOOL, I CHALLENGE YOU TO PROUDLY ACCLAIM
THE GREAT AMERICAN EAGLE AS **YOUR** MASCOT SYMBOLIC OF POWER,
COURAGE, DIGNITY AND INDEPENDENCE.

THIS "KING OF BIRDS" — STRONG, SWIFT, MAJESTIC, MAKING HIS
PLAYGROUND IN THE CLOUDS AND DEFYING THE STORM — HAS
THROUGH THE CENTURIES BEEN CROWNED BY THE GLAMOUR OF
LEGEND AS THE UNDISPUTED RULER OF THE SKY AND MADE THE
EMBLEM OF FREEDOM, THE INCENTIVE TO VALOR AND THE PLEDGE OF
VICTORY. THE GRANDEUR OF ITS FLIGHT INTO THE CLOUDS, ITS
PRETERNATURAL KEENNESS OF VISION AND ITS FREEDOM-SOUNDING
SCREAM NOT ONLY HAVE STIRRED THE IMAGINATION OF MEN IN EVERY
AGE, BUT HELPED TO LEAD OUR OWN ASPIRATIONS TO THE CLOUDS.
NO LONGER DOES ITS GRACEFUL FIGURE ADORN ONLY THE GREAT
SEAL AND INSIGNIA OF A FREEDOM-LOVING COUNTRY TO SIGNIFY ITS
PROWESS AND WORTHINESS, IT HAS ALSO FOUND A PROMINENT PLACE
IN EACH OF OUR HEARTS SO THAT WE WHO ARE SO EARTHBOUND
PHYSICALLY CAN ASPIRE TO NEW HEIGHTS SPIRITUALLY AND SEIZE
UPON THIS SYMBOL TO HELP US SOAR TO EVEN GREATER HEIGHTS OF
SPIRITUAL AND ACADEMIC FREEDOM.

J. HAROLD ZOOK
TEACHER AND ADMINISTRATOR, 36 YEARS

feelings about Indian Valley, the Eagle, and my appreciation for being given the opportunity for thirty-six years to make a contribution to the constituents of Harleysville and others.

Most persons in retirement look forward to filling their lives with activities related to their own interests—their own pleasure. Harold did not spend retirement in this manner. His first loyalty was to his school and former students. In his own words he describes his contribution to his successor:

I spent the entire first summer going back and orienting the new assistant principal. Usually an administrator would train a new person the last two or three months before retiring, but I was too busy with students. Usually the end of the year is so busy with closing out things. I asked the principal and the school board if they would mind if I just continued my work right up to the end. Then during the three summer months I trained the new assistant principal and got my files in order. I reduced four files down to one. I redid the whole key system since they had built a new addition to the building. I made a complete key file for the entire building like I had done in my first years of administration. At that time I couldn't find the keys I needed. There were hundreds and hundreds of keys in a box, so I spent one entire summer with a secretary just trying every key in every door, and then made a large graph. We identified all the keys making sure we had a key for every door. Each key was put into a filing system that I updated with the new addition to Indian Valley, so nobody had to do those things again.

I spent September, October, and November going back and helping the assistant work with some of the students I had begun to work with. Frequently, when working with difficult students who aren't making proper choices, it takes two to three years to really bring about a permanent change. The new assistant asked me to help her, as she was completely new to the district.

Harold's interest in and concern for students and others did not end with retirement:

After I retired, there were an overwhelming number of people to thank. I'm one of those who feels a thank-you note is in order and I literally took that first year to write hundreds of personal thank-you notes to students who had written to me—some students I hadn't heard from in thirty years. Somehow they found out about my retirement and wrote letters to me, and in those letters I discovered that I had no idea how I had touched lives. A disabled child was in my class and I never knew that my disability influenced her as it did. She had difficult times, but she was determined that if I could be a teacher, so could she. After struggling through college, she struggled to get a job, much as I had done. It wasn't easy for a disabled person to get a job in the early sixties. Therefore, she wrote in this letter how my disability and my courageous outlook on life had inspired her beyond any realization I ever had. I wrote hundreds of thank-you notes and letters. I don't recall how many parents there were to whom I needed to respond.

One board member, the lady who put into motion that the library should be dedicated in my honor, asked me out for dinner about six months ago. Every two months she would write a two-page letter about how things were going in school and some of the difficulties they were having as a board; she also always told me about her family. I had both of her children in school. We just kept in touch. It was those kinds of things that occupied my time.

There is still an eighty-year-old lady who writes about a two-page letter to me every two weeks, faithfully without fail. My first year of retirement was basically that—letter writing. My father was also right at the point where he couldn't be left alone, so caring for him worked out well. I was able to take care of him, take him visiting, and do all those kinds of things. I was really set to get my affairs in order since I never had time to do that. I wanted to get a whole filing system that I never had time to do. I was just in the process of doing that—in fact, I had everything laid out on the table—when I was taken to the hospital.

My first three years of retirement, before I went to the hospital, were spent writing letters. I would follow the newspaper since I still had students who were going through high school and I'd watch for their achievements. If they were recognized for some achievements, I'd fire off a letter of congratulations to them. I enjoyed that. It's basically what I did. It kept me busy. I wrote an average of three or four letters a week to students who were in college or high school. I only learned later the impact even that had when students received things that were unexpected. So my retirement years were productive and enjoyable.

By the time he found time for his own interests, his muscular deterioration was so advanced there was no time for them:

There were many things I wanted to do in retirement. I had bought a new computer system at school for the office since we only had one. We had two secretaries and my secretary didn't have one, so I bought a computer that I tied into the district computer system so that we wouldn't have to rely on one computer with two secretaries. My first goal was to come home and learn the computer, since I never learned that. I always sent my secretary to school and various conventions to learn every aspect of the computer, but I never learned it myself. I just gave them the information and told them to set it up to my liking. I learned to work with the computer during my first year of retirement.

My goal was to set up a small business out of my home that would be making greeting cards. I have some kind of affinity with that. I wanted to get into a market that dealt with children's greeting cards. If you've ever noticed, there's not really a good source out there for children. I was going to design and write specific cards for children to send to parents, to teachers, to friends, to grandparents, to aunts, to uncles, to all those folks. I was in the process of setting all that up. I even had a printer lined up who would do the printing and designing. We had things pretty well set to go. All I needed to do was learn the computer so I could do that. However, that happened just as I went to the hospital, so I never got that achieved. Parents were asking me what my goals were in retirement, and when I told them, they were very enthused about the prospect of having cards designed for children.

I had numerous opportunities for developing other vocations. Parents pleaded with me to set up a counseling service in Harleysville, but I wasn't certified for that. That didn't really matter to me, but at that point I wanted a break. I wanted more time to care for my father, which I did. I started to get my own things in order at home when life took another dramatic turn.

12

Miracle of Life

My last operation involving a tracheotomy procedure has had a major impact on my life. I had a living will. I never wanted to be kept alive by mechanical means, and this certainly would have been included in that. I was pulled back to life, and my youngest brother, Don, was very involved at that time. He stayed at the hospital for many hours to learn about my care and to learn about the ventilator. It was a brand-new ventilator, one that none of the doctors or nurses had ever seen. I was fortunate that my brother Mervin's personal friend was the first distributor of this type of ventilator on the East Coast. The other ventilators weighed more than forty pounds, were big and very cumbersome.

When Don and his wife, Robin, took me to the emergency room, Don was becoming very frustrated because he knew how uncomfortable it was for me to lie on my back and was trying to tell the emergency personnel what to do. Finally, a friend of Don's took him by the shoulders and said, "Don, this is a matter of life or death. You need to let these doctors do what needs to be done or he won't make it." The doctors were already frantically pulling people together to help.

I don't remember much about being in the hospital the first several days, except having tubes down my nose and my throat. I couldn't talk, eat, or do anything. I was uncomfortable at times. By the fourth day, it was becoming very critical to make a move to get me off life supports. I was in and out of consciousness. The doctor in charge read my living will that my attorney and I had previously put together. I hadn't realized it, but the living will contained a clause indicating if there was a chance that I could have a quality of life, the doctor should initiate life supports. My doctor felt that with an operation I could have some quality of life.

On that assumption, my doctor called my family together—all my brothers and sisters, plus my school nurse friend, Eleanor—who sat down before coming to the hospital and developed a list of questions. They all gathered in my hospital room along with the doctor and discussed my situation. I strained to listen to the discussion, managing to hear parts of it as I slipped in and out of consciousness.

I remember someone asking the question of how long I would live if they removed the life support. I heard the doctor's reply: "Maybe a minute, maybe an hour, perhaps a day at best."

I heard the question about how long I would be hospitalized if I had the operation. By this time I had my fill of hospitals. The doctor answered, "If we do the operation, it would be two weeks here in Saint Joseph's Hospital, and then he will be moved to a rehabilitation hospital."

"How long will he be in rehab?" someone asked.

"Perhaps six months," was the doctor's reply.

I thought about that for a minute. I had no desire to go through that again, remembering all my discomfort, being poked with needles to keep me going, the machines going off, et cetera. About that time my second youngest brother fainted, causing a bit of a stir, so he was given a chair next to my bed.

After all the questions were asked, one of my brothers asked me if I would be willing to have the operation. My only way of communicating was to write on a tablet, which was very laborious. "Why should I? I have no responsibilities," I wrote.

My sister Ruth said, "Your nieces and nephews need you." I dearly love every one of my nieces and nephews. There isn't a thing I wouldn't do for them. Ruth's children were my first two nieces and nephew with whom I was very close. I had just been working with a niece who was involved with drugs. All of a sudden I realized my work wasn't finished here. Many times I brought other nieces and nephews into my home to enjoy activities together as well as to discuss the importance of living clean lives, et cetera. I guess my brothers and sisters appreciated my being this kind of uncle to their offspring. As I lay back on my pillow, I thought about my nieces and nephews and what we meant to each other. I finally wrote on my tablet, "I'll give it my best shot." And my family was so relieved.

His sister Ruth remembers: "When Harold was taken to the hospital, I asked if I should come home from Indiana. Later they called asking me to come because things didn't look good for Harold. I wondered how I could get an airline ticket so quickly, but when I called the airlines they told me that if I could get to the airport within two hours, they would put me on a plane and give me a reduced price for the ticket. Unfortunately, Harold doesn't remember my being at the hospital even though I spent twelve-hour days with him every day for a week. We communicated by him writing on a tablet. When the doctor told him without a tracheotomy operation he might live an hour or a day, he asked his family to help make the decision because he knew it would be a big responsibility on the rest of us. There was no doubt on the family's part that we wanted him to live. I don't recall, but he says he asked me in writing why he should choose to live. He says I told him his nieces and nephews needed him. It was a very special week for me even though I'm sorry Harold has no memories of it. It was a special time of bonding. I'm so proud of our family because we're so fond of him and want the best for him. We give credit first of all to the Lord, and then to all the caregivers and those responsible in any way for his care. I have never heard Harold say he wished he wouldn't have chosen to live. He does say he wouldn't want to go through it again, but he's grateful to be here. He loves life, maybe even more than he did before. It hasn't always been easy to see

274

Harold suffer; there were many tears. It is Harold's determination that has made him progress as he has. His speech therapist was amazed at how soon he learned to speak again. The adjustment to speaking with or around a tracheotomy tube is often very difficult or not accomplished at all."

Harold continues: I was immediately taken to the operating room after the doctor's meeting with my family. Recuperating was a long, enduring experience—I couldn't eat; I couldn't do anything; I needed constant care. At Saint Joseph's Hospital, I got so many letters about prayer chains being formed all over this country. I got hundreds of pieces of mail telling me people were praying earnestly. Even my financial adviser and his wife wrote letters telling me they were praying for me every day. It was the first time in my life when I really felt the power of prayer. I can't even begin to explain it. I felt such a force that was generating through me. I felt weak, but I still felt strong. It gave me immense hope for the future. A Lutheran pastor at Saint Joseph's Hospital came every day praying powerful prayers that gave me a lot of courage and strength to face whatever was ahead. I had no idea what I was facing. All I knew was that I had chosen to live rather than die—that I wanted to make the best I could of the situation. I decided to take it moment by moment.

The nurses and staff at the hospital were tremendous, going out of their way to help make me comfortable. When the time came to leave Saint Joseph's Hospital after two weeks, I was just becoming accustomed to the staff. I was frightened about going to a new hospital. I had no idea what was ahead of me. I loved my nurses. I was frightened and I didn't want to go. I again began questioning whether or not I had made the right decision.

The day I was to leave, the Lutheran pastor came early because he heard I was leaving to go to a new hospital. He said, "I want to see you one more time and to say a prayer for you." We visited for five minutes; then he laid his hand on my shoulder and prayed the most powerful prayer I think I ever felt in my life. He prayed for God to lift my anxiety and that God would lead me through these turbulent waters, asking God to protect me in my journey. The long drive to the rehabilitation hospital was a serious concern because they had to manually ventilate me all the way. I dreaded to think of lying on my back for the hour's drive. I had discussed all these fears with the reverend, and when he was finished with his prayer I immediately lost all my fear and apprehension. I was totally at peace with myself.

I wish I could put into words the feeling of the power of prayer, the power of knowing so many people being behind me. I can't explain it. I can only say it's a tremendous feeling. I think that's when I really got serious about my faith and my religion. It was more than just words. It was a life with meaning.

I made the journey with two ambulance attendants and two nurses who worked hard to make me as comfortable as possible. The admission process at the rehabilitation hospital was very painful and inconvenient because of all the tubing attached to me. The area around my tracheotomy tube was very sore at that point. I was finally placed in a nice room with pleasant people going out of their way to make me comfortable. A majority of the people at Vencor Rehabilitation Hospital never left there alive. Patients either died there or were sent to another facility. I understand I was only the seventh patient since 1978 to go directly home from there. My roommates were very pitiful cases, simply existing, and I kept thinking, *This could be me.*

Everyone on the staff was very dedicated, especially Tammy, my respiratory therapist, who was a very beautiful person with a wonderful warm personality. She spent time at my bedside when I began questioning the wisdom of my decision to live. She kept encouraging me, giving me hope, strength, and a reason to live. Some people have that ability and some don't. She had it. I worked so hard because of Tammy and another one of my nurses. I wanted so much to please them, to show them I was worth their care. I wanted to make them happy and feel good about being a nurse. I strove to please others rather than myself. When I saw a smile because of something I did, it invigorated me so that I could hardly contain myself sometimes.

I recently was privileged to return to Vencor for a visit. Tammy told me she thought about me almost every other day since my leaving the hospital two years earlier, wondering what had happened to me. She recalled the time just prior to my leaving the hospital how they tried to get me on my feet. Someone stood on a chair with a belt around my waist; there were crutches under my arms and a person at each shoulder, with still another person on his knees pushing my knees back. Even though it was very painful and I was so weak, it was an accomplishment to stand just for half a minute. She was so delighted to see me in my condition. She couldn't stop holding my hand, telling me how good it was for me to come back to visit her in such good condition.

I could see that my visiting the people at Vencor was inspiring to them. They were awed with my progress, my ability to speak, my emotions. Tammy learned I was walking as much as 200 steps a day with crutches. All she could remember was it took five people to help me stand for thirty seconds.

My family did so much for me. My one brother, Don, took two weeks off from work without pay to be with me. I tried to fathom all that love shown to me. My nieces and nephews surrounded me with visits, as well as my other brothers and sisters. I always knew I had a loving family, but I never understood the degree of importance of family, of love, and of the strength that can be derived from loving brothers and sisters. I kept getting better and better.

I was looking forward so much to going home, but when I did arrive home there were dozens of people there—speech and physical therapists, nurses, a respiratory therapist working with my brother Don, setting up the ventilator, someone trying to get twenty-four-hour nursing coverage, none of whom had been trained. Don spent many nights at my home those first weeks training nurses and giving me comfort. I remember Don being called out at three o'clock one morning because the ventilator kept malfunctioning and the nurse didn't know what to do. I had a hunch what was wrong, but I couldn't speak or turn over in my bed to show her, so I finally motioned for her to call Don. Another time at one o'clock, the ventilator went berserk and Don came to solve the problem. How he ever gained all the knowledge about this machine I'll never know.

My homecoming was a lot of hard work. I had many great nurses who helped keep me from getting discouraged. I tried not to show it, but I guess there was evidence of my being discouraged at times, which I suppose can't be helped. They would talk with me, helping me make it through those times of frustration. It took about a month to work out schedules for all the medical people coming in, including speech therapists, physical and respiratory therapists, nurses, caregivers, social workers, and others trying to make my stay at home workable. I couldn't even have visitors because of all the medical people in the house. I learned later that very few people expected me to live beyond six months. I was so weak I couldn't have fought off any kind of flu or colds. Everything had to be so sterile. Anyone who came through the door was required to remove their shoes and scrub their hands.

The hardest part for me was becoming a total receiver. I had tremendous difficulty with that my first couple months. However, my nurses helped me a lot in dealing with it. All my life, I was always giving of my talents and that's what made me thrive. All of a sudden I couldn't even lift my hand by myself. I could barely write. Someone had to put my hand on a pad and let me scribble my note because I couldn't talk. You can't imagine what it's like to not be able to do as much as raise your hand. I couldn't even blow my nose; someone had to hold the tissue for me.

Ruth recalls, "The first two years, I came to be with him one week each month. Each time I came, I was amazed at the progress he was making. One of the funniest things I remember was when the speech therapist was at the house working with him on five-syllable words. He was trying to help Harold say the word *hippopotamus.* Harold kept saying, 'Hip-hip-o-pot-pot-a-mus,' which sounded funny to me, so I burst out laughing. Harold had to laugh, too. I would tease him by mimicking his efforts, which always brought lots of laughter."

Harold continues: I made it through the first winter with flying colors. It's miraculous. I'm in better health than any of my doctors expected me to be. I was never expected to be able to speak like this. That took a lot of work with loving, caring people. I never expected to eat a sandwich or a hamburger, since everything was pureed. It was too dangerous to drink through a straw. I had to sip a little at a time.

When I left the hospital, several people gave me their addresses, asking me to let them know how things were going. Somehow these addresses were lost and I was unable to get in touch with them for two years. This was especially true for a therapist named Tammy. I felt really bad about this, but when I called the hospital they wouldn't give me the home addresses of therapists or nurses who worked there.

Terri, my caregiver, said, "I began thinking of ways to contact Tammy. Finally, I decided to call the hospital, telling them I was a respiratory therapist, too, and I needed to talk to Tammy. They patched me right through to her. It seemed she was at a point in her career where she was burning out. Seeing Harold was something she needed at the time. I told Harold he can't even imagine how it feels to have a patient come back to you and say, 'Thank you.' They all mean to, but it seems the hospital experience was such a painful one for them that they would rather not go back to that time. It was a good thing for Tammy at that point for Harold to go back and let her see him as he was two years later. The timing was just right for both Tammy and Harold."

When I visited Tammy, she just could not believe how good I looked. All the people who had worked with me in that hospital—there were about nine of them—remembered a tremendous amount of detail about me. Tammy said I was the first patient who ever came back to thank her for her care. Most people who go there either die or remain in very bad shape.

The hospital workers just couldn't believe how I looked and that I could talk, because when I left the hospital I couldn't speak at all. I couldn't eat except for pureed foods. I couldn't even use a straw. That's why I wanted to go back. I wanted to tell Tammy, in particular, as well as other nurses and aides, how much I appreciated what they did for me. I guess I was by far the best patient there, both physically and mentally. They told me it was a tremendous inspiration to them for me to want to come back after two years and personally thank each one. They couldn't stop talking about it for two weeks because they knew I was coming. I told Tammy how she had inspired me during those times when I wasn't sure whether I wanted to live or die.

Just three months before my returning to see her, Tammy had serious thoughts about leaving her position, but she didn't. I tried to explain to Terri how it felt to have this gnawing in my heart for two years and then all of a sudden find that person. I can only imagine how it must feel to put a child up for adoption and then, after thirty or so years, finally find that child about whom you have been thinking all those years.

I can't begin to describe the feeling of ease that came to my heart when I finally found Tammy. I was very concerned about becoming emotional; I didn't want that. It never happened. We embraced each other, exclaiming how good we both looked. After reminiscing and chatting for about an hour, Tammy took me around the hospital to meet other people who remembered me. It was a great experience and I have Terri to thank for that. Being a respiratory therapist, Terri was almost as excited about it as I was.

Harold's brother Don described the events that placed Harold in the hospital:

"Our sister Fern had called telling Robin, my wife, that Harold was having trouble. On other occasions, Robin came over and talked to him, but he seemed to be fine. We thought Fern was just overly concerned. Several days later, Fern called again. Robin asked to talk to Harold. As soon as she began talking to him, she knew he was in trouble because he wasn't responding properly—just moaning, et cetera. He was sitting at the kitchen counter in his wheelchair, marginally responsive and basically incoherent. He was leaning forward, mumbling without much control.

"We called the ambulance, but we questioned whether he could lie on the gurney on his back. He had always told us he couldn't lie on his back because it was so uncomfortable. We waited for about thirty to forty-five minutes after the first ambulance came trying to get a wheelchair ambulance where he could stay in his chair on the way to the hospital. Exeter has such a unit, but they were unable to get in touch with it. Eventually, we decided to put him in his van in his chair. By that time, he acted just as though he was sleeping. I kept asking, 'Harold, can you hear me? Are you all right?' It was amazing to me that he didn't fall over. He stayed sitting in his chair. An EMT (Emergency Medical Technician) from the ambulance gave him oxygen. On the way to the hospital, another ambulance brought a second oxygen tank. The entire way to the hospital, which was about fifteen minutes, Harold was totally unresponsive.

"At the hospital, the doctor said Harold's oxygen and carbon dioxide levels were not compatible with life. He was practically dead. The emergency room people couldn't insert the ventilator tube into his throat, because to do this they had to tilt his head way back. An anesthesiologist finally was able to insert the tube. As soon as the tube was in place, they let me see him. He was lying flat on the gurney and he was frantic. He had told us earlier that if he ever went to the hospital, we shouldn't let them have him lie flat on his back. I was trying to tell the emergency workers he couldn't lie flat on his back. Harold was trying to pull out the tube and motioning like he had to get up. The emergency staff was trying to hold his arms down. We slid him down to the end of the gurney where he tried to sit up a little bit, again trying to pull out the tube. Finally the anesthesiologist basically said, 'Look! He needs this or he isn't going to live.' Although he was very uncomfortable, they finally got him to his room. He was given a shot of something to help him relax.

"He was at Saint Joseph's Hospital in Reading, Pennsylvania, for about two weeks. The insurance company was pushing to get him released to a rehabilitation hospital, but the one they wanted to send him to had no vacancies. He was then sent to Vencor, where he spent four weeks. After several weeks, it became apparent they weren't able to do much for him. They were mostly into custodial care, where people went to die. They didn't have the therapists or the man-hours or staffing to provide the type of care Harold needed. The insurance company began pushing them to have him discharged, and then they started pushing us as a family to get people to the hospital to be trained to take care of him in his home. It was October—the harvest season and the busiest time of year for farming families, such as Harold's. They wanted any caregivers who would be responsible for Harold's care to be there for five eight-hour days—five or six people! That just wasn't going to happen.

"We finally talked to one of the caregivers who had worked with my dad and who had some experience with respiratory equipment to go for training. My wife, Robin, agreed to help out as much as was needed. I took off work and went to be the main one to be trained. As it turned out, they didn't quite know what to do with me. They were unaccustomed to helping laypeople with no medical background learn how to care for people on a ventilator. The therapist gave me all kinds of technical information that put me in a whirl. He was talking about 'peeps and pips.' It was a mess. I wasn't sure I was going to be able to do this, but the options weren't very good. It meant either my staying there and learning or

Harold going to another hospital that wouldn't have done him any good.

"We set a release date. We had an agreement with a respiratory therapist who would supply the necessary equipment for the home. The hospital personnel tried to get nursing help through the Home Visiting Nurse Association but weren't very successful since they were all overworked and overbooked. I had taken two weeks off from my teaching job, and it was nearing the end of the two weeks. The closer we got to the release date, hospital staff began saying, 'Yes, but what about this, and you don't have enough people, and you need a doctor near home to take care of Harold.' I called the doctor who had cared for him at Saint Joseph's Hospital, but he wouldn't care for him since he didn't take ventilator patients. Somehow we got in touch with another doctor who reluctantly agreed to be Harold's pulmonary doctor. That was a last-minute glitch. Harold was scheduled to leave the hospital at 10:00 in the morning, and I wasn't told about needing a doctor until 9:00. That's how inept they were at that hospital. I was on the phone almost two days working on getting everything set up. They kept throwing up roadblocks, and the social worker was adamant that Harold couldn't go home. They wanted to send him to Good Shepherd, another hospital, but he didn't want to go.

"Nobody would listen to me—the respiratory therapist and the social workers wouldn't listen to me; they were afraid to release him because they didn't want the liability. I finally made an appointment with the hospital administrator, a young fellow from a farm background. He listened to me. I told him, "My brothers are farmers; they can't come down here since they don't have that kind of time. Furthermore, it's not necessary, because the respiratory people from the Home Medical Supply House will do the training on-site to better accommodate my brothers' schedules.' The agreement we worked out was that for twenty-four hours I would do all the care for Harold while the respiratory therapists, nurses, and everyone involved would watch to make certain I was competent. I felt like they were checking me off!

"I think when I told the administrator that we were farmers accustomed to fixing things and figuring things out, he understood since he was from a similar background. 'We're willing to accept the responsibility and the risks,' I said. 'I know he might not live, but he does not want to be here. He's not progressing, and he might do a lot better if he's in familiar surroundings with people who know him.' Finally, he was released on schedule. He was brought home by ambulance, so I took his wheelchair to the car. As I put his chair in the car, I said, 'Yes! We're out of prison!' There had been so many obstacles we had to overcome, but we finally got out!

"The first days at home were not much fun. There were small things—like his oxygen. In the hospital he was on a four-liter flow, and when they released him for some reason they said he had to be on a six-liter flow. The enrichers only provided up to five liters, so we had two enrichers hooked together. The respiratory therapist didn't even show me an enricher. They didn't deal with the equipment we would have at home.

"We had to work out various adaptations to make the equipment work in his house. Harold wasn't supposed to be without oxygen at any time; we didn't know what would happen if he were without his oxygen for any length of time. Getting him in and out of bed with a Hoyer lift was even difficult and dangerous; everything had to be figured out.

"A lot of people showed up at his house the first few days. I was trying to figure out how to care for him when the nursing people would show up wanting an hour or two to interview him. The physical therapist, the respiratory therapist, and the home health people were all trying to find out what he needed. It was a zoo!

"The first trip to Dr. Shuman's office was quite a trip. When I called him from the hospital, he reluctantly agreed to care for Harold although he had never seen him. Because of this he wanted to see Harold as soon as possible. On this first trip, I was carrying his battery, the ventilator, and the emergency bag while walking next to Harold. On the second trip, Harold suggested setting the battery on his wheelchair footrest; we hung the ventilator on the chair. Every time we went somewhere in the van, something would go wrong, such as the ventilator would stop working. We would pull to the side of the road, get out, and fix it. There was always a driver and a nurse accompanying him.

"During the early days, as caregivers were being trained, when the ventilator stopped working or there was another emergency, I would be called in the middle of the night to figure out what had gone wrong. Frequently, the nurses couldn't even figure out what was wrong, panicking in their efforts to help. For example, the first night at home, a hose came off the back of the ventilator. The nurse panicked, not knowing what to do. She was trying to find where the problem was while Harold was trying to tell her to check the hose. However, Harold couldn't speak and was too weak to tell her what to do. He began to hyperventilate and finally, through his gestures, the nurse understood she was to call me. I told her to always check the hoses when a problem occurred.

"One night when my brother Ken was on duty, a part of the apparatus was turned to the side, causing the alarm to sound. Moisture had gotten into one of the tubes and Ken didn't know what to do, so he called me and together we found the solution. To this day, Harold always keeps his hand on the apparatus lying on his chest to be sure it is turned correctly. Another night Harold's heart went from seventy to eighty beats a minute to one hundred and forty beats a minute and I was again called. It took about two hours to put him to bed and two hours to get him up in the morning, and even to this day each of those takes one hour.

"One of those first days, my brother Mervin took care of Harold for several hours, so I could just take a walk across the fields. I still recall how good it felt just to go outdoors for that walk. Several days later a nurse cared for Harold while I went to one of my

285

son's school functions. What a relief it was to get out and do something with my family. Those first days were just plain tough.

"Gradually my brothers Ken and Mervin learned how to care for Harold. Mervin took off work for a week to provide care during the gaps when nurses weren't available. Ken helped out a lot at night. The nurses didn't think Lloyd could care for him because he has only one hand, but he wanted to try. They all worked together, improvising when necessary, and Lloyd was able to help out, too. For example, Harold would put a glove on Lloyd's hand. Somehow they all worked together to handle Harold's needs."

Lorraine, the wife of Harold's favorite cousin, comments; "When Harold was hospitalized and we thought he wouldn't make it, I was devastated. I had always known he meant a lot to me, and I thought I could not do without him. I cried my heart out many times thinking he wouldn't make it. I soon realized this was very selfish of me, because when we visited him in the hospital I saw how he was clinging to life. After seeing him, I could no longer pray that God would spare him because I didn't want him to be suffering and struggling just to breathe. I had to resolve my feelings and let it all up to God. I knew he had already made a big impact on my life, whether he was with us or not. It was such a miracle to watch him recover, due to what I truly believe was the love he received in return for the love that he had given all his life. His family and his nurses love him. I know of no one else who has the team of nurses he has. He praises his nurses, but it's easy to see it works both ways—that he is very special to them as well. I just thank God he is still with us today.

"I remember taking Harold to several weddings of students whom he had helped when they were in school. It felt so good to be a part of that. There were many students he could just have let fall through the cracks. His whole life has made such a tremendous impact on so many lives."

Some of Harold's caregivers describe their experiences working for Harold. Terri and Harold discuss their impressions:

Terri: I personally feel that I was brought to Harold to experience his patience, his compassion and perseverance. I have been a health-care worker nearly twenty-five years, and while I have become close to people and had good relationships with them, I have never known anyone who has been through so many hardships and is so selfless. He is still totally focused on everyone and everything around him. It's almost as if all the things he's been through didn't even happen. He seems to have glided right through them, focusing on others around him. One was Tammy, the respiratory therapist from Vencor. During those first two years as I was caring for Harold, he would frequently speak about the heartache he felt not being able to find Tammy so he could properly and personally express his appreciation for the loving care and encouragement she provided during those early days of his recovery in the hospital. This is just one of many examples. His suffering and intensive care could have been very traumatic to his health-care workers, but he chose to focus on those who were caring for him, which, in turn, helped him cruise right through the toughest times. I don't think most people handle their adversities in the way he does.

Harold's family is exceptional in the way he interacts with them and they with him. It is obvious that his father helped the family establish a strong work ethic. They work like dogs to get things done; they're very focused; but they are also very caring and compassionate. It just comes right out of them. They are also very focused on helping everyone they can. If I were to mention a need, even though I wasn't asking for something, I feel that Harold especially would find a way for that need to be taken care of. His whole family is like that.

I have been with Harold since November of 1999. Several months before I met him, Harold witnessed my family struggling to get out of a crash-landed hot air balloon in his brother Lloyd's field near Harold's house. I worked for the company where Harold had been hospitalized. The day after I was laid off, I received a phone call from Harold's family looking for caregivers. Since I live only a few miles from Harold's home, I feel we were destined to be together.

Harold: The timing was just right, because Terri now coordinates all of us to keep everything going smoothly.

Terri: We've become a family now. Even the caregivers who are no longer employed here rally around when we have a get-together. Everyone who can possibly come will be there.

Harold: I had twenty-eight care-givers when I first came home. The respiratory supplier, who works with many home-care people, said he never saw anything like this where so many, especially women, can work together in one house and be at peace with one another.

The supplier of Harold's respiratory equipment, Manny Esh, states: "I have known Harold for about two years. Harold's character is very interesting. He is the type of person I like to be around because he always cheers me up. While you might think he needs cheering up, whoever is around him gets a lift. He makes people feel good. His strength seems to come from his ability to figure things out. He wants to know how everything works and to do as much for himself as possible.

"His family's support also helps him persevere. His situation is so much easier because his brothers and sisters have accepted him just like he is. They make it look like taking care of him is fun.

"Harold speaks highly of all his caregivers. He never speaks negatively about one of them; of course, I've never heard him speak negatively about anyone. It's never hard for him to get nurses to care for him, because he shows appreciation. I've learned from him to be sure to show support to my employees and to say good things about them to others. If something goes wrong, he is right there helping to discover what needs to be fixed. He makes people want to care for him, and he wants them to feel comfortable. If I need to be cheered up, I come to see Harold. He stays upbeat because he is a religious person, which gives him an extra power. I think Harold enjoys being a manager, since he is running a 'business' and it gives him a challenge.

"The first day I met him, I was impressed because he brought out a paper he asked his lawyer to draw up that says he will never sue anyone. That says a lot about Harold's character, saying right up front that all he asks is for people to do the best for him they can and he will accept whatever happens. This has always been fascinating to me, because many patients I see struggle to get care, but Harold never does. I don't know if it's because of that paper or not, but it definitely has to do with the idea behind the paper. There's something to be said in the area of health care. Some nurses fear not knowing enough and getting sued. I have given this idea to other people and they would never do what Harold did. [See the appendix for a copy of this legal paper.]

"At one time, I asked Harold to visit a graduating college class of nurses I was teaching to talk about his situation. I could readily see the experience bringing out the teacher in Harold. He knew there would be some young nurse who could learn from him and then during her career provide the best care possible. He just knows how to bring out the best in people. He was beaming because of the opportunity it provided him.

"Nearly two years after visiting and speaking to that first graduating class of nurses at Alvernia College, Harold happened to meet one of those nurses who was now working in the emergency room at the Reading Hospital. He had gone there to have his tracheotomy tube changed, as is customary for him every eight weeks. The attending nurse immediately said, 'I know you!'

" 'How's that?' asked Harold.

" 'You spoke to my senior class of nurses at Alvernia two years ago,' she responded.

"She then went on to tell Harold how much she appreciated his personal message and the demonstration concerning his ventilator—its various functions and how it benefits the patient. Harold, in turn, was pleased to find out how rewarding she was finding her career as a nurse—and, he added, 'She's a good one!' "

Terri and Harold continue their conversation:

Terri: I have never been in a work situation where there isn't a weak link somewhere causing problems. This is totally a good group.

Harold: I think it's because everyone is focused on helping me become the best I can. I feel all the doctors and nurses have tried to develop all my abilities. There were times when I didn't feel like trying, but they helped me stay focused on what I needed to do. It was wonderful to have such a large team working together. Terri helps keep us focused. She has a researching mind, helping others find ways and means to do things. She keeps our family of nurses and caregivers together. Every other month we all get together for a picnic, a dinner or special function.

Terri: Harold's influence filters out to others when they see him being so helpful and positive; they then help others, too. Harold is such a perfectionist, but he is very relaxed in dealing with all these different personalities that have been plunked in his lap, saying, "Here we are!" We're all very different with our silliness and idiosyncrasies, and Harold takes that all in stride like it's simply part of the package. He doesn't expect us to be the perfectionist he is. It's OK that we're different and that we're unique personalities. That's one of my favorite things about him. Knowing his perfectionist personality, I would think he would want me to line things up just like he does, but he just doesn't.

Harold: When you become reliant on someone, you'd better flex a little bit.

Terri: Yes, but you're in charge here, although you never try to force us to be anyone but whom we are.

Harold: That's what helps make things go.

Terri: Hearing how many lives he's touched, I've told him several times that's probably why he never married. He wouldn't have been able to touch the lives of all the children, to spend the time he spent at school and maintain a marriage relationship. Now, with his health needs, we've become another family here because of the adversity he's had to face. I think all the caregivers feel that way. I often hear lots of thanks: "Thanks for giving that party. Thanks for giving us a chance to come to see Harold again."

Harold: We go out to ball games together. Terri and I work together sending out the invitations, et cetera. At our parties, we usually honor someone. For example, we threw a welcome-back party for my niece Janelle when she returned to the States after spending a year in Mexico as a missionary nurse. She had spent three weeks with me during her Christmas vacation while in nursing school and the nurses loved her. It was a marvelous experience for her because my nurses trained her all about my care—how to care for a tracheotomy, how to suction me, how to heal my wounds, et cetera. By the time she went back to nursing school she could say, "I know how to do that!" After graduation from nursing school, she went to Mexico, where she had far greater experiences than she would have had in the States. She's just a gem. The nurses kept in touch with her while in Mexico with cards and letters and care packages.

Shelly is another of Harold's nurses: "Considering I was a pediatric nurse for over eight years, I got away from geriatrics because people didn't have that spark anymore; they just wanted to give up. I was leery about coming to care for Harold, but I thought I'd give it a try, knowing that if I didn't like it I could call the agency telling them this is not for me. I soon saw that Harold has a zest for life. It's amazing to see what he has gone through and how he still goes about his daily living even with his tracheotomy and ventilator. He lives like everyone else does, and even more so. I enjoy coming to work, even though this will be my last month. Circumstances in my home make it necessary to work only part-time, so I'll be filling in where I'm needed.

"I think many times Harold could slack off or complain. I never hear him complaining. He just moves forward with a posi-

291

tive attitude and deals with what needs to be done. Many times people in his situation don't take care of themselves, because it's too much to suction when necessary, but he faithfully writes down what he eats, because of his diabetes, and watches his blood sugar.

"I have learned so much from Harold. When he tells me things about the kids he worked with in school, I try them with my kids and they actually work. He makes it easy to work here. He doesn't complain or give us grief about anything—and he could! But he is very generous and caring, which makes us want to do more than is required. I think I chose pediatrics because children don't complain, but Harold doesn't complain, either. It's not only the nurses; it's the quality of the patient that makes a nurse want to do the extras.

Barb, another caregiver, has been with Harold from the beginning: After working as a church secretary for twelve years, I decided to do something different with my life, and that was to attend travel school. I needed some extra cash, so I was looking for part-time work in the evening. One evening, Harold's brother Don called saying, 'I heard you're looking for a part-time job. How would you like to work for my brother?'

" 'Doing what?' I inquired. 'Tell me what I would need to do.'

"When Don told me about Harold and the kind of care he needed, I was hesitant. 'Don, my stomach gets pretty queasy. I'm not sure I can do that, but I'll give it a try.'

"Don set up a time for me to meet with him and to learn what Harold needed. Harold was still becoming accustomed to the equipment, and Don was performing a suctioning. Harold's face was beet red, he was gagging, and tears were flowing down his cheeks. At that time, my tears started flowing down my cheeks, and I grabbed a tissue to wipe the tears off Harold's cheeks. Harold told me later how that movement with me wiping his tears touched him. When I asked him about those tears, he said, 'They are tears of joy.'

"I responded with, 'I guess I'll be crying a lot of tears of joy right along with you.'

"I truly believe God led me to this job because I was going back to school during the day and looking for a part-time job in the evenings. This was a great atmosphere, because it was quiet and with having three children at home, I could study and work on my projects while sitting next to Harold. He even worked on one of my projects and helped me with my English class.

"I don't know what had caused me to stay. During that first visit when Don was suctioning Harold, his dad was sitting at the kitchen counter. We heard a thump and looked over to see their dad lying flat on the floor. We think he was probably overcome with seeing the suctioning process and passed out. Rushing around the kitchen counter to get to him, I asked, 'Shall I call nine-one-one?'

" 'No!' exclaimed Don. 'Don't ever call nine-one-one!'

"I'm thinking, *What kind of people are they? This man has fallen and hit his head and they don't want to call nine-one-one?* I wasn't sure I could work for these people. Don explained to me later it was his father's desire not to call nine-one-one if anything happened to him. His father soon woke up, so we helped him back to his chair and he was fine. He didn't remember anything and life went on!

"It's been two years since I've been with Harold and he has been a blessing to me, because he's a good listener and a very compassionate man. We all come to him with our problems. He's been my counselor for the past two years. We have also grown in our spiritual lives together. I was dealing with some personal problems while Harold was dealing with his failing father and his own inner feelings. We spent many nights talking over our problems. He claimed I helped him find resolution to his problems, and I claim he helped me resolve mine. We began reading devotionals. We also began reading the book *Tuesdays with Morrie.*

"Ever since Harold's father passed away, Harold doesn't let

the grass grow under his feet. We're out and about, whether it's grocery shopping, dining out, going to productions, or whatever. He has been so good to each and every one of us. I can never repay what he has done for me—and he pays me on top of that.

"Harold is such a great listener, very compassionate and nonjudgmental. He has an open mind, so I can feel the freedom to talk without feeling I'll be judged. We can tell Harold has never been married. Sometimes he needs a woman to boss him around a little bit. At the same time, he has done a wonderful job, because he has about seven different women—most of us are women—come into his house and each of us does things differently. We even drive his van differently—some go too fast; some drive slowly; some ride the brakes. He has to be very open-minded and flexible to adjust to that many personalities. We all cook, use the dishwasher, wash and dry the clothing, and of course we all have our own ways of doing those things. Even how each nurse does the personal care is different.

"My spiritual life has grown both through reading devotionals and through conversation. I consider myself as being nonjudgmental, but Harold is someone with whom one can be truly open and speak your mind. He has reassured me in my mind that I love life, I love God, I love people. We have talked numerous times about life in general, about forgiving, about how life is so short and we should make the best of it, taking it a day at a time. I don't know if I could be the person Harold is if I were in his situation. He's usually upbeat. I admire him for that.

"Harold's strength comes from his faith and the family he came from, because they are all there for him. He appreciates them realizing how lucky he is. I often tell him he's very lucky he got his education and had the job he did, that he is as well off as he is with his gorgeous home, with the modern equipment, et cetera. There are many people in similar situations who can't afford the modern equipment he has. He is very appreciative of all that is done for him.

"There is a little joke we have between us that goes back to when Harold would forget to say please; his boss at school would say, '*Please* understood.' We joked about that when Harold would direct us to do something. We would say, 'OK. *Please* understood!' Then we would laugh together.

"I'll always admire him for who he is. I can never pay back what he has done for me. He loves his women fat! I have gained so much weight working here. His family are all such good cooks. There wasn't a week that went by when there would not be a cake or pastry on the counter. However, this past year Harold was diagnosed with diabetes, so the sweets disappeared. He takes us out to eat and he really spoils us. He has been so encouraging throughout my schooling, and the first day on my new job an arrangement of flowers in a lovely cup and saucer showed up and guess who it was from—Harold.

"For speech class one day, I needed to do a demonstration. Harold willingly came with me as my demonstration when I showed the class what I did at my part-time job. He was so happy to do that for me. He made quite a hit with the class."

Harold reflects on his hospitalization: My recovery was a miracle; it was a lesson. It made me wonder, *Why me? Why was I spared?* I kept telling myself, and my nurses reminded me, there was a purpose. They gave me a purpose, telling me how much I meant in their lives. I think it made my family value life and the importance of family. Their rallying around me created all kinds of inner feelings. Maybe this book is the reason I'm still living. I was fearful that reviewing my life would touch some nerve centers for me, but I don't mind if it helps somebody else. I can't imagine how my life might inspire someone, but I'll have to leave that in the hands of the Author, Almighty God. My hope is that the efforts put into it will bring dividends, not for me but for someone out there who needs some words of encouragement.

Epilogue

Today Harold's life depends upon the proper functioning of a ventilator and his oxygen supply. In the past two years he has had twenty-eight different caregivers, one of whom must be with him twenty-four hours a day. They drive his van to take him places and use his kitchen to prepare his meals. All have different ways of driving and approaching their duties. It takes four hours each day for his personal care. An hour is required just to help him get in and out of bed. Yet Harold has remarked to his caregiver Terri that the last two years have been among the best years of his life since he has met so many wonderful people.

Harold goes to ball games, public activities, and restaurants and visits many friends. He has bought a Toro lawn mower, has installed a lift in his garage to help him get on the mower, and is again mowing his own lawn. He serves as a counsel to his nurses and caregivers. His thoughts are not centered upon himself but on others. He is able to say, "This new life is even better since I have made new friends, touched new lives, and have a new family." His new family of nurses and caregivers organizes periodic get-togethers at Harold's house.

Harold also says: I always knew that I had a great family and lots of friends, but when you go through something like this, you learn who your friends are. My family is even more beautiful to me than they ever were before, because I know how much I mean to them and how much they mean to me. My quality of life has been enriched. This book has brought back many emotions, things I have forgotten or purposely pushed aside. To hear the love these people are pouring out during interviews for the book is overwhelming to me. I hope and pray this book will mean something to somebody, perhaps somebody who is depressed or ready to give up. If so, I'll be more than pleased with the effort that has been made. At first, I was reluctant to have anyone write my story because I couldn't imagine reading about myself. It hasn't been an easy task, but I pray someone will be blessed and encouraged to make the most with what he or she has in life.

Henry Wadsworth Longfellow penned the following words, which relate to Harold:

> Lives of great men all remind us
> We can make our lives sublime;
> And, departing, leave behind us
> Footprints on the sands of time;
>
> Footprints that perhaps another,
> Sailing o'er life's solemn main,
> A forlorn and shipwrecked brother,
> Seeing, shall take heart again.
>
> Let us, then, be up and doing,
> With a heart for any fate;
> Still achieving, still pursuing,
> Learn to labor and to wait.

The Eagle continues to soar to even greater heights.

Harold was selected by his alma mater, Eastern Mennonite University, to receive the 2002 Alumnus of the Year Award.

All proceeds from the story of J. Harold Zook go to the Conflict Transformation Program (CTP) at Eastern Mennonite University, his alma mater. Established in 1994, CTP encourages the building of a just peace at all levels of society, in the United States and abroad. CTP is committed to a mutual learning community that values the diversity and rich experience of students, faculty, associates, and staff. The program prepares reflective practitioners for a life of nonviolence, witness, service, and peace building, equipping students to understand conflict and to engage in action to transform it. The program reflects the manner in which Harold handled discipline during his teaching and administrative career at Indian Valley.

For more information concerning the Conflict Transformation Program:

Conflict Transformation Program
Eastern Mennonite University
Harrisonburg, VA 22802-2462
Phone: (540) 432-4490
Fax: (540)432-4449
E-mail: *ctprogram@emu.edu*
Web Site: www.emu.edu/ctp

Appendix

Appendix

DAVID F. SPANG
ATTORNEY AT LAW
12 WEST MAIN STREET
FLEETWOOD, PENNSYLVANIA 19522

TELEPHONE (610) 944-6870   FAX (610) 944-6893

ASSUMPTION OF RISK AND RELEASE

THIS AGREEMENT, Made this _____ day of _____, 200__, between J. HAROLD ZOOK (Patient) and _____ (Caregiver).

WHEREAS, Patient's health has deteriorated to the point that he can no longer take care of his physical needs without the assistance of others; and

WHEREAS, some of Patient's health requirements include procedures which involve some risk to Patient; and

WHEREAS, Patient has requested and employed Caregiver to provide him with the assistance that he requires which include procedures involving risk; and

WHEREAS, Patient agrees to assume all risks attendant to the services to be provided by Caregiver and wishes to release Caregiver for all liability arising out of the delivery of services to Patient; and

WHEREAS, Patient desires that this agreement be binding on his estate as well as on his heirs, executors and administrators.

NOW, THEREFORE, KNOW ALL MEN BY THESE PRESENTS That Patient hereby agrees with Caregiver that all risks with respect to the services to be provided by Caregiver to Patient are assumed fully and completely by Patient and Patient hereby fully and completely releases and discharges Caregiver on account of all liability arising out of the delivery of services to Patient. This agreement shall be binding on the estate, heirs, executors and administrators of Patient.

IN WITNESS WHEREOF, Patient and Caregiver have hereunto set their hands and seals the day and year first above written.

_____ (SEAL)
(J. Harold Zook)
PATIENT

_____ (SEAL)
CAREGIVER

Harold, age 2 with sister Ruth, age 3

Harold as a junior with other high school public speaking contest winners in 1954

Harold in 1952 at age 15

Harold as a high school senior in 1955

Harold won second prize in a college public speaking contest in 1957

Harold as an English teacher in 1968

Harold in 1975 when he
became assistant principal

Harold and his seven siblings in 1978

Harold, his five brothers, and his dad, August 1996

Harold on his Amigo at a former student's wedding, 1993

Harold presenting the Student of the Month Award

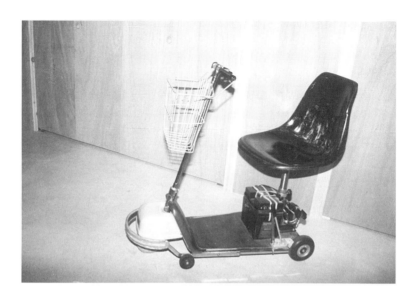

Harold's Amigo, used to get around the school

Harold conducting Christmas carols at school, 1995

The new library was dedicated to Harold

Harold with parents at a surprise retirement party, 1996

Renee with Harold and her "Spirit of the Eagle" award

Harold and the Indian Valley Middle School

Harold on his Toro lawn mower, May 2002

Harold and his lawn mowing shows his penchant for precision!

Credits

Cover: Photo of Harold: permission received from Scholl Photography

Photo: Page ii; Photo: Harold with "Spirit of the Eagle" Plaque; permission received from John Rowe, Photographer

Dedication: Page v; Photo: Harold and His Family, 1978; permission received from John Rowe, Photographer

Foreword: Page x; Photo of Harold with Heritage Clock and President Lapp; Courtesy of Marian Payne

Acknowledgments: Page xv; Photo: Harold with Marian and James Payne, Courtesy Marian Payne

Chapter 1, Page 2: Photo: Sara on Her Wedding Day: permission received from Wendy L. Miller, Photographer

Page 6; Quote from Indian Creek Foundation publication; permission received from the Executive Director, Indian Creek Foundation.

Page 9 & 11; Photo of Christ and Letter from the Artist; permission granted by Dorothy Hermansader, widow of Allen F. Hermansader

Page 20; Photo: Jennifer on Her Wedding Day: permission received from Phaze II Photography & Video

Chapter 7, Page 138: Quote from THE REPORTER of Lansdale, PA, October 4, 1986; permission received from Phil Freedman, Executive Editor of THE REPORTER

Page 139; Quote from the READING EAGLE of Reading, PA, January 20, 1991; permission received from the READING EAGLE

Page 159; Quote from the READING EAGLE of Reading PA, January 20, 1991; permission received from Chuck Gallagher, Managing Editor of THE READING EAGLE

Chapter 9: Page 177–179: Quote from the SOUDERTON INDEPENDENT of Souderton, PA, June 7, 1989; permission received from Barbara A. McClennen, Managing Editor of the SOUDERTON INDEPENDENT

Chapter 11: Page 252 & 253; Poem: "How to Conduct The Eagle Spirit"; permission received from Nadeen McShane and Carole Darragh

Page 256; Quote from the SOUDERTON INDEPENDENT, February 19, 1997; Permission received from the SOUDERTON INDEPENDENT

Page 263; Painting; permission granted by Dorothy Hermansader, widow of Allen Hermansader

Page 265 & 266; Song: "Teaching: A Legacy of Love" permission for publication granted by Virginia Bernd, AKA Hilary James, Instar Productions (A CD of the song is available from Virginia Bernd, 602 Melvin Road Telford, PA 18969)

Appendix: Page 308; Photo: Harold and His Seven Siblings—1978; permission received from John Rowe, Photographer

Page 314; Photo: Harold and the Indian Valley Middle School; permission received from John Rowe, Photographer